ENABLING CREATIVE CHAOS

Joe,

Thank you for your
help with this research
project. Good luck
with law school!

Best,
Katherine
8/30/09

PS see yourself
in index.

ENABLING CREATIVE CHAOS

The Organization Behind the Burning Man Event

KATHERINE K. CHEN

The University of Chicago Press | Chicago & London

KATHERINE K. CHEN is assistant professor of sociology at The City College of New York, The City University of New York (CUNY).

The University of Chicago Press, Chicago 60637
The University of Chicago Press, Ltd., London
© 2009 by The University of Chicago
All rights reserved. Published 2009
Printed in the United States of America

16 15 14 13 12 11 10 09   1 2 3 4 5

ISBN-13: 978-0-226-10237-5   (cloth)
ISBN-13: 978-0-226-10238-2   (paper)
ISBN-10: 0-226-10237-8   (cloth)
ISBN-10: 0-226-10238-6   (paper)

Library of Congress Cataloging-in-Publication Data

Chen, Katherine Kang-Ning.
    Enabling creative chaos : the organization behind the Burning Man event /
Katherine K. Chen.
        p. cm.
    Includes bibliographical references and index.
    ISBN-13: 978-0-226-10237-5 (cloth : alk. paper)
    ISBN-13: 978-0-226-10238-2 (pbk. : alk. paper)
    ISBN-10: 0-226-10237-8 (cloth : alk. paper)
    ISBN-10: 0-226-10238-6 (pbk. : alk. paper)   1. Burning Man (Festival)—Management.
2. Black Rock City, LLC—Management.   3. Art festivals—Nevada—Management.
I. Title.

    NX510.N32B6335 2009
    394.2509793'54—dc22

                                                                    2009009143

⊗ The paper used in this publication meets the minimum requirements of the American National Standard for Information Sciences—Permanence of Paper for Printed Library Materials, ANSI Z39.48–1992.

Contents

List of Illustrations   *vii*
Preface   *ix*
Acknowledgments   *xi*

1   Introduction: The Perils of Under- and Overorganizing   *1*
2   Context: The Development of the Burning Man Event
    and Organization   *24*
3   "Do-ocracy": Acting on Suggestions and Criticisms   *42*
4   "Radical Inclusion": Attracting and Placing Members   *64*
5   "No Spectators": Motivating Members to Contribute   *84*
6   "Immerse Yourself": Managing Relations in the Pursuit of Legitimacy   *112*
7   Conclusion: Sustaining Creative Chaos   *152*

Appendix 1. Ethnography and Qualitative Research   *165*
Appendix 2. Interview Protocols   *173*
Notes   *179*
Reference List   *207*
Index   *229*

Illustrations

Figures

2.1 Burning Man event population by year   *36*

Tables

1.1 Bureaucratic vs. collectivist practices   *6*

1.2 Outcomes associated with underorganized, moderately organized, and over-organized bureaucratic and collectivist practices   *20*

2.1 Members of the 2000 LLC board and senior staff   *39*

6.1 Relations between the Burning Man organization and governmental agencies, the media, and commodifiers   *120*

Photo gallery follows p. 110

Preface

Most people spend significant time and effort dealing with organizations, including the government, workplace, and voluntary associations. For some, these experiences feel unpleasant and unrewarding, or even dehumanizing and exploitative. Popular culture such as the *Dilbert* comic strip, *The Office* television series, and *Office Space* and *Brazil* films satirize the frustrating, alienating, and even psychosis-inducing aspects of the workplace. Citizens groan about inflexible, entrenched bureaucracies and worry that these organizations no longer demonstrate accountability to their constituents. Critics decry organizations that pollute, produce unsafe products and services, and mislead investors and consumers. These perspectives portray organizations as unresponsive and even malevolent forces.

Yet most of us have difficulties imagining life without organizations. By organizing collectively, we can realize goals that are difficult to accomplish by individuals. While organizations often seem to enforce the status quo, they can also serve as catalysts for change. Rather than accepting the dark side of organizations as inevitable, why not reshape organizations, so that our organizational experiences and efforts more closely reflect what we desire?

This book examines the Burning Man organization to show how we have the agency to mold organizational experiences more to our liking. Although members of the Burning Man organization produce an unusual output of a temporary arts community, the challenges that they have faced are shared with many organizations: how to integrate different perspectives on organizing, how to recruit, retain, and motivate members, and how to deal with external entities. In addressing these challenges, Burning Man members sought to maintain meaning, responsiveness, and flexibility while still allowing for stability, fairness, and efficiency. Like any collectivity, the Burning Man organization has had its share of flaws. Nevertheless, the Burning Man organization's development can help readers rethink possibilities for their own organizations, whether these involve the workplace, government, political or social mobilization, recreation, voluntary work, or spiritual matters. It is my hope that readers will use this book to brainstorm ideas about how to approach organizing.

Acknowledgments

Several people have asked what I consider as my contribution of "art" to Burning Man. Thanks to a vast community of support throughout the years, here is my contribution. First and foremost, this book would not have been possible without the help of past and current members of the Burning Man organization and community. In particular, organizer Marian Goodell ensured my full access to the organization. Others too numerous to name here assisted with necessities such as rides and temporary housing, while others granted interviews and access to personal archives.

David J. Frank, J. Richard Hackman, and Peter V. Marsden were especially helpful in supporting my efforts to understand how a seemingly unusual organization shed insight into organizing issues in general. Dr. Frank provided fast feedback, made timely inquiries, and offered constant encouragement. When I was making sense of my field notes and initial drafts, Dr. Hackman demonstrated the art of discerning findings from the noise. Dr. Marsden rigorously reflected on my findings, helping to sharpen my theoretical claims; he also suggested relevant literature on collectivist organizations and other topics. In addition, Joseph Galaskiewicz shared his uplifting, wry guidance; Barbara Reskin suggested provocative comparisons. Neil Fligstein, Doug Guthrie, and members of the Corporation as a Social Institution group formed by the

Social Science Research Council (SSRC) and Sloan Foundation workshops contributed feedback on presentations of this research.

On subsequent revisions of the manuscript, Barry Cohen, Mario Small, and Dana Weinberg made insightful comments that honed the introduction. Rakesh Khurana and Joel Podolny also made comments on an oral presentation that helped with the framing of issues and clarification of terms. Collaborative analyses with Siobhán O'Mahony on data collected from our respective field sites allowed for further comparison of organizing issues (Chen and O'Mahony 2006, forthcoming). During later drafts of the book, Howard Lune, Jacqueline Olvera, and Stacey Sutton offered detailed suggestions that helped me rework the introduction and chapters 5 and 6; Howard Lune, Jacqueline Olvera, and Daniel Beunza also made suggestions on the concluding chapter. William Paterson University students Kassandra Barnes and Lesleigh Campagnale graciously provided several citations.

Two anonymous reviewers read two full drafts of the book manuscript. Their extensive comments and suggestions improved this book from start to finish, particularly in the introductory chapter's typologies and charts and the sequencing of chapters. In addition, Doug Mitchell and Tim McGovern at the University of Chicago Press gave valuable editorial support, and Carol Saller provided her detailed copyediting expertise. However, any errors in this book are mine.

The National Science Foundation funded three years of graduate study. Harvard University also provided the Graduate Society Fellowship, and the Sociology Department allocated two grants toward attending conferences. The Harvard Graduate Student Council assisted with summer research and conference funds. The Derek Bok Center for Teaching and Learning granted a postdoctoral position, and the Social Studies program provided yet another opportunity to continue writing while at Harvard. At William Paterson University, discussions with students reinforced the difficulties of organizing. My current position at The City College of New York, The City University of New York (CUNY), enabled me to finalize revisions to this book.

My family offered their unwavering support for my project, even when research and writing encroached upon my time with them. Friends and colleagues, including Yomi Ayeni, Alex Barker, Bayliss Camp, Joe Chen, Gwen Dordick, Nana Kirk, Natasha Lepore, Rob Oliver, Todd Pittinsky, and Alexandra Vega, accompanied me through this arduous journey. Sergei deserves special mention for his patience and humor, as well as his intrepidness in cheerfully preparing us for Burning Man during recent years.

This book is dedicated to the Burning Man community.

Introduction

The Perils of Under- and Overorganizing

ON LABOR DAY of each year, Black Rock City shuts down in the Nevada Black Rock Desert Playa.[1] As the city's pirate radio stations broadcast their farewells, the mass departure of dust-covered cars, recreational vehicles (RVs), converted buses, and trailers recreates the caravans of wagons and cattle that once traversed the desert on an ill-advised shortcut to Oregon and California.[2] But unlike the mid-1800s travelers who crossed the desert to pursue their fortunes, contemporary travelers have found their El Dorado in the desert: an evanescent arts community known as Burning Man. In 2007, more than 47,000 individuals converged upon this annual week-long event. Their activities culminate with Burning Man's namesake, the bonfire of "the Man," a forty-foot-tall wooden and neon sculpture that anchors the temporary city's center. While current attendees can look forward to regular Burning Man events, Burning Man did not always have such a certain future. As this book shows, over the years, both disorganization and excessive organization have threatened to curtail Burning Man. Without concerted organizing efforts, this event, now in its third decade, would have not survived its teens.

Little of that past uncertainty is evident in the current event, where countercultural norms, participatory art, and a striking location set Burning Man apart from other events and festivals. First, "participants," as attendees are called, are responsible for creating, rather than passively consuming, the event. Some volunteer for the infrastructural services that support Black Rock City. Other individuals participate by forming theme camps that host interactive activities: visitors can spar with foam-padded bats in a replica of Mad Max's Thunderdome, ride a mini roller coaster doused by fire, roller-skate to disco music under the stars, or relax in shaded "chill spaces." Since Burning Man tenets prohibit vending, commercialism, and spectating (i.e., gawking), participants must bring their own food, water, and shelter for the week. However, under the gift economy, they may receive or bestow art, trinkets, Burning Man memorabilia, or shared experiences. Adherents claim that these activities reinvigorate community relations by offering an alternative to a cash-based economy of paid performers, products and services, and corporate sponsorship.[3]

Second, the Burning Man event breaks conventions about who can make art and how to experience art. The event encourages both artists and lay-persons to create and share art. Much of the art demands audience interaction; people can taste, smell, manipulate, and alter art in ways prohibited or discouraged elsewhere.[4] Participants chip away at a massive ice ball to make snow cones, crawl through an ammonite-spiraled maze, recline upon a bed of imported grass, listen to a band perform in a stained-glass-like cathedral made of recycled plastics, swing inside a seventeen-foot-tall birdcage, animate a "Laughing Sal" by peddling an exercise bike, and dedicate a memento in a latticed temple that burns on the event's last evening.[5] To explore these art installations, performances, and theme camps, some participants roam the over four-square-mile city in art cars decorated as a Spanish galleon, a fire-breathing dragon, a red-eyed whale, a trio of cupcakes, and other fantastic designs.[6]

Third, Burning Man attendees build and dismantle a fully functional city under physically challenging circumstances. Extreme temperatures, tent-flattening winds, blinding dust storms, and torrential downpours may jolt campers from their reveries. To help the Burning Man collective thrive in this remote area, the organization behind the event coordinates resources and services, including shelters for infrastructural services, portable toilets, and medical and fire protection teams. After the event's end, workers and volunteers restore the event site, knowing that they will return next year to the flat, grayish-white desert ringed by mountains and capped by a domed expanse of sky.

Like other collectives, Burning Man started as an informal, ad hoc group of individuals. The first five Burning Man events required relatively few organizing efforts to carry out their small evening bonfires on a San Francisco beach. After the event relocated to the Nevada Black Rock Desert and transformed into a booming temporary city, it needed increasingly complex efforts to handle legal and political issues, secure resources, and coordinate individuals. In 1997, to facilitate organizing, event cofounder Larry Harvey and other organizers created the Black Rock City Limited Liability Company, hereafter referred to as the Burning Man organization or Project.[7] Organizers head efforts to plan the event and secure resources via ticket sales and donations that generate an approximately $10 million budget.[8] They also coordinate with governmental agencies, local officials, and other groups such as the media, all of which pose demands that have escalated with the event's growth. An estimated two thousand volunteers contribute on a year-round or limited basis, making this organization a largely volunteer-fueled operation.[9]

When referring to this organization's efforts, I use *members* as a general term to include those who work for the Burning Man organization as volunteers or employees. I use the term *organizers* for those who head the organization. Following Burning Man parlance, I use the terms *coordinators* and *managers* for department or committee leaders and the term *staff* for both paid and unpaid members. The terms *participants* and *event attendees* refer to those who attend the event; a small percentage of these persons also volunteer for the organization. While the Burning Man leaders consider those who organize or participate in the event's theme camps and art projects as part of the Burning Man organization, my analyses focus on those who contribute time to the organization and its activities.

Burning Man members establish conditions where thousands can, as organizer Michael Mikel, a.k.a. Danger Ranger,[10] describes, surf the edge of creative chaos: "Our event is just on the edge of chaos sometimes. With that, there is a tremendous amount . . . of creativity and a tremendous amount of freedom, but we [as organizers] try not to be overbearing in our control. . . . We try to give people as much freedom [as possible]."[11] Mikel's characterization underscores the two extremes that threaten the Burning Man event. If the Burning Man organization does not provide enough structure for the event, then the ensuing chaos could overwhelm attendees. On the other hand, if the organization imposes too much structure, the event's creativity and vitality could suffocate.

Members face a similar dilemma in developing and maintaining the organization behind the Burning Man event. If members underorganize, their organization does not have enough structures, such as designated rules, positions, or procedures, or enough coordination to support members' efforts. If members overorganize, structures and coercive control constrain rather than enable organizing efforts. Skeptics might argue that for creative or meaningful endeavors like Burning Man, members will have positive experiences irrespective of their organizations. But research has shown that even organizations devoted to artistic endeavors and social change can suffer from under- and overorganizing (Dubin 1987; Fisher 2006; Freeman 1973). The unintended consequences[12] of under- and overorganizing can adversely impact members' experiences and abilities to achieve collective goals. As a result, members' commitment may wane. If an organization, particularly one that depends upon volunteers, cannot sustain members' commitment, then the resulting withdrawal of members' support can hasten an organization's closure (Duckles, Hager, and Galaskiewicz 2005; Knoke 1981).

By examining how the growing Burning Man organization dealt with under- and overorganizing, we gain insight into the development of organizations more generally. To this end, this book examines how Burning Man members navigated several challenges as they shifted from ad hoc to formal organizing. I focus on how members enacted—that is, developed and carried out—organizing structures. I draw on data collected during repeated, intensive participant observations of organizing efforts among Burning Man members.[13] During annual periods of three to eight months between 1998 through 2001, I volunteered for several departments, and I observed organizational activities such as meetings, orientations, and mixers. I also interviewed eighty-one past and present members about their experiences. I followed up in subsequent years by monitoring e-mail lists and visiting the annual Burning Man events through 2008. During one such follow-up visit to the 2004 Burning Man event, a desultory chat with a Burning Man volunteer turned into a discussion about organizing extremes.

This discussion highlighted concerns that other members had regularly expressed about possible under- or overorganizing. Rob Oliver, a friend and a volunteer manager, described what happened when a fellow volunteer broke a rule while helping a participant. On the last day of the event, an attendee had sought assistance at Playa Info, an information service manned by volunteers. He had accidentally locked his keys in his car and needed a locksmith or tow truck.[14] Since the event lacked pay phones or cell phone service, a volunteer lent his personal Internet phone so that the stranded person could call for help in the nearest city, a several-hours drive away. In doing so, the volunteer violated an official ban on the use of Internet phones in Playa Info and other public areas. This rule was intended to curb event attendees' expectations that the Burning Man organization would provide Internet services.[15] Unluckily for this volunteer, a Burning Man employee had witnessed the volunteer's transgression and was furious. Although the volunteer claimed that he didn't realize the policy still applied to the last day of the event, the employee recommended barring him from camping near Playa Info in future events.

As I listened to this account, I wondered how others would react to this incident. I didn't have to speculate for very long, as an acquaintance who had overheard our conversation shared his views. A San Francisco resident exclaimed in a gentle voice, "That's why I'm an anarchist!" His assertion echoed a belief espoused by other Burning Man aficionados who distrusted formal organizations and preferred unregulated individual action. Surprised by this unsolicited statement, I asked the self-identified anarchist to explain his views. After a few minutes of conversation, I discovered that we were concerned about the same issues regarding the Internet phone incident. We both saw organizational rules not as iron-clad, but as context-dependent guidelines. In my opinion, the angry employee had overlooked the context under which the volunteer had lent his phone, as well as the potential consequences of punishing his actions. I wondered whether the volunteer, who had donated hundreds of hours of computer expertise and other help, would quit the organization. Would others dismiss this incident as an unfortunate, one-off exchange between a well-meaning volunteer and an overworked, cranky employee? Or, would they view it as proof of overorganizing, as my anarchist companion claimed?

Burning Man members regularly had such conversations about the appropriateness of organizing practices. Such discussions revealed that some members preferred practices that enhanced fairness, stability, and efficiency, while others were comfortable with less certainty and wanted more flexibility, responsiveness, and meaning. Some reasoned that an event that celebrated creativity, spontaneity, and participation should rely upon unconventional and unregimented organizing practices. These persons equated formal organization with overorganizing; they viewed the designation of rules, routines, a division of labor, and hierarchy as crushing rather than enabling efforts. For instance, Burning Man cofounder Jerry James worried about whether organizing diminished participation: "Like most big organizations, . . . the main obstacle they face is how to maintain the essence of people wanting really to participate in what [is] becoming a bureaucracy."[16] Critics also fretted that the developing organization concentrated power in the hands of a few organizers, rather than representing collective interests.[17]

In contrast, other Burning Man supporters, including several event organizers, viewed formal organizing as a crucial step in enabling a creative community to develop and thrive. From their perspective, underorganizing contributed to the debilitating chaos of past events, where people were too preoccupied with their survival to engage in creative activities. In fact, several interviewed members speculated that insufficient organizing indirectly contributed to accidents that killed one volunteer and severely injured others during the 1996 event. Thus, members sought to reliably produce an annual Burning Man event, especially given the increasing demands by resource providers and governmental agencies. However, most members did not want to overorganize and risk reproducing the strict, top-down control, routinization, division between active "cast members" and passive "guests," and mission fanaticism evident in venues such as Disney amusement parks.[18] Rather, as specified in the Burning Man mission, members strove to establish a community that nurtured individuals' participation and self-expression. In short, members sought conditions that enabled creative chaos without debilitating chaos and totalitarianism.

Organizing Practices

As informal, ad hoc groups formalize into organizations, their members make decisions about how to handle organizing matters, including the recruitment and retention of members and the coordination of activities with other groups such as resource providers and regulatory agencies. Table 1.1 compares two particular types of organizing practices that members might choose: bureaucratic and collectivist.[19] Traditionally, researchers categorized organizations by their use of these practices (e.g., Bordt 1997; Rothschild and Whitt 1986).[20] While previous research focused on organizations that exclusively use one type of organizing practice over another, recent research

Table 1.1 Bureaucratic vs. collectivist practices

	Bureaucratic Practices	Collectivist Practices
Allocation of tasks	Fixed division of labor	Rotating system of tasks
Form of decision making	Hierarchy of offices	By consensus, democratic decision making
Form of guidelines	Set of general rules	Flexible rules
Allocation of organizational property	Separation of personal from collective property and rights	Melded personal and collective property, personal stake in ownership
Assignment of responsibilities	Positions and promotion based on technical expertise, skills, and experience	By interest, members can learn and teach skills
Connection of members with organization	Employment as a career	Belief in the ethos or mission of the organization
Source of organizational authority	Legal-rational authority, or authority vested in position	Value-rational authority, or authority vested in collective beliefs and mission

Note: Table based on Rothschild and Whitt (1986: 62–63).

has elaborated an additional category of organizations that blend practices. Such organizations have been described and categorized as hybrid organizations (Bordt 1997), interactive organizations, postbureaucratic organizations (Heckscher 1994), organic organizations (Burns and Stalker [1961] 1994), and adhocracies (Mintzberg 1993).

While categorization helps distinguish among organizations, it has several disadvantages: it reduces organizations to static classifications, downplays members' agency, and sparks unproductive debates about whether to lump together or split apart phenomena. Researchers argue that instead of focusing on categorizing organizations into typologies, we should examine the consequences of particular organizing practices, and we should explore possibilities for minimizing noxious consequences (Coleman 1990; Jasper 2004; Martin 1990; Reinelt 1995; Staggenborg 1995). These opportunities can promote learning, innovation, and change (Clarke 2006). Therefore, this book examines under what conditions members can avoid the "undesirable externalities" or consequences of organizing practices.[21]

Bureaucratic practices

Table 1.1's middle column describes bureaucratic practices that correspond with organizing aspects listed in the left-most column. Bureaucratic practices specify expedient ways of reaching predetermined ends; these practices also uphold fair rather than particularistic treatment of individuals. A fixed division of labor allocates responsibilities among members. A hierarchy designates who is in charge and who should follow, while rules and goals help direct members' activities. Personal property and rights are separated from those of the collective. As individuals gain experience, they can ascend a career ladder, and they are assigned their positions according to their demonstrated competency or expertise. Authority is derived from one's position, rather than personal charisma or ties (Scott and Davis 2007). These specifications aim to impart certainty, impartiality, and expediency (Jackall 1988). In addition, these practices can promote innovation by increasing coordination and providing a basis for experimentation and improvisation (Adler and Borys 1996; Craig 1995; Feldman and Pentland 2003).

Most researchers categorize the majority of modern, complex, and large organizations as bureaucracies.[22] According to the German sociologist and economist Max Weber ([1946] 1958), the bureaucratic form first spread because of its superior efficiency over other organizational forms. Researchers attribute the contemporary proliferation of bureaucratic practices to two related factors: the institutionalization of bureaucracy as a widely accepted, legitimate form, and organizations' tendencies to reproduce accepted and successful forms (DiMaggio and Powell 1983; Zucker 1983). In other words, bureaucratic practices are so ingrained that they are viewed as *the* way to organize, and people have difficulties imagining alternative organizing practices. If people introduce alternative practices, other institutions, including governmental agencies and organizations that provide resources, will pressure them to adopt standard bureaucratic practices (DiMaggio and Powell 1991; Pfeffer and Salancik 1978).

Collectivist practices

To a lesser extent, people have also experimented with what are known as cooperative, collective, democratic, or collectivist practices. In particular, the 1960s–1970s countercultural movement inspired the spread of collectivist practices. These practices were often deliberately antithetical to the bureaucratic practices of dominant institutions. Rather than privileging expediency, collectivist practices focused on increasing organizational responsiveness to constituents and cultivating democratic principles of participation. Collectivist practices tried to reflect members' interests in organizing processes and collective goals, so that members could also realize personal goals (Rothschild and Whitt 1986). Otherwise, organizational maintenance issues, such as efforts to recruit members and secure resources, could override substantive goals and members' interests (Zald and Ash 1966).

Some collectivist organizations provided mental health, alternative medicine, legal services, education, and shelter services, while others produced and sold labor-intensive or skill-intensive goods like artwork, architecture, clothing, food, machinery, and software (Farrell 2001; Jackall 1984; Jackall and Crain 1984; Kanter 1972; Kleinman 1996; Martin, Knopoff, and Beckman 1998; Newman 1980; Riger 1984; Rothschild and Whitt 1986; Sager 1979; Schwartzman 1989; Swidler 1979; Taylor 1979; Thomas 1999; Wharton 1987; Whyte and Whyte 1988; Zwerdling [1978] 1980). Other groups have used collectivist practices to pursue social movement agendas, including women's rights, civil rights, AIDS activism, and global justice (Chetkovich and Kunreuther 2006; Knoke 1981; Levi and Murphy 2006; Lune 2007; Oerton 1996; Ostrander 1995; Polletta 2002; Riger 1984; Sirianni 1984). Communes, or self-sustaining groups devoted to religious or lifestyle principles, also organized with collectivist practices (Kanter 1972; Zablocki 1980).

Table 1.1's right-hand column lists collectivist practices. These practices attempt to incorporate and express members' values. In contrast with bureaucratic practices' privileging of fairness, efficiency, and stability, collectivist practices emphasize flexibility, responsiveness, and meaning.[23] Rather than motivate members with monetary incentives or career advancement, collectivist practices support guiding members' actions with normative control.[24] In other words, members are bound together and directed by their commitment to a shared mission or goals, or what Weber ([1922] 1978) termed "value-rationality."[25] Collectivist practices also empower members as co-owners, rather than just the hired hands, of their enterprises. Rather than restrict decision making to the top of a hierarchy, members participate in consensual or democratic decision making. Furthermore, collectivist practices favor looser, context-dependent specifications that enhance responsiveness to individuals' interests. Instead of being assigned to specialized roles, members can rotate responsibilities for tasks irrespective of their expertise or experience. Thus, members can develop a variety of skills and pursue their interests. In addition, flexible rules and policies govern members' activities. Members collectively interpret and modify rules as needed, rather than adhering to rules without question (Rothschild and Whitt 1986).

Whether an organization adopts bureaucratic or collectivist practices tends to coincide with particular goal orientations and legal forms.[26] For example, a business usually incorporates as a for-profit. This legal form helps members to pursue the goals of minimizing liability by protecting assets against claims or lawsuits while maximizing profits from the sale of products or services. Typically, firms rely upon bureaucratic practices to help members coordinate increasing scale and conform to organizing conventions. In contrast, a charity, or an organization expressly intended for religious, philanthropic, scientific, public safety, literary, or educational purposes, usually incorporates as a nonprofit (Brody 2006; Simon, Dale, and Chisolm 2006). Unlike the for-profit form, a nonprofit form does not allow for the redistribution of profit or loss among members (Frumkin 2002; Galaskiewicz and Bielefeld 1998). A charity's goals are also oriented toward a specified mission, such as supporting education, health care, or housing for a particular population. In running its daily operations, a charitable organization may depend upon collectivist practices, which allow members to hone skills and participate in decision making (Ostrander 1995).

Much of past research has emphasized the development of organizations that rely upon either bureaucratic or collectivist practices. However, recent research has documented how organizations are increasingly adopting both bureaucratic and collectivist practices. Based on such findings, several researchers have posited that particular practices can help address certain tasks and stages of an organization's development (Polletta 2002; Riger 1994; Schmid 2006). For instance, feminist organizations often mix bureaucratic and collectivist practices (Ashcraft 2001; Bordt 1997; Disney and Gelb 2000; Iannello 1992; Reinelt 1995; Riger 1994; Thomas 1999). The mixing of practices can increase as an organization grows and as external and internal demands for particular practices intensify (Martin 1990). In fact, among women's non-profit organizations surveyed in New York City, organizations that blended collectivist and bureaucratic practices were more numerous than organizations that relied upon either form alone (Bordt 1997).

A growing number of organizations in the for-profit and nonprofit sectors have introduced collectivist practices to promote member participation in organizing and production processes (Heller et al. 1998; Kalleberg et al. 2006).[27] Data collected from a statistically representative sample of organizations in 1996 indicated that 37 percent of for-profits and more than 60 percent of nonprofits used teams. In addition, "somewhat smaller percentages" of these organizations' teams were responsible for "deciding on tasks and methods, solving problems, or selecting leaders" (Kalleberg et al. 2006: 283). While studies have shown how such hybrid organizations have difficulties mixing bureaucratic and collectivist practices (Rothschild 2000; Vallas 2003b, 2006), these blends have demonstrated promising results for both members and their organizations (Cappelli and Neumark 2001; Zell 1997). For instance, studies have shown that in workplaces where employees are involved in work process decisions, employees are more likely to spend extra time and effort on work, and they are also more likely to experience pride in their work. Moreover, such participatory workplaces have more peaceful management-employee relations than workplaces that do not rely upon participatory practices (Hodson and Roscigno 2004). In addition, participatory practices can promote members' organizing efficacy (Lopez 2004; Warren 2001), enabling members to take charge of pursuing complex goals.

Besides combining bureaucratic and collectivist practices, organizations are blurring the boundaries between mission and profit. Even though nonprofits' primary goal is not oriented toward profit, nonprofits are focused on securing resources (Galaskiewicz and Bielefeld 1998). As governmental subsidies and grants decline, nonprofits expend more efforts on raising funds (DiMaggio 2006). Some nonprofits have turned to commercial activities to raise funds—for example, museums run gift shops; universities form alliances with firms to market discoveries (Grams 2008; Tuckman and Chang 2006). Such a focus can divert efforts away from pursuing substantive goals. These can lead to undesired changes, such as diminished member participation (Powell and Friedkin 1987). Nonprofits have also adopted practices and standards from the business sector, which can exacerbate mission drift (Rothschild and Milofsky 2006; Stone 1989).

For-profit firms now carry out activities and missions that are similar to those of nonprofit organizations (Fennell and Alexander 1993). For example, for-profits provide services that have been traditionally associated with the nonprofit sector, such as culture, education, health care, and social services

(Dees and Anderson 2004; DiMaggio 2006; Gumport and Snydman 2006; Marwell and McInerney 2005; Scott et al. 2000). Increasingly, for-profit missions emphasize environmentally responsible practices, products, and services, as evidenced by the Body Shop skin and hair care chain, the Whole Foods Market grocery, and petroleum and chemical firms (Besharov 2008; Hoffman 2001; Martin et al. 1998). For-profit missions also include social concerns, such as fair labor practices, as advertised by apparel firms' claims of "sweatshop-free" clothing. Understandably, skeptics wonder whether such activities serve as window dressing that enhances organizations' legitimacy while objectionable business practices continue behind closed doors (Forbes and Jermier 2002; Frynas 2005; Meyer and Rowan 1977; Pfeffer and Salancik 1978; Tolbert and Zucker 1983).[28] Nevertheless, it is clear that for-profits are being held accountable for responsibilities and standards beyond pursuing a profit.[29] Given the eroding distinctions among the for-profit and nonprofit forms, researchers suggest that it would be more fruitful to examine organizations' practices, rather than focus on their legal forms (Dees and Anderson 2004; Gumport and Snydman 2006).[30]

Such cross-over in practices and goal orientations raises a practical question about organizing: how can a growing organization mix practices and goal orientations without triggering under- or overorganizing extremes? As I describe in the next section, organizations risk underorganizing if they fail to set up sufficient structure and coordination. At the other extreme, organizations risk overorganizing if they wield organizing practices with coercive control.

Unsupportive Underorganizing and Repressive Overorganizing

Underorganizing can occur under two conditions: (1) if an organization lacks sufficient structures such as goals, rules, and procedures; or (2) if members' activities are not sufficiently coordinated or integrated across positions and departments.[31] Without adequate formalization and coordination, an organization does not have the capacity to act as a "tool" that enables members' efforts (Adler 1999: 38; Adler and Borys 1996).

New and expanding organizations often have difficulties establishing sufficient formalization and coordination. A lack of specified structures can embroil organizations, particularly ones that rely upon the collectivist practice of decision making by consensus, in constant, excruciating debates about appropriate goals and practices (Davidson 1983; Polletta 2002). To supplement scarce organizational resources such as labor, supplies, equipment, and workspace, members may contribute superhuman efforts and personal resources. This can foster burnout and undercapitalization, or the exploitation of individuals' labor (Swidler 1979). External pressures, such as state repression or difficulties obtaining resources, can further erode an organization's capacity to survive and produce (Rothschild and Whitt 1986). As members quit in frustration, organizations decline (Newman 1980).

Even more established and well-funded organizations struggle to sufficiently formalize and coordinate activities. For instance, the Department of Homeland Security (DHS), a federal agency responsible for domestic security in the United States, recently drew fire for its insufficient structure. A Senate committee report characterized the DHS's Science & Technology (S&T) unit as "a rudderless ship" and demanded that it produce a five-year plan and assessment standards.[32] Highly regimented organizations like the military can also suffer from underorganizing. If units are inadequately coordinated, groups may revert to their individual routines rather than working together to adapt to complex, changing circumstances. In the military, these conditions can generate "friendly fire," or maneuvers against fellow troops (Snook 2000). In the workplace, more instances of worker revolt and supervisory bullying of workers occur in underorganized workplaces than well-organized workplaces (Hodson, Roscigno, and Lopez 2006; Roscigno and Hodson 2004), suggesting that insufficient coordination and formalization can also allow abuse and mismanagement to proliferate.

On the other hand, if sufficient organizing practices are in place but are coupled with coercive control, then groups can experience overorganizing. Under these conditions, organizations are no longer accountable to members' interests; organizations instead give preference to other imperatives such as productivity or survival. Such shifts can occur when bureaucratic practices are reinforced by overzealous or excessively centralized managerial control (Adler 1999; Adler and Borys 1996; Braverman 1974; Burawoy 1979; Gouldner 1954). When coupled with such tight control, organizing practices can hinder rather than enable members' efforts. If higher-ups use rules and procedures as a "weapon" to elicit compliance from members and clients (Adler 1999: 38; Gouldner 1954; Jackall 1978) or to build personal fiefdoms (Jackall 1988), then members cannot express dissent or initiate action without risking censure by superiors (Jackall 1978). If operations are overly centralized, employees cannot share information and innovative practices across units. For example, Federal Bureau of Investigation (FBI) agents complained that information was funneled between field agencies and headquarters but not *among* field agencies (Cunningham 2004). Similarly, the National Weather Service, a governmental agency, introduced rules intended to promote consistency across its offices, but these rules constrained offices' abilities to deal with local challenges (Fine 2007). When enforced by the state, bureaucratic practices and coercive control can endanger individuals' civil liberties and well-being. Past examples include the detainment of more than 100,000 Japanese Americans by the U.S. government at internment camps during World War II (Robinson 2001) and the systematic suppression of political dissent by the FBI during the 1960s (Cunningham 2004).

If coupled with coercive control, collectivist practices can also generate overorganizing. For example, collectivist commitment to a cause can inspire extraordinary achievements, but it can also be used as peer pressure to punish individuals and suppress dissenting views. Members report being intimidated into conformity in their workplaces and voluntary associations (Barker 1993, 1999; Lalich 2004; Mansbridge 1983). If members raise questions about the use of practices, their concerns are dismissed or belittled (Kleinman 1996); individuals are ostracized and their contributions marginalized (Freeman 1973, 1976). Under these circumstances, collectivist practices do not fulfill their participatory intent. In effect, overorganizing severs an organization's accountability to members while demanding members' unquestioning compliance.

Unintended Consequences of Under- and Overorganizing

Drawbacks of underorganized bureaucratic and collectivist practices

In general, underorganizing can sap organizing activities with excessive ambiguity. Without sufficiently specified organizing structures and coordination, members lack the means to accomplish goals, much less pursue their interests (Freeman 1973). Underorganizing inflicts the undesired consequences of dissipated efforts, privileged informal relations, masked hegemony, misdirected activities, and reinforced underorganizing or triggered overorganizing.

Dissipated efforts. Without structures such as specified guidelines, goals, or a division of labor, members may dissipate efforts on endless discussions of who they are as a collective, what they want to achieve, and how to accomplish aims (Freeman 1973; Kanter 1972; Swidler 1979). Without a cohesive identity, norms, and direction, individual members may also experience anomie. These consequences can lower productivity and accelerate an organization's closure. For example, after a personnel shuffle, a student intern constantly had to ask her new superior for assignments. After several lackluster responses, the intern gave up and either slept or played games, activities that did not contribute to her hoped-for learning experience.[33] Instead of realizing that underorganizing accounts for organizational problems, individuals may blame themselves for personal shortcomings, thus overlooking possible organizational reforms (Popkin 1978). Members of the Student Nonviolent Coordinating Committee (SNCC), a college student organization that advocated the civil rights of African Americans, argued for months about how to organize and which organizing direction to take. Their indecisiveness about organizational structure, along with insufficient resources and FBI pressure, contributed to membership decline and difficulties with maintaining the organization (Polletta 2002).

Privileged informal relations. Groups, including those that depend on collectivist and bureaucratic practices, often use informal relations to recruit and acculturate newcomers and facilitate tasks such as decision making. Under such relations, members are expected to engage in emotional labor, in which they elicit or repress particular feelings when interacting with others, to further organizing and production (Hochschild 1983; Martin et al. 1998). If informal relations are overly privileged, then informal ties rather than superior qualifications can help people advance up the career ladder in ostensibly bureaucratic organizations (Dalton 1959; Jackall 1988). While members welcome social contact (Hodson 2001), they may use informal relations to gloss over problems and inequities among members. This can reduce organizational accountability to members unless someone protests. For instance, one member of an alternative health organization refused to initiate a solidarity-building ritual, a meditative circle formed by linking hands, with the critique, "It's a nicey-nicey way to hide conflict" (Kleinman 1996: 71).

Informal relations can also generate cliques that exacerbate inequalities (Pearce 1993; Polletta 2002; Sirianni 1984). If newcomers have difficulties joining established cliques, they will not be able to participate in decision-making matters (Freeman 1973; Graham 1995; Polletta 2002). Members also avoid participating in decision making because they are conflict-adverse, or they fear appearing uncooperative if they voice dissenting views, or they feel less skilled in public speaking (Hernandez 2006; Polletta 2002; Sirianni 1984). As a result, those elected to leadership positions may not be the most technically competent, but have the strongest friendship ties and charisma (Hernandez 2006). Practices meant to facilitate participation may thus unintentionally curtail member involvement.

Masked hegemony. Unclear decision-making policies and diffuse accountability can mask control by a few or allow abuses to proliferate (Freeman 1973). In the absence of formal authority, members must tap personal charisma to advance their efforts, which can hasten member burnout (Swidler 1979; Vallas 2003a, 2003b). Articulate, aggressive, or well-connected individuals and subgroups can dominate proceedings and thus alienate other members (Freeman 1973; Leidner 1991; Mansbridge 1983). Worse, without set goals and procedures, members may turn to controlling each other. For example, members of feminist groups disparaged individuals as not being sufficiently feminist because their class, occupation, marital status, personality, or sexual identity differed from ideals (Freeman 1973).

Misdirected activities. Without specified structures, members expend efforts on navigating disorganization rather than fulfilling goals (Hackman 2002). In particular, without guidelines on how to propose ideas and reach agreement in decision making, members risk continual misunderstandings. Ambiguous decisions can fuel counterproductive efforts, as members may act on incorrect interpretations of decisions (Jones and Schneider 1984), forcing members to revisit issues. In generating consensus, members may resort to lowest-common-denominator, suboptimal decisions (Freeman 1973; Greenwood and Santos 1991; Jones and Schneider 1984; Mansbridge 1983; Rothschild and Whitt 1986; Schwartzman 1989). Furthermore, without procedures about how to express dissenting views, individuals lack full say in matters (Freeman 1973), unless they have personal connections or exceptional communication and influence skills. At the Body Shop, a manager complained about having to use showmanship to advocate proposals: "You don't just make a proposal. You have to pitch it—be emotional and argue it. There aren't clear channels and structure" (Martin et al. 1998: 450). Alternatively, members may capitalize on disorganization for their own ends. For example, as a firm underwent a merger, managerial direction diminished, and employees indulged in long, business-expensed lunches and nonwork activities.[34]

Reinforced underorganizing or triggered overorganizing. If members view particular practices as central to their organization, they may resist change, even if proposed changes could redress underorganizing. For instance, some members may reject introducing certain practices, such as rules or a division of labor, as ideologically inconsistent with their beliefs and founding practices (Borland 2005; Clemens 1993; Deckard 1979). Or, they may resist fine-tuning existing practices. By not addressing underorganizing, members can undercut goals and hasten organizational closure (Freeman 1973; Polletta 2002). For example, when deciding on how to expand, members may eschew new practices as incompatible with founding principles of participation. For the People Express airline, this refusal to change practices hastened the company's demise (Hackman 2002). In such situations, the organization would have benefited from flexibility in implementing new practices, rather than preserving existing practices as defining features (Weick 1996).

On the other hand, underorganizing can inadvertently trigger overorganizing. For example, most research (e.g., Rothschild and Whitt 1986) has suggested that growing organizations, including those with collectivist practices, will formalize as they encounter underorganizing problems. This conversion process could lead to complete bureaucratization, such that few or no collectivist practices remain (Kanter 1972; Milofsky 1988; Newman 1980; Oerton 1996; Rothschild and Whitt 1986). Such changes can displace goals and reduce accountability to members' interests (Matthews 1994).

Drawbacks of overorganized bureaucratic and collectivist practices

To maintain an organization and its production, members may tighten controls over organizing and work processes. However, this can introduce undesired consequences, crushing activities with too much structure and coordination. When wielded coercively, bureaucratic and collectivist practices can deplete meaning; ignore, suppress, or co-opt informal relations; conceal hegemony; stifle performance; and intensify overorganizing.

Depleted meaning. Bureaucratic practices can serve as enabling tools for reaching desired goals (Adler 1999; Adler and Borys 1996). But when backed by coercive control, bureaucratic practices can become ends in themselves. This inversion of the means and ends can trigger an "inexorable iron cage" of escalating routines and rules; organizational members follow and enforce bureaucratic practices without considering their applicability to the circumstances. For some, this increasing rationalization robs participation of desired meaning, "magic," and "enchantment" (Weber [1946] 1958). As escalating rules and routines restrict their autonomy, members undergo stress, boredom, depression, and anger against their organizations, coworkers, supervisors, and clients (Burawoy 1979; Ehrenreich 2001; Hamper 1991; Jackall 1978; Leidner 1993; Raz 1999; Roy 1959). To ease the drudgery of routines and tyrannical authority, workers seek meaning through improvised games, rituals, and interactions. For instance, Disney amusement park employees developed games that punished difficult customers by lurching rides to a jerking halt or crunching stray limbs with doors (Van Maanen 1991). Administrative workers spread gossip that could make or break their supervisors' careers (Ogasawara 1998; Shulman 2007). While such acts demonstrate individual inventiveness and agency (Hodson 2001), they afford limited subversive relief, as individuals continue to comply, for the most part, with top-down directives (Scott 1990; Van Maanen 1991).

Like bureaucratic practices, collectivist practices can build enabling structures—in this case, a sense of meaning—by creating solidarity among members. These practices contribute to a substantive rationality, or collectively held values that are "morally binding" (Barker 1999: 74). However, when administered with coercive control, substantive rationality can override individuals' interests (Barker 1999) and dissipate meaning. To control production, members may engage in excessive formalization such as rule making (Barker 1993, 1999) and peer surveillance (Sewell 1998). These measures foster ill will, as members resent those who do not uphold norms. Workers also report experiencing more stress from peer and internalized pressure than they did under bureaucratic control, when only managers supervised their efforts (Barker 1993, 1999; Graham 1995; Mumby and Stohl 1991; Sewell 1998).

Ignored, suppressed, or co-opted informal relations. The hierarchy, rules, and roles of bureaucratic practices can overlook or suppress informal relations, or relationships that are not based on formal positions (DiMaggio 2001; Heckscher 1994). However, authority based on one's formal position may not be enough to elicit cooperation. In such cases, a skilled manager curries favor with solicitous inquiries, gifts, and lunches with subordinates (Ogasawara 1998). Other managers squelch informal relations to maintain control, as evidenced by Wal-Mart management's chastising of employees for committing "time theft" by chatting with coworkers while on shift (Ehrenreich 2001: 181).

Some organizations, particularly those that rely upon collectivist practices or corporate culture, attempt to enhance control and productivity by building member commitment through informal relations and common values. However, practices intended to promote group cohesion can also trigger resistance and cynicism from those who resent such overt manipulation (Biggart 1989; Graham 1995; Kunda 1992; Weeks 2004). In addition, participatory practices such as teamwork can form the basis for worker solidarity against managers (Vallas 2006; Videla 2006). Moreover, informal group norms may encourage employees to violate rules, generating undesired consequences (Hodson 2001). For instance, group norms encourage police officers to exert excessive force against civilians. Officers who deviate from these norms are shunned by their coworkers and may not receive sufficient support to carry out their responsibilities (Hunt 1985).

Concealed hegemony. Seemingly impartial bureaucratic structures can conceal hegemony, or the domination of the majority by a few. Given the taken-for-granted nature of hierarchy and rules, leaders can consolidate and legitimize power with little resistance (Perrow 1986). Using their power and access to resources, leaders can direct organizing activities toward personal rather than collective interests (Michels [1915] 1962) and punish those who do not support their agendas (Jackall 1988). For example, a Hewlett-Packard (HP) board member reportedly suggested his novel as required reading for employees and offered to sign his books in the corporate cafeteria; he later allegedly scolded the HP chairperson for not extolling the quality of his book before other managers (Stewart 2007).

Hegemony can also arise at the group level, especially when members face external pressures from competitors or regulatory agencies. Internal demands for conformity can induce groupthink. Rather than assess available information and options, members engage in decision-making processes that affirm group cohesiveness and suppress dissent (Janis 1982). Such group hegemony can contribute to undesired outcomes that reduce accountability and performance (Heller 1998). For example, by ignoring individuals' repeated warnings about safety, NASA normalized deviance that led to the disastrous launch of the *Challenger* space shuttle (Vaughn 1996).

Like bureaucratic practices, collectivist practices can tighten the "iron cage" of control as individuals internalize norms that serve organizational interests but neglect individuals' interests (Barker 1993, 1999; Foucault 1995; Graham 1995; Sewell 1998). Such effects are particularly apparent when members use collectivist practices, such as commitment to an ethic or mission, to avoid acknowledging inequalities among members (Darr 1999; Kleinman 1996; Vallas 2006). Or, members use collectivist practices to censure others for not sufficiently adhering to the collective's espoused ideology or norms (Freeman 1973, 1976; Jackall and Crain 1984). Such activities can increase a group's cohesiveness and identity (Dentler and Erikson 1959). However, the systematic suppression of individuals' interests can lead to destructive outcomes. At an extreme, mass murder and mass suicide have been committed by religious groups such as Peoples Temple, the Branch Davidians, and Heaven's Gate (Hall et al. 2000; Lalich 2004) and extremist groups (Stern 2003).

Stifled performance. By circumscribing members' activities, overorganized structures can stifle performance. When combined with coercive control, such rules, procedures, and roles demoralize members and curtail possible improvements to performance and experiences (Heckscher 1994; Perrow 1986). These issues are most apparent in organizations with such strict top-down authority that front-line members have little control over their work. For example, at a manufacturing plant that endorsed participatory practices, line workers could not make changes to the machinery without managerial authorization. If workers fixed problems without that consent, they could be censured for new problems, even if these were unrelated to their fixes (Vallas 2006). In other workplaces, when members openly addressed performance issues, their articulated concerns and suggestions were ignored, repressed, and even punished (Rothschild and Miethe 1999).

Members can also subvert performance using organizing practices. For example, members fixate on enforcing rules without considering their relevance, as demonstrated by the Burning Man employee and the Internet phone incident. While rules can benefit the collective—for instance, by increasing work safety (Gouldner 1954)—in other cases, they can undercut collective interests (Crozier 1964; Weber [1946] 1958). For example, citing other work responsibilities, employees in a large Japanese bank overlooked requests for their assistance and thus slowed organizational performance (Ogasawara 1998). Concerns about ensuring that practices are carried out may, ironically, displace the intent of practices. When collecting information needed for decision making by consensus, workers may resort to informal, behind-the-scenes communication with undisclosed sources. By failing to maintain transparent exchanges, members "violate the principles of the participatory process to ensure the survival or maintenance of the participatory system" (Stohl and Cheney 2001: 363).

Intensified overorganizing. If organizations do not update rules to incorporate changing circumstances or relevant know-how, rules can overproliferate, and members have to break these rules to do their work. For instance, line workers may disregard protocols that were designed by those without applicable front-line experience (Adler 1992). Rule making can trigger even more overorganizing when members formulate rules to address every possible scenario (Barker 1993, 1999). Escalating rules can spark continual disagreement among members about how to carry out organizing activities, introducing more rules and regulations (Burns and Stalker [1961] 1994; Crozier 1964). The desire to establish control can induce panoptic surveillance, ranging from intrusive, hovering supervisors (Perlow 1998) to charts and other visual flags that broadcast individual transgressions for all to see (Barker 1999; Sewell 1998).

Blending Practices to Avoid Under- and Overorganizing Extremes

These undesired consequences highlight the salience of understanding how organizations can more effectively use bureaucratic and collectivist practices. The growing number of organizations that blend collectivist and bureaucratic practices further underscores the importance of conducting empirical research, especially since comparatively less research has examined such organizations (Bordt 1997). As a revelatory case, the Burning Man organization allows us to closely examine how members mixed a legal form, goal orientations, and two types of practices while coping with challenges posed by growth and external groups. As the next chapter recounts, Burning Man organizers decided to incorporate as a for-profit form. However, their primary goal was forming an arts community, rather than making money. Over time, the growing organization also mixed collectivist and bureaucratic practices. When addressing practical concerns, such as how to accomplish tasks, Burning Man members relied upon bureaucratic practices that enhanced fairness, efficiency, and stability. Yet they also endorsed collectivist practices that supported flexibility, responsiveness, and meaning.

At times, members had to contend with countervailing expectations about appropriate ways of organizing—should they adopt a bureaucratic practice, a collectivist practice, or some mixture of the two? By assessing the possible consequences of practices, members can anticipate how an organization might change with a particular practice. Some changes can invoke under- or overorganizing, as depicted in table 1.2.[35] Without adequately specified organizing structures and coordination, underorganized collectives may ex-

Table 1.2 Outcomes associated with underorganized, moderately organized, and over-organized bureaucratic and collectivist practices

		Bureaucratic		
		Underorganized	Moderately organized	Overorganized
Collectivist	Underorganized	Disabling chaos	Bureaucracy	Oligarchy
	Moderately organized	Collectivist organization	Enabling organization	Disempowered teams
	Overorganized	Culty collective	Feel-good collective	Totalitarianism

perience such *disabling chaos* that they cannot produce, much less effectively organize. Such groups may decide to either shut down, or they may formalize. Groups that adopt only collectivist practices, that is, *collectivist organizations* (e.g., Rothschild and Whitt 1986), may become overorganized, generating a *culty collective* that subsumes individuals' interests to the collective "good." Some voluntary associations have demanded such unquestioning obedience from members (Freeman 1973; Lalich 2004). If groups introduce only bureau-cratic practices, they develop into a *bureaucracy* (Weber [1946] 1958). However, if these bureaucratic practices become overorganized, they can introduce rule by a few, or *oligarchy*. With their expertise and control over organizational resources, leaders can subvert organizing efforts for their own ends, thus overriding collective interests (Jackall 1988; Michels [1915] 1962).

Organizations that blend bureaucratic and collectivist practices can also experience the negative consequences of overorganizing. The bureaucratic practices of hierarchical authority or a division of labor mixed with coer-cively applied collectivist practices can reinforce problems such as structural inequalities among members (e.g., Kleinman 1996). Members thus create a *feel-good collective* that avoids addressing issues. If coercively controlled bu-reaucratic practices blend with collectivist practices, *disempowered teams* can result. Members cannot carry out participatory practices, much less effectively produce, because bureaucratic practices restrict decision-making authority and other responsibilities to management (e.g., Vallas 2006).

When coercive control mixes with both bureaucratic and collectivist practices, *totalitarianism* may result. Members are expected to carry out or-ganizational imperatives, yet members do not have the means to demand organizational accountability to their interests. Such extreme outcomes are manifested in members' complaints about excessive top-down organizational control within a therapeutic counseling community (Strand 2007) and truncated career mobility and exploitation in workplaces and progressive social movement organizations (Boltanski and Chiapello 2005; Fisher 2006). These characteristics are also evident in despotic nations where a bureaucratic apparatus reinforces the authority of those in power and demands unquestioning obedience from citizens.

These outcomes indicate the difficulties of finding the "sweet spot" in combining bureaucratic and collectivist practices. If members can sufficiently specify collectivist and bureaucratic practices but avoid exercising coercive control, they may be able to form an *enabling organization*.[36] Using the development of the Burning Man organization, I show how bureaucratic and collectivist practices can help a growing organization mediate between under- and overorganizing in order to develop an enabling organization. Bureaucratic and collectivist practices not only help compensate for each other's weaknesses, but also reinforce each other's strengths. In short, *bureaucratic practices afford fairness, efficiency, and stability; collectivist practices allow for flexibility, responsiveness, and meaning.*

By making the implicit explicit, formalized bureaucratic and collectivist practices can stave off the undesired extremes of underorganizing. Continual discussions of how to organize with both of these practices can help keep organizations accountable and responsive to members' interests and organizational goals, thus warding off overorganizing. Such discussions not only help members understand organizational actions, but also further develop their communication skills and commitment, thus aiding goal attainment (Freeman 1973; Milofsky 1988; Polletta 2002; Viggiani 1997).

While the Burning Man organization may be considered an unusual or extreme case because it produces a temporary arts community, it shares similar developmental challenges with other organizations. Burning Man members' discussions provide insight into organizing processes that are either taken for granted or repressed in conventional organizations. By examining the conversations and debates that fuel organizing decisions, we can understand how organizations are created (Jasper 2004; Suddaby and Greenwood 2005). That is, we see how an organization develops through interactions among members and with other groups. Understanding how these interactions shape and are shaped by organizations is particularly important as organizations dominate society with more power and rights than an individual person (Coleman 1990).[37] At the same time, understanding how organizations can adopt collectivist practices is increasingly relevant as individuals demand more say in running their organizations (Freeman and Rogers [1999] 2006; Zell 1997).[38]

In addition, this study shows how individuals can cooperatively act in a society that has been criticized as disintegrating into isolated and passive individuals.[39] By organizing together, individuals form and sustain ties with others.

Such ties circulate information, cultivate trust and reciprocal relationships, and develop a larger collective identity beyond individual self-interest—what social scientists call "social capital" (Putnam 2000). Since organizations help individuals coordinate such collective action (Marwell 2004, 2007; Sampson et al. 2005; Scott and Davis 2007), we need to know how organizations can simultaneously develop and promote—rather than suppress or ignore—their members' interests (Cloward and Piven 1984). This would help us design organizations that can achieve both collective and individual ends, rather than privileging one end at the expense of another. By examining these organizing issues, this book helps us reimagine organizations and their place in everyday life.

Context

The Development of the Burning Man Event
and Organization

AT THE CORNER of Third and 16th streets, a gentrifying industrial stretch of the San Francisco waterfront, individuals converge upon the Burning Man headquarters to prepare for the annual Burning Man event. Inside a converted warehouse, posted maps depict the upcoming site for Black Rock City, a horseshoe-shaped series of streets curved toward the signature sculpture of the Man. Displayed artwork, such as oversized photos and hand-painted props, immortalize art projects from previous events. The scattered furnishings demonstrate creative reuse of scavenged materials: a tall vitrine that once hawked watches now displays Burning Man memorabilia; a squat flat file intended for architectural drawings stores art proposals; a dining table supported by a stack of buckets hosts volunteers' meetings.

Amidst these reminders of the past and plans for the future, Burning Man members work in offices, conference rooms, and a common area dubbed the "Zocaló."[1] In one office, administrative staff process ticket orders mailed in hand-decorated envelopes from around the world. As they sort the mail, they answer phone inquiries about the ticket sales that fuel the organization's approximately $10 million budget. In a nearby room strewn with hardware, information technology (IT) specialists ensure that the server and intranet are up and running. They manage the graphics, content, and Web cam for the www.burningman.com Web site, which received almost eight million hits and entries per month during 2005.[2] In another room, human resources administrators gather information on affordable health benefits for the small staff.

While these activities sustain the Burning Man organization, other activities contribute to the Burning Man mission of supporting art and community. In one room, the art curator examines proposals and meets with artists about their progress on large-scale installations and performances.[3] In another area, a volunteer categorizes items for the organizational archives, while an artist, a prominent figure in the San Francisco art scene, finalizes plans for a local event. In an adjoining conference room, the head organizers, who are known as the senior staff, meet to discuss their budget; recruitment and management of members; relations with the media, governmental agencies, and interest groups; and other issues. The limited liability company's (LLC) board members, whose ranks include some senior staff members, also assemble here to decide financial, staffing, and policy matters.

Unlike in other offices, activity at the Burning Man headquarters does not slow down in the evenings or on the weekends. Instead, the pace quickens as local volunteers gather for meetings, orientations, and workshops. These individuals, part of an estimated two-thousand-volunteer force, and the small full- and part-time staff carry out a mission of fostering creative community. A mission statement for 2000 and 2001 articulates their aims:

> Our practical goal is to create the annual event known as Burning Man. Our purpose . . . is to generate an experience that encourages participants to do three things: (1) creatively express themselves, (2) fulfill an active role as members of our community, and (3) immediately respond to and protect that environment.

Members help create the conditions that enable over 47,000 individuals to gather at the Nevada Black Rock Desert, some 325 miles away from the Burning Man headquarters. Their year-round efforts help "create a unique environment which focuses on creativity, art and freedom of expression."[4]

The Burning Man organization has not always operated under these conditions. During the two previous decades, members dealt with insufficient organizing structures, staffing, and resources, as well as pressures from interest groups and regulatory agencies to end the event.[5]

Minimal Organizing: 1986-1990

The first Burning Man event, held in 1986, arose from rather modest origins. Friends Larry Harvey, an underemployed landscaper, and Jerry James, a carpenter, built an eight-foot-tall figure out of scrap wood. They then transported and burned the unnamed figure on San Francisco's Baker Beach, where a gathering of twenty friends and family had assembled. According to media accounts, the event started as an exorcism of an ended romance. Organizers' accounts claimed that the event continued a tradition of summer solstice festivities that were hosted by fellow San Francisco denizen Mary Grauberger.[6]

In the earliest years, the event was so small and informal that it did not require a formal organization, nor did it have a formal name.[7] According to one founder, the first event's gathering was like a family barbecue or picnic. The organizers' young children built and burned their own sculpture of a dog next to the wooden figure of a person.[8] The latter sculpture, albeit in a larger-scale form, anchored subsequent annual events on the beach. Word-of-mouth and announcements in local newsletters, mainly those distributed by the underground group Cacophony Society,[9] attracted over three hundred attendees by 1989.[10] The growing event also drew local media coverage and the local art community's involvement.

Not everyone appreciated the event's increasing popularity. Video footage of a confrontation between a law enforcement officer and an attendee foreshadowed the event's bumpy relationship with authorities:

OFFICER: You must be in charge of [the bonfire], right? Let me see some sort
    of identification. What kind of group is this?
ATTENDEE: I'm just playing my drum.
OFFICER [*speaks sarcastically*]: You have nothing to do with the fire. Do you
    think I was born yesterday or this morning? Get out your driver license.
    Do you want to talk to me about this? About the whole deal, yeah?
ATTENDEE: I just heard it was a party called Summer Solstice.
OFFICER: So you guys brought out your drums. You guys are just hanging out.
    I told you to put your drum down.
ATTENDEE: Oh sorry, I'm just playing my drum on the beach, I'm not hurting
    anyone.[11]

The Start of Formal Organizing: 1990–1995

Governmental officials finally caught up with the event in 1990; their intervention catalyzed the event's transformation and relocation. Citing safety concerns about burning large items on the beach, a Golden Gate National Recreation Area ranger stopped organizers from igniting the event's signature sculpture. Organizers negotiated with officials to allow the eight hundred disappointed revelers to enjoy the forty-foot sculpture without the bonfire.

To avoid disputes with authorities, a few attendees suggested relocating the event to the isolated Nevada Black Rock Desert, where they had previously participated in small events like a 1989 wind sculpture festival.[12]

With the event's move to Nevada, the summer solstice beach bonfire transformed into a Labor Day weekend desert camping trip. *Rough Draft,* the Cacophony Society's newsletter, billed the September 1–3, 1990, event as "Zone Trip #4—Ascent into the Black Rock Desert."[13] At the event, participants joined hands and stepped over a line drawn in the desert's surface, signifying their collective entry into another zone of experience.[14] With this ceremonial crossing, ninety members ushered in a new era, one that significantly expanded the span and scope of organizing behind the event.[15]

By this point, experienced underground event organizers John Law and Michael Mikel had joined the organizing team.[16] These organizers strategically placed the 1990 event in an area that they predicted would be difficult for local authorities to monitor. Nevertheless, a concerned local called the authorities to report that Satan-worshippers from San Francisco had descended upon the desert. An officer from the Bureau of Land Management (BLM), a federal agency responsible for managing some 264 million acres, including the Black Rock Desert, subsequently visited the campers. After a guided tour of the event site, the BLM officer left satisfied that the ninety attendees seemed relatively harmless. This visit initiated the event's first sustained relationship with a governmental agency. From 1991 onward, the BLM required that the Burning Man organizers apply for special recreation permits. The BLM also demanded that organizers purchase insurance for the event, submit a plan of operations, and pass a postevent cleanup inspection.[17] Such requirements, when coupled with disagreements with officials about how to run the event, intensified organizing efforts.

The event's relocation to a remote site in another state posed other organizing challenges. Organizer John Law had made some event preparations, such as renting a portable toilet and circulating a detailed map and directions to the difficult-to-find site.[18] Nonetheless, attendees of the first Black Rock Desert events arrived unprepared for the rigors of desert camping. Mikel recalled how campers rested under their cars to evade the harsh sun until nightfall, when temperatures became bearable:

> We didn't know anything about the environment. . . . By the time the sun came up at 10 or 11 o'clock in the morning, it was so hot that you couldn't stay in the tent. . . . So during the hottest part of the days, we all crawled under our cars like lizards; we were . . . lying down underneath the cars to stay cool. But in the evening, it was really wonderful. We'd have our party, and there wasn't a lot going on particularly at that time, there was no theme camps, no real organiza-

tion, just hanging out and drinking because we had nothing to do, and partying in the evening, and we had set up the Man, and the last evening of the weekend, we burned it [the Man].[19]

As attendees gained experience, they organized efforts to enhance their own and others' enjoyment of the event. In 1991, organizers produced the *Survival Guide* to assist the two hundred fifty event attendees' preparations for camping in the desert. In 1992, Mikel formed the Black Rock Rangers, a volunteer group modeled on the Texas Rangers. The Rangers assisted with search-and-rescue missions for attendees lost in the desert. In 1993, Mikel initiated the *Black Rock Gazette,* the official newspaper of articles about event activities, tips, and humor composed and distributed during the event.[20]

By 1992, organizers were publicizing the event as the Black Rock Arts Festival, elevating the gathering's legitimacy beyond its bonfire origins. The event's population broke the one-thousand mark by 1993. Attendees started the first on-site radio station, and a few brought art cars, or vehicles that they had decorated according to a motif. Several people, including Jerry James and Peter Doty, also introduced theme camps, or collectively organized camps with activities that invited interaction with passers-by.[21] Former public relations manager Naomi Pearce described how Peter Doty dressed up as Santa and dispensed eggnog and fruitcake as holiday carols played endlessly at his Christmas Camp, inspiring others to reimagine elements of everyday life:

> You've got to give the man [Doty] some serious credit for wearing a Santa suit in the middle of the desert at the end of August. . . . Pretty soon you've got people using stuff that's familiar to them, like the armed disgruntled postal workers were actually armed disgruntled postal workers, so they had the uniforms already. . . . They happened to be people that had guns, and [disgruntled postal workers] was a big joke at the time in society, and so they . . . created the theme camp based on what they knew already.[22]

Theme camps helped orient the activities of the growing numbers of attendees.[23]

The organization behind the event also started to solidify, but its operations were limited. Organizers waited until the month before the event to start planning. Lacking a headquarters, they met in the apartment of P. Segal and other members to discuss matters.[24] Nevertheless, media like the *New York Times Magazine* commented with surprise, "The festival is anarchy so well organized that there are registration forms, a media contact and a press kit."[25] In 1994, the organization unveiled an official Web page on the WELL, a community site predating the World Wide Web and commercial online services.[26] With this new forum for communication, attendees coordinated efforts and cemented friendships via e-mail discussion lists.

In 1995, the Burning Man event took on an additional identity as Black Rock City. John Law, Michael Mikel, and Larry Harvey formed a legal partnership, in which the partners assumed liability for the event of four thousand persons. The partners also recruited their friends Dana Albany, Harley Dubois (then Bierman), Joegh Bullock, Vanessa Kuemmerle, Dan Miller, Stuart Mangrum, and Crimson Rose, to assume responsibilities as the senior staff.[27] This constituted the group's first self-described "division of labor."[28] Even with these formalized structures, the organization still operated like a group of friends.[29] Although most of the organizers lacked extensive business or conventional organizing experience,[30] their aspirations and persistence shepherded the event through expansive growth.

Rectifying Underorganizing: 1996-1997

Most organizers and attendees marked 1996 and 1997 as pivotal years in the development of the event and organization. Ironically, the 1996 event featured Dante's *Inferno,* or Hell, as its theme. To some, the "scary" and "edgy"[31] atmosphere indicated that the event had tipped too far over into disorder and chaos. Since people could camp wherever they wanted, they scattered their camps throughout the site. Some individuals drove their cars at high speeds between encampments, risking accidents with pedestrians, camps, and other vehicles. Just before the event's official start, a motorcycle-truck accident killed one worker. Shortly before the event's end, an under-the-influence driver crashed his car into a few tents and severely injured several campers.[32] Looking back, several interviewees expressed surprise that the event did not have even more serious accidents.[33] Cofounder Jerry James claimed that "people were rioting more or less, it was like a muted riot. . . . it was really exhilarating but very dangerous."[34]

The unanticipated population growth to eight thousand attendees overwhelmed the 1996 event's infrastructure. With hindsight, John Law realized that organizing efforts suffered from insufficient experience, manpower, and funds: "We should have had twice to three times as many people [helping] in there, but we didn't have the money . . . for the infrastructure, and we really weren't professionals."[35] Jennifer Holmes, who was the volunteer liaison with the contracted emergency services personnel, explained that the population growth and medical emergencies outstripped preparations: "We weren't expecting that ten thousand people would show up, and we weren't expecting that we would have all of these really bad accidents."[36] Likewise, local agencies argued that the event drained their limited resources. A 1996 *Los Angeles*

Times article quoted Pershing County sheriff Ron Skinner's view: "I think there's a general consensus . . . that the Burning Man Festival has outgrown itself. My whole entire staff is just totally burned out from the last five days. We're a small department that serves 4,700 to 5,000 people, and we're just not equipped to handle 10,000 party-goers."[37]

Organizers wondered whether authorities and locals would continue to tolerate the event, given its reputation of conflagrations, explosions, guns, reckless driving, and substance abuse.[38] Media coverage of the event's activities drew unfavorable attention. Christian fundamentalists, for example, seized upon the 1996 event's art performances and images of attendees cavorting about as devils as evidence that Burning Man encouraged paganism and immorality. More importantly, governmental agencies increased their jurisdictions over the event, forcing organizers to comply with additional regulations and higher fees. For instance, the BLM asked the state, district, and county health agencies to oversee the event's toilets and sanitation in 1996.[39]

At meetings during and following the 1996 event, organizers and members bitterly argued over how to cope with these issues. Organizer Crimson Rose remembered that "'96 was sort of the year when things divided—we were either going to implode totally, and Burning Man was going to die, or it had to go to the next level."[40] Organizers rowed over whether the event should continue and, if so, how much it should grow.[41] John Law opined that the event had run its course and should cease: "I was convinced in '96 [that] the event couldn't continue."[42] Like-minded members argued that continuing the event endangered lives in a selfish exercise of "ego."[43] A less extreme group suggested that the event continue, but with attendance limited to selected individuals. Others argued that the structurelessness of the 1996 event called for more formal organizing, rather than an end or restriction to the event. This faction, led by Larry Harvey, believed that the event should not only persist, but also accommodate significant population growth.[44]

Harvey's faction prevailed in continuing and expanding the event, but at the cost of an irrevocable rift among organizers. John Law's departure dissolved the three-person partnership. In 1997, the remaining organizers incorporated as a limited liability company, a for-profit form.[45] To continue running the event, organizers realized that they needed to rectify underorganizing. In a memo circulated among the organizers, Naomi Pearce recommended that the organizers consider getting professional help as other growing events had done:

> This "project" has never been run professionally[,] and it's getting to the size where the lack of organization is starting to really get annoying. . . . It's time to seriously consider going pro. . . . It's time to "sell or partner." . . . In other

words, "when the going gets weird, the weird turn Pro." . . . It is possible to be professionally savvy, and still be as "radical" or weird or whatever ([like] the Grateful Dead). Business doesn't *have* to mean Helco.[46]

Pearce emphasized that with formal organization, the event would not lose its distinctive nature or be derailed by corporate interests, as satirized by the thwarted takeover of the 1996 Burning Man event by Satan and his "Helco" corporation.[47]

Rather than relinquishing operations to professionals, organizers revamped organizing efforts themselves. To recruit prospective volunteers, the organization unveiled a Web site that facilitated user navigation and contact with the organization.[48] Organizers also overhauled the 1997 event, with the aim of facilitating creativity while curbing the chaos of previous events. The redesigned, pedestrianized city could accommodate up to ten thousand occupants on its preset grid and labeled streets. In addition, theme camps could coordinate to form a village, a new concept. A village could build an internal infrastructure, such as a community entrance, and determine village-wide policies, such as whether they would allow media coverage. Organizers also upgraded medical and communication services and prohibited guns, vending, and driving.[49]

Most importantly, organizers redirected the event away from the anarchist activities and ideology that were popular with some eventgoers. To civilize the wild "frontier," organizers placed greater responsibilities upon individuals and the community. In a somewhat facetious description, Michael Mikel commented on how eventgoers could no longer do as they pleased, although they still had certain freedoms:

> In the early days, people used to take drugs, drop acid, drive . . . at 90 miles per hour in their car with their headlights off while they were drinking wine and shooting guns out the window [laugh], and we just can't do that anymore. At the time, it was open frontier. It was freedom basically, but as we've become a community, there now is a responsibility to other members in the community. There are limits to what you can do, and we've made changes, but [there's] still a tremendous amount of tolerance for nudity and acceptance for individuals to do what they want with their bod[ies].[50]

Mikel noted that oversight by authorities and the norms of surrounding local communities still created tensions about the event's activities:

> Many of the communities around there and local authorities and law enforcement are used to small community . . . and we come up and set up a global

community where our standards are different, and there is a tremendous amount of conflict and disagreement [between us and them], and there's always this push to impose their standards, their style of morality, and their laws on our community.[51]

Clashes over values threatened the Burning Man event's future. For the first time, the organization faced concentrated opposition from organized interest groups. Public Research Associates, an environmental lobbying group, pressed for ways to bar the Burning Man event from using the Black Rock Desert.[52] This group sought an environment impact statement on the event site; the expenses of this assessment would have been charged to the Burning Man organization.[53] Citing a lack of resources and the Burning Man event's incompatibility with "the values of Pershing County citizens," sheriff Ron Skinner also advised county commissioners to formally request that the BLM not reissue the permit for 1997.[54]

Prompted by these roadblocks to the permit process, organizers moved the 1997 event from the BLM-managed land in Pershing County to private land in Washoe County. Although this move circumvented previous problematic relations, the Burning Man organization had to contend with two new actors: Washoe County officials and private land managers. Harvey lamented how organizers spent their efforts negotiating with new actors instead of supporting artists' projects:

> In '97, if you broadly define political, I'd say two-thirds of my time was taken by that, it was long, long hours. . . . That's why in that year we had no proper art team—there was no time. We couldn't be bothered with art, to hell with art, it's politics, and I felt like I had landed into wilderness [*laugh*] in the name of self-expression, how did I end up doing this crap?!![55]

Washoe County officials made several demands, including that local contractors provide services like fire protection. They also imposed regulations that organizers argued were financially unreasonable and inapplicable to an event located in the desert. Organizer Mikel recounted their efforts to navigate these regulations:

> They [Washoe County officials] assumed that we were like some other festival or fair, so they immediately produced their 270-page book of instructions and regulations . . . which were all designed for a fair taking place in Reno on asphalt. So many of the things that were in there were somewhat ridiculous, like having striped parking lot telephones every 500 yards [and] flush water toilets.[56]

In addition, Washoe County conducted criminal checks on the organizers' backgrounds, actions that organizers viewed as personal insults. Furthermore, county officials asked that the organization pay fees up front, a financial hardship, given that most tickets were purchased at the event. Organizers viewed these actions as a thinly veiled attempt to regulate the event to death, or at least out of the bounds of Washoe County.[57]

Relationships with private land managers about access to the event site involved similar frustrations. Negotiations about the rental fee extended to a nerve-wracking twenty-four hours before the event's start. Even after reaching an agreement, land manager Annie Westerbeke sued the organization for more money.[58] These protracted negotiations and delays in the permit process by the BLM contributed to uncertainty about whether the event would take place. Organizers worried that these delays discouraged would-be eventgoers from buying tickets and attending. Fearing that the hefty agency fees would not be paid because of the lower than anticipated attendance, Washoe County ordered its sheriffs to confiscate ticket proceeds from the admissions gate.

These issues saddled the already financially strapped organization with a $200,000 debt.[59] Organizers canvassed event attendees, who had already paid the admission fee, to help defray these unanticipated costs with donations. Harvey recalled how attendees donated about $50,000 in response to organizers' pleas:

> At the event, we asked people to give money as they went out of the Gate, [and] we prayed that the police wouldn't take that money. [The attendees] gave us quite a lot . . . which is a tribute to what Burning Man meant to them because I can't think of any commercial event where the people would do that, if the producers said, "we're broke, help us out." . . . I don't think the participants have ever felt so close to us as they did that year.[60]

Several individuals hosted benefit events in their local communities that raised an additional $35,000 toward alleviating the organization's debt. Washoe County officials also eventually refunded $45,000, a portion of the originally demanded fees.[61]

Maturing the Burning Man Organization and Event: 1998–2001

In 1998, organizers moved the event back to BLM-managed land, where the event continues to be held. Organizers also expanded the event's duration from five to seven days and revamped its identity as an arts community. To support these changes, organizers escalated their coordination efforts and quit their jobs to work full-time and year-round managing the Burning Man operations.[62] In March 1999, the organization rented its first San Francisco headquarters, at 3450 Third Street. In a warren of offices sandwiched in a narrow warehouse space, organizers were able to work together, hold meetings, maintain phone lines and servers, and store items and equipment.[63]

This move allowed organizers to establish everyday operations, triggering dramatic organizational changes. For instance, they replaced ad hoc budgeting with standard budget processes that projected expenditures and mapped possible ticket costs.[64] In addition, organizers tried different ways of structuring meetings and making decisions. Rather than attempting to do everything themselves, as they had done in the past, they hired professionals to assist with technical tasks such as bookkeeping, administrative work, and meeting facilitation. This organizational expansion increased capacity for placing more volunteers and tapping a wider variety of individuals' motivations for contributing. Although not all members supported increasing formalization, their questions and concerns facilitated more reflective organizing and strengthened organizational accountability.

Unanticipated roadblocks threatened to curtail the organization's access to resources. For example, credit card companies froze assets collected from the first quarter of the 1998 ticket sales in case event attendees demanded refunds for their tickets. This disrupted the organization's cash flow until organizers and a volunteer who worked for a bank convinced officials to gradually release the funds.[65] Organizers also fended off repeated attempts to limit the event's use of the Black Rock Desert. To do so, they rallied supporters to influence political processes, and they formed relations with state and local officials to expedite permit processes and address concerns.[66] For instance, organizers mobilized supporters to oppose two legislative proposals that sought to limit recreational use of the Black Rock Desert. After brokering with interest groups and lobbying lawmakers, organizers secured an exemption for the Burning Man event in legislation that designated the Black Rock Desert as a National Conservation Area.[67]

Organizers continued to negotiate with law enforcement authorities about their activities at the event, including arrests and citations. Whereas previous events had had no arrests, there were thirty-eight during the 2000 event, and participants reported instances of entrapment and search and seizure without warrants.[68] The following year, citing an "indecency to women and children" statute, sheriff Ron Skinner asked a theme camp to remove a large, cartoonish depiction of two men having sex. Such incidents sparked furors about due process and freedom of expression among event attendees.[69] Organizers negotiated behind the scenes to convince law enforcement not to take similar actions at future events.[70]

Diffusion of Burning Man Organizing beyond the 2000s

As illustrated by figure 2.1, the Burning Man event population has increased exponentially over two decades. During the early and mid-1990s, the population size doubled. By 2001, population growth had slowed, mitigated by the softening economy, the dot-com bust, and annual increases in ticket prices. Nevertheless, growth continued, reaching 47,097 by 2007.

As the Burning Man organization and event ages, various challenges could affect its continued existence. Practical considerations, such as the limited supply of portable toilets and vendors and the narrow roads accessing the event site, place constraints on future growth.[71] In addition, mounting costs, which have been passed onto attendees via increasing admission prices, may decrease the event's appeal. Some past event attendees have claimed that they and others have been "priced out" by the increasing admission prices. Organizers have tried to rectify these inequities by providing scholarship, discounted, and "comp" (complimentary or free) tickets.[72] A few worry that a highly mobilized and organized opposition group, such as a religious or an environmental group, could threaten the event's use of federally managed land.[73] In addition, as Burning Man members age or lose interest, the organization will experience turnover and possibly lose the knowledge needed to continue the event.

With such eventualities in mind, organizers implemented alternative ways to grow. Rather than just increasing the scale of the organization and its event, organizers facilitated the development of local communities and

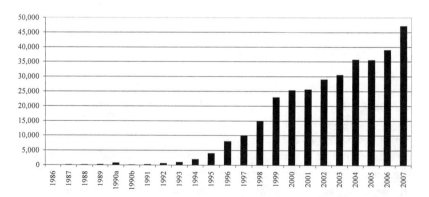

Figure 2.1 Burning Man event population by year.
Note: 1990a was the last Burning Man event held in San Francisco, and 1990b was the first Burning Man event held in the Nevada Black Rock Desert. *Source:* Population numbers from http://www.burningman.com/whatisburningman/about_burningman/bm_timeline.html#2007

organizations, known as regionals, by providing links, information, and advisory support as needed. Several regional groups, including overseas groups in the United Kingdom and Japan, have hosted their own events.[74] A few, such as the Austin and New York City regionals, have even formed their own LLCs and nonprofits.[75] Given the enthusiasm of Burning Man adherents, it seems likely that this event will continue to grow through such local communities and organizations.

The Structure of the Burning Man Organization, circa 2000

Although the Burning Man event started in 1986, leaders did not establish a formal organization until 1995. Initially, organizers did not recruit enough help to undertake responsibilities, and they lacked sufficient structure and coordination to assist the small group of volunteers. After the accidents and chaos of the 1996 event, organizers formalized departments, norms, procedures, and the recruitment of volunteers. These changes helped Burning Man correct for underorganizing.

Currently, the Burning Man event involves some 47,000 persons. Event attendees compose the largest segment of Burning Man members, much like a church congregation who attend services and contribute money.[76] In an e-mail newsletter, organizer Marian Goodell depicted the Burning Man organization as including event attendees who build artwork, develop theme camps, and volunteer before and during the Burning Man event:

> The Org[anization] is a nebulous entity to many. . . . Anyone who takes responsibility and follows through with a commitment to the organization that brings the event to fruition is part of the "Org." Counting Theme Camps, Art Projects and Volunteers, probably nearly ⅓ of Black Rock City ARE the Org! Ideally, everyone would be part of the Org. :-)[77]

Many of these persons enact the Burning Man experience, even though their activities do not directly support the Burning Man organization.

Organizers, a small paid staff, and volunteers labor on a year-round basis to support both the Burning Man organization and its event. The LLC board, also known as the Black Rock City Council, decides financial and legal matters. Larry Harvey described the board as deliberating on "legal actions—anything that affects the survival of a project, certainly monetary stuff, any allocation or investment of funds, or basic economic policy."[78] Harley Dubois opined that years of working together eased the group's process of decision making by consensus:

We have been through so much together that we really do think very much alike. We all have our own opinions, of course, but it's fairly easy for us to come to a place of commonality because our goals are so much the same . . . that it's not that hard for us to come to consensus.[79]

Although organizers decide matters by consensus, the board has a designated leader. As the executive director, Larry Harvey exercises the final say in decisions. He assigns senior staff members their responsibilities and assesses their performance, chairs meetings, and supervises the finances, which includes determining ticket prices, approving large checks, and setting senior staff salaries. Harvey also acts in a creative capacity by conceptualizing the event's annual theme, overseeing funded artists and their art, and monitoring the development of Black Rock City and the Burning Man sculpture. In addition, he and fellow organizer Marian Goodell represent the organization when negotiating with various public and private agencies. Furthermore, Harvey and others engage in public relations by granting interviews with the media, lecturing at public forums, and writing and editing feature articles for Burning Man publications.

The LLC board includes five other organizers who oversee different areas of organizational operations, as depicted by table 2.1. Most were invited to join the board during the mid-to-late 1990s.[80] Individuals were selected for their trustworthiness, experience working with the Burning Man organization, and expertise. Members claimed that they were not interested in expanding or changing the board's composition. Unless a member departs, the board composition is unlikely to change.

While the LLC board determines particular legal and financial matters, the senior staff, which reports to the LLC board, forms policies and procedures relevant to the organization and event. The senior staff also supervises those within their departments of responsibility. Unlike the LLC board members, not all members of the senior staff work full-time for the Burning Man organization; several volunteer part-time and hold full-time jobs elsewhere.

These individuals lead growing departments that started with a few overworked volunteers and ad hoc practices. For instance, interviewees reported that in the past, organizers disbursed cash for expenses from their own pockets and from garbage bags stored in their residences.[81] Observations indicated that organizers tried to teach themselves bookkeeping and budgeting skills. Starting in 1999, professionals were hired to handle cash flow with accounting, bookkeeping, and auditing, and to negotiate legal contracts for services; these professionals joined the Business Management Department. The Business Management Department also oversees several operations that serve

Table 2.1 Members of the 2000 LLC board and senior staff

Member	Area of responsibility
LLC Board members	
Larry Harvey	Executive director/art
Harley Dubois	Community Services
Marian Goodell	Communication/business
Michael Mikel (a.k.a. Danger Ranger)	Black Rock Rangers
Will Roger*	Department of Public Works (DPW)
Crimson Rose	Administration/art
Senior staff members	
Dana Harrison*	Business affairs
Duane Hoover*	Black Rock Rangers director
Flynn Mauthe*	DPW operations director
Dave Thornton	Finance
Joe Fenton*	Black Rock Ranger, playa operations manager
Joseph Pred	Black Rock Ranger, emergency services manager

*Individuals who have since changed positions or departed the organization as of the early 2000s. Additional individuals, some of whom hold new areas of responsibility, have joined the senior staff since 2000.

participants and workers during the Burning Man event. At its inception, the commissary fed 31 volunteers; by 2000, the Commissary served up to 16,708 meals a day, effectively becoming Nevada's seventh largest restaurant.[82] As one of two places where event attendees can exchange money for goods, the Center Camp Café serves coffee and tea and hosts performances. Once a nondescript stand of hay bales propped against a freezer truck, Camp Arctica transformed into a fifty-foot igloo theme camp where event attendees can buy ice blocks and cubes to cool their food and drinks.[83]

Likewise, Community Services encompassed departments devoted to helping participants.[84] Several of these departments were initiated by volunteers and were later absorbed into the Burning Man infrastructure; all of these departments still depend on volunteers. Greeters welcome newcomers and returnees to the event. Check Point Salon[85] (later renamed Playa Info), Bulletin Boards, and Directory disseminate information. Theme Camp Placement and

Villages place theme camps and assist villages. Earth Guardians and Recycling encourage environmental conservation. Lost and Found matches lost items with their owners. Lamplighters light the city's streets each night.

By distributing press kits to media covering the 1993 event, volunteers inaugurated what is now known as the Communications Department. This group shares information with participants, media, government agencies, interest groups, and the general public. The Communications team, more popularly known as Media Mecca, interfaces with the approximately two hundred major international, national, and local news agencies and independent groups that cover the event in print, radio, video, documentary, digital, and Internet forms. Until its closure in 2005, the *Black Rock Gazette* newspaper composed and distributed "propaganda" articles, humor, and coverage of breaking issues for event participants. Formal technical support and development for electronic communication did not start until 1999. The initial team of volunteers, known as the "Tech team," spun off into a Database team to focus on the massive data-processing needs of the organization, an Extranet Team to design online communications tools for internal use, Network/Desktop Support, System Administration, and Burning Man Organization Support to develop organization-specific software. The Internet Web Team supports the www.burningman.com Web site, which hosts an extensive print, photo, and text archives and a collection of documents and Web-site and e-mail links.

The Black Rock Rangers is one of the most visible departments, as its khaki-attired volunteers patrol the event for medical emergencies and other problems. To ease cooperation with the multiple medical, fire, and law enforcement agencies at the event, the Rangers have adopted standardized protocols and procedures. However, this department's mission maintains that its Rangers serve as a buffer between event attendees and governmental agencies: "The Rangers are a non-confrontational mediating entity dedicated to the safety, welfare, and quality of experience of the participants of Burning Man and the citizens of Black Rock City."[86] The Rangers also include several smaller subunits. The Coast Guard patrols the city's perimeter to discourage gate-crashers, while the Department of Mutant Vehicles (DMV) registers art cars that can drive in the otherwise pedestrianized city. The Gate collects tickets from participants and makes official population counts.[87]

Once a loose band of "misfits,"[88] the Department of Public Works (DPW) coordinates the manual labor and materials needed to build, maintain, and disband the physical infrastructure for the Burning Man event. The DPW sets up the miles of trash fence surrounding the event site, the temporary streets pressed into the desert surface, and the shade structures that shelter various event services. By 2000, this department had subdivided into a management team, operations team, construction, and cleanup team. Its units have several tiers of management, a strict code of conduct and schedule, and a wage system. One DPW subdivision includes a fully operational airport where, barring inclement weather conditions, small aircraft can take off from and land on a temporary runway located on the Black Rock Desert.

The Art Department promotes artists' efforts. These volunteers fund, schedule, and place projects at the event site, and they handle pyrotechnics and fire safety. They also oversee the organization's art archives for posterity and arrange additional art shows.[89] In addition, under Larry Harvey's direction, this department elaborates on the event's changing annual theme.

At the time of my study, Burning Man's departments were in different stages of development. Approximately half had formed during the late 1990s, and most have subsequently expanded in size and responsibilities. Follow-up visits indicated that these departments have undergone further changes, although two of the observed departments have since disbanded.[90] Next, I show how the Burning Man organization matured its once underorganized collective and avoided overorganizing.

"Do-ocracy"

Acting on Suggestions and Criticisms

IN MAY 2003, Media Mecca volunteers buzzed about an acrimonious exchange forwarded to their e-mail discussion list. A volunteer had asked an eBay seller to drop the Burning Man name from the title of his advertisement on the auction Web site. The volunteer pointed out that the listing's title violated a norm prohibiting the use of the Burning Man name to sell products or services. The would-be seller responded by contesting this policy and the Burning Man organization's authority to make such requests. Among other complaints, the respondent dismissed formal organization as counter to the Burning Man endeavor. In a lengthy post on his personal Web page, the self-identified "'socially-conscious' anarchist" advocated "self-organization" as the preferable way to produce an authentic Burning Man event:

> If the original spirit of Burning Man were still alive, there would be no official "Burning Man Organization." Instead Burning Man would [be] self-organized by its participants through a complex web of coordinated, decentralized actions and spontaneous contribution—a self-directed, self-forming order, rather than one imposed by some officialdom with its official rules of procedure, permanent hierarchies, and standing bureaucracies.[1]

The critic then argued that the prohibition against using the Burning Man name to sell products privileged organizational interests over constituents' abilities to make a living. His complaints suggested that insufficient collectivist practices, too many bureaucratic practices, and coercive control had created oligarchy, a form of overorganizing. This rumble of discontent echoed others' concerns about organizing changes.

If Burning Man members adopted such suggestions, they risked triggering another form of overorganizing or regressing into underorganizing. If members shunned bureaucratic practices and implemented collectivist practices with coercive control, they could establish a culty collective that suppressed individuals' interests for the collective "good." On the other hand, if members eschewed all organizing practices, then they risked underorganizing and reproducing the disabling chaos that nearly ended Burning Man during the late 1990s.

Given such possibilities, members were cognizant of the consequences associated with organizing changes. At times, organizers expressed ambivalence about the effects of increasing formalization. During a senior staff meeting, transportation coordinator Michael Carpenter, a.k.a. Tex, introduced a one-page "Bill of Lading Form" for items trucked from the San Francisco headquarters to the Nevada event site. Carpenter intended these labels to curb the misplacement of items, as departmental heads often complained that they found missing shipments in another department's possession. After the presentation, organizer Larry Harvey joked to Carpenter, "You've created a hideous, faceless bureaucracy, and we love it!"[2]

As Harvey's satiric exclamation showed, organizers sympathized with concerns about whether efforts to alleviate underorganizing could inadvertently foster overorganizing. Since the Burning Man organization not only depended on volunteer labor, but also encouraged members to actively participate in organizing matters, organizers could not ignore members' opinions about how to organize. Organizers thus faced two intertwined challenges: determining what to do with suggestions and critiques, and justifying organizing practices to skeptical members.

By examining how organizing practices incorporated members' input, we can understand the extent to which the Burning Man organization changed in blending bureaucratic and collectivist practices. This chapter focuses on two particularly controversial areas of organizing: (1) the organization's legal form and practices, and (2) decision-making processes. In the former area, critics warned against the consequences of overorganizing; in the latter area, confusion about where members could apply their input indicated possible underorganizing.

To address these issues, organizers introduced practices designed to increase organizational accountability to members' interests and encourage member participation. In particular, organizers added practices that enhanced financial and organizing transparency. These changes thus combated the over-organizing excesses associated with oligarchy. Organizers also clarified where and how people could participate in decision making. These specifications helped ward off underorganizing consequences, including activities misdirected by ambiguous decisions. Although members could not fully resolve all areas of contention, their discussions and actions illustrated the iterative and experimental processes of organizing.

Revamping a For-profit Legal Form and Organizing Practices

Several interviewees suggested that underorganizing had incapacitated the growing event, particularly during 1996. Even years later, they spoke in strained, even angry, tones about how insufficient organizing practices and coordination exacerbated the "chaos" of the 1996 event. Former organizer John Law remembered how emergencies overwhelmed their small volunteer ranks: "There were all these accidents, and no one knew how to deal with them. . . . There were too many people. . . . It was hellish."[3] Former volunteer Jennifer Holmes recalled that with the event's unexpectedly large population, the few trained medical and Black Rock Ranger volunteers could only react to, rather than prevent, problems: "Our M.O. for that weekend was let whatever is going to happen, happen out there, and we will just pick up their broken bodies when the dust clears. That was all that we could do." At the event's end, Holmes had to beg contracted medical personnel, who had already prepared to leave, to start treating those seriously injured by a car accident:

> I run over to medical . . . and I said, "We need you to go to [the accident]," and they were like, "well, we're packing, we're leaving." . . . I finally convince them to . . . go, it was like ugh! Pulling teeth, you know? We have people bleeding out their heads—someone . . . [with a] second-degree burn . . . down her back. It was very difficult.[4]

Law explained that organizers had neither the numbers nor the expertise to handle the growing event: "We had a tiger by the tail as it [the event] got bigger."[5] Based on these experiences, a small contingent, including Holmes and Law, vowed never to return or support the event again.

In contrast, the remaining organizers decided to reorganize and intensify their organizing efforts so that the event could continue. Organizer Larry Harvey recalled, "I made the case . . . of how do we expect us to make this [the Burning Man event] to scale unless we form a more organized group?"[6]

Reorganizing included dissolving a recently formed legal partnership. Although the partnership had lent legitimacy to Burning Man and facilitated logistics like equipment rentals,[7] this legal form did not sufficiently protect personal assets against lawsuits,[8] as organizers discovered when an individual who was severely injured during the 1996 event sued Burning Man and other parties for negligence.[9]

At this point, the remaining leaders decided to regroup as a limited liability company. Michael Mikel explained that they selected the LLC form for its flexibility and protection against liability, even though their primary purpose for organizing was not for profit:

> It [the LLC form] provides more protection legally than a partnership . . . and it also gives a tremendous amount of freedom and flexibility. . . . We don't want to be locked into a nonprofit, because we need more flexibility . . . and we didn't want to be a business because we weren't going for profit per se, and we looked at tax reasons, so it was for a multitude of reasons, and it just seemed like the best organization.[10]

Similarly, organizer Larry Harvey emphasized that they had chosen a for-profit form because it allowed them to exercise direct control over organizing, whereas a nonprofit form required conceding oversight to a separate board.[11] Incorporating and formalizing helped stabilize organizing efforts, allowing organizers to build relationships with entities such as banks and governmental agencies.

Even with these changes, the nascent Burning Man organization faced perilous conditions, in particular, difficulties with securing resources. For example, organizer Harley Dubois recounted how the 1996 event's *Inferno* theme fueled locals' perceptions of eventgoers as "pagan devil worshippers." These perceptions impeded organizing efforts: "People wouldn't do business with us. . . . We couldn't get porta-potties almost one year. When they did do business with us, they charged us twice as much money."[12] Organizing efforts focused on survival activities, such as paying off debts and recruiting help to replace those who had quit. Black Rock Ranger Joe Fenton, a.k.a. Boggmann, remembered the struggle to reorganize with remaining members: "The organization took a major hit in 1996 when John Law left. . . . They had to reinvent everything . . ."[13]

Organizers faced internal opposition over the extent to which a formal organization should coordinate planning for the event. For instance, critics complained that the organization cramped their freedom by introducing rules that restricted event activities. Such complaints often relied on comparisons with the "good old days," when the event lacked formal organization and allowed activities such as shooting firearms. Although critics admitted that formal organization enhanced the event's survival prospects, they mourned the passing of structurelessness. Former organizer John Law commented, "Organizers went from free-spirited to bureaucracy out of necessity." He lamented the shift away from anarchy, which he considered essential to the event: "It's more like a corporation than it is like a bunch of anarchists in the desert doing whatever they want."[14] Member John Rinaldi, a.k.a. Chicken John, expressed similar regrets about how ad hoc organizing had turned "corporate," thus eroding the event's distinctiveness:

> It's run more like a business, it's run more like a corporation. . . . As a result, that's the feeling that you get out of the event now, which is, it's a little stale, it's a little sedate, it's a little safe, there's a lot of rules. . . . But it's grown, and in order for it to grow like that, it had to evolve in order to survive. It had to evolve into a corporate manual thing, it had to evolve into meetings and an office that probably costs $30K a month.[15]

Such ambivalence and even antipathy toward the corporate form were often evident in art projects' satirical portrayals of corporations,[16] as well as in the event's emphasis on providing an alternative space that eschewed corporate sponsorship and interests.

In addition, critics attacked the organization's for-profit legal form as incompatible with volunteer labor and the collectivist norm of participation. They charged that individuals were duped for organizational ends under the guise of taking responsibility for a collective enterprise. In a 1999 San Francisco neighborhood newsletter, an anonymous critic's article satirized Burning Man as a cult-like corporation that expropriated volunteer labor:

> Just a few short years ago, Burning Man was little more than a rag-tag, desert gathering of . . . anarchists, bohemians, and other riffraff. Its transformation into Burning Man LLC, a profitable corporation offering a trendy, postmodern vacation for young, high-tech professionals, is largely due to the marketing genius of Larry Harvey, Burning Man's visionary co-founder, and CEO.

The author ribbed that Burning Man capitalized upon the labor of "a large number of bohemian slacker types" to maximize profit: "By using these less desirable demographic elements as an unpaid workforce, Harvey is able to keep overheads to a minimum, thus ensuring maximum profitability." The article also portrayed Harvey as taking advantage of volunteers' desire for self-actualization: "To recruit the free labor that is central to Burning Man's unique business model, Harvey has succeeded in convincing work-shy bohemians that toiling long hours in the desert heat can somehow lead to personal fulfillment."[17]

In a similar vein, former organizer John Law accused the organization of reproducing a class-based system of labor:

> They [Burning Man] can attract volunteer labor for months! Like people will go back to their lives after the event, and they're broke, sick, and don't have any money, and can't get a house. . . . These are the poor people who go out to support the rich . . . dot-com kids and hippies who come in their RVs.[18]

Another long-time event attendee grumbled that the organizers were like "Tom Sawyer" in convincing volunteers to do work.[19] In a bulletin board thread titled "Burned by Burning Man LLC," an event attendee claimed that she had been overworked, threatened, and eventually thrown out of the 2002 event when an arrangement to exchange dishwashing work at the commissary for entry into the event soured.[20] Such criticisms reflected tensions about whether the organization had demonstrated adequate accountability to members, or whether it had become a culty collective by taking advantage of members' enthusiasm for organizational ends.

Some criticisms depicted the overorganizing excess of oligarchy, as well as an unresponsive and moribund bureaucracy. For example, an anonymous post on a cult watchdog Web site razzed Burning Man's chain of authority and rules: "Major decisions require the permission of Larry Harvey . . ." and "The rule book for Burningman [sic] is thick and intricate. Every project is micromanaged."[21] While Burning Man organizers dismissed this post as a prank and made humorous allusions to the post's jabs, e-mails from dedicated members raised criticisms that were not as easily dismissed. For instance, in an e-mail addressed to organizer Larry Harvey, Burning Man artist Russell Wilcox described his negative experiences with a new department. Wilcox cautioned, "Bureaucracy substitutes procedure for human interaction, depersonalizing and dehumanizing the whole process."[22] Before making specific recommendations to increase organizational accountability, a volunteer's e-mail to the staff listserv alluded to "complaints of micromanagement, consolidation of power among a few decision makers, . . . absence of empowerment to senior volunteers, the growing sense of entitlement by some senior staff and the lack of interest in taking input from participants."[23]

A few critics agitated for extreme changes, such as disbanding the organization, changing its legal form, or replacing bureaucratic practices with collectivist practices. They urged Burning Man members to emulate groups like the Rainbow Family, which produced countercultural events without an official organization.[24] Critics also demanded that the Burning Man organization adopt only collectivist practices or incorporate as a nonprofit. For instance, the critic quoted at the beginning of this chapter called for "the reorganization of the LLC into a non-hierarchical not-for-profit form of legal entity, with consensus decision making, regular rotation of officers, the ability of constituents to recall officers, and the equality of decision-making power for all of the Burning Man community written into its charter."[25] Such recommendations claimed that these changes would increase the organization's accountability to its members.

Similarly, proponents of adopting a nonprofit form, such as a 501(c)3, argued that this would accord greater organizational legitimacy, credibility, and accountability to the community than a for-profit form provided. Black Rock Ranger Jim DeLaHunt argued that the LLC form did not require enough financial transparency: "They [organizers] don't publish their budgets, they don't publish their financial statements . . . so they don't take responsibility. One of the ways that you can tell what's really going on is that you follow the money, and they don't take responsibility for making that transparent."[26] DeLaHunt explained that a nonprofit form's constraints on allocations offered "better credibility" than a for-profit form. He worried:

> As a LLC, they [organizers] can . . . do whatever they want to do that's not illegal. They're welcome to pay themselves huge salaries, . . . to keep their financials secret, . . . to take money from Burning Man and invest it in assets that they can control and serve their interests and not the interests of the future Burning Man festival. There are very few checks and balances on them, and that gives them a lot of freedom, and that's what causes a credibility problem . . . why do they need all of that freedom?[27]

Not all critics demanded that the organization switch to a nonprofit form, but they did question what their money and labor supported, especially as ticket prices for the event increased each year. For example, volunteer Earl Stirling, a.k.a. Dodger, e-mailed Larry Harvey with his questions and concerns about financial expenditures: "[Burning Man is] a privately owned company just like any other commercial concert or festival promoter. I think that's fine. But as soon as they start asking me for money and sympathy for escalating costs, I want to know the full story. Where the heck is all this money going?"[28] Other members, such as P. Segal, recognized that "huge financial challenges" necessitated formal organization:

> The organization has become so huge, it needs . . . a year-round staff. It can't be Larry [Harvey] doing it out of his bedroom anymore. To maintain a staff, you need . . . salaries, you need an office, you need archives, they now have all

of these wonderful art pieces. . . . They need a facility . . . all of those things are very expensive. They need . . . to have the financial cushion so that they can start paying for the things that need to be done next year now and not just constantly running in the red.[29]

Rather than ignoring criticisms, organizers considered whether the expressed concerns were valid and merited action. For example, during a staff meeting, organizers discussed reactions to the 2000 newsletter distributed to Burning Man supporters. While past newsletters used a simple, monochromatic format, this newsletter looked more professionally produced, with photo-quality glossy print. Organizers worried that readers would view this change with disfavor:

LARRY HARVEY: Any word from them [the Burning Man community] on the newsletter?

MICHAEL MIKEL: They loved it, the color.

JOSEPH PRED: I received negative feedback on the newsletter. People felt it was real slick.

MIKEL: Expensive.

HARVEY [*speaks with a sarcastic tone*]: That's local [criticism]. We should reproduce the mimeograph at greater cost.[30]

As demonstrated by this exchange, organizers' reactions to feedback varied. Organizers sometimes resorted to ironic humor that acknowledged criticisms. For example, Crimson Rose recounted how she and other organizers "were joking . . . about turning Burning Man into a consumer event and then the people that say that we've 'sold out' can stop sniveling about it."[31] But in an e-mail to the staff list, art curator Christine Kristen, a.k.a. Lady Bee, cautioned against dismissing criticisms as irrelevant: "Too many times . . . people who have intelligent criticism of our organization [are] written off as 'whiners' when in fact they are truly concerned with what they see going on around them." Kristen argued that as part of a collective, organizers had a responsibility to consider such concerns: "As we are a community, not a corporation, we are bound to respond to each other, and, I think, to take people's feedback seriously."[32] In an e-mail that seconded Kristen's plea, volunteer Ggreg Taylor advocated for constructive dialogue across the organization:

It is critical that you as Staff discuss what all of us as a community are concerned about, and to discuss it honestly and openly. I think it is additionally critical that it be discussed as a group . . . and not left to the top of the hierarchy. . . . Loads of folks on staff are scared of dissenting because they fear retribution, or having their opinions discounted. There needs to be an open forum for speech right now.[33]

Such entreaties elicited organizational responsiveness to members' concerns and validated member feedback as legitimate. Such expressed concerns could have been ignored if the organization relied only upon bureaucratic practices.[34]

In discussing organizing possibilities, members explicated rationales for particular practices, as well as paths not chosen. In an e-mail, one volunteer rejected a recommendation to make all decisions by consensus as unsustainable, averring "[Burning Man] would have died long ago if we tried to run it like a Rainbow Gathering."[35] In responding to critiques about Burning Man's reliance upon volunteer labor, organizers highlighted the centrality of such involvement to the Burning Man endeavor. Organizers stated that in a volunteer-dependent organization, "no one gets paid what they're worth," and that Burning Man could not exist without the "gift" of volunteerism.[36] Borrowing from Lewis Hyde's ([1979] 1983) work, organizer Larry Harvey reframed Burning Man's dependency on volunteer labor with the gift economy:

> We tell people to regard themselves as a gift, to commune with their own reality, that essential inner portion of experience that makes them feel real. Then we ask them to project this vision out onto the world in the form of a gift that can be shared with other people. . . . This ethos has led participants to bestow an incredible array of gifts on Black Rock City. . . . It nourishes an abundance of art, of course, and people make millions of spontaneous contributions to our city's social life. But we also organize a public service sector: the Black Rock Rangers, for instance, or the people at Media Mecca, the Artery, Playa Info, the Lamplighters, even our ice concession and coffee house—all these folks who work for institutions at our civic center. Almost all of them are volunteers. They're giving gifts.[37]

Harvey argued that members had a civic responsibility and duty to contribute, and that such giving strengthened ties and pooled resources among members.

In some cases, leaders made changes that addressed criticism and suggestions. In particular, leaders increased organizational accountability: they added a nonprofit arm, modified their LLC's redistribution agreement, and increased financial transparency beyond the LLC form's requirements. Experts helped organizers launch the Black Rock Arts Foundation, a nonprofit arm for gathering and distributing grants, in 2001.[38] Organizers retained an LLC form for the main Burning Man organization, arguing that they needed to maintain control.[39] However, LLC members signed away their rights to organizational property. With this change, they could not sell their stake in the organization. As Larry Harvey explained:

> We divested [the Burning Man organization] of property interest. . . . If any member of the LLC quits, they're entitled to a golden parachute amounting to $20,000 to $25,000, and that's it, good-bye. That they can't transfer their interests, . . . they can't claim a sixth share of the capital or the worth of it, they have no rights whatsoever. . . . So now people can't say that even though we collect fairly large salaries, that we're building masses of equity.[40]

Harvey publicized this change on the Burning Man Web site in the hopes that it would assuage concerns about organizers' interests.[41]

Organizers also increased financial transparency by publishing organizational expenses. Starting in 1993, organizers selectively disclosed financial expenses for medical services, donations, and Larry Harvey's salary in print and e-mail newsletters.[42] However, organizers like Marian Goodell hesitated about releasing a more comprehensive financial disclosure. They worried that readers might not understand the high cost of labor and overhead, which dominated expenses among most organizations. Furthermore, organizers feared that sharing such information would expose them to additional pressures about efficiency when they were still struggling with handling finances.[43] Nevertheless, organizers conceded to members' repeated requests for financial transparency. Starting in 2002, they posted an annual financial report and general budget on the event's Web site.[44]

In addition, organizers stressed that the organization's primary objective, despite having a for-profit form, was to produce the Burning Man event. In a financial report posted on the Burning Man Web site, organizer Larry Harvey joked, "We are more aptly termed a 'no-profit,'" and explained that the organization's intent was not to make money: "Burning Man is not a product and our goal is not to profit." He pointed out that the organization prohibited several activities that could have generated income: "We have never had investors. We accept no commercial sponsorships, endorse no products, and we have disallowed vending except for the sale of coffee and ice at the event. All of these activities are typical sources of income and funding for a normal business that exists to create a profit."[45]

Members' attitudes and activities further reflected this distinction of the Burning Man organization as an unconventional, "no-profit" business. Black Rock Ranger director Duane Hoover depicted the difficulties of handling the organization as a business endeavor: "I've never encountered an environment that was [*laugh*] like Burning Man. . . . Working with a group of artistic people who just at a very basic gut level just don't give a shit about business and organization, and yet they're compelled [to] because of their responsibility to run the organization as a business, is a source of continued frustration and/or amazement to me sometimes."[46] Members avoided becoming too business-like with cautions against an overzealous pursuit of efficiency. Organizer Michael Mikel recognized that their endeavors were not optimal, especially given their self-taught business skills: "As a business, we're very inefficient and poorly run."[47] Nonetheless, he claimed that by accepting some inefficiency and ineffectiveness, organizers avoided creating a bureaucracy that overlooked members' interests. Mikel equated an efficient bureaucracy with the Nazi's approach to genocide, one of history's most extreme episodes of coercive control: "If we were so efficient, if we were so effective at managing our business and spending money, it might be like a train going down the track, we couldn't get off in time. The Third Reich was very effective—maybe we don't want to go there. Maybe it's ok to be wasteful."[48]

Like Mikel, some members accepted some inefficiency to support a more inclusive, risk-taking art event. They recognized that practices should be responsive to members' interests, rather than privileging business concerns. For instance, volunteer Chase Lehman commented that too much focus on a budget could detract from the organizational mission: "You would be thinking more about the budget . . . than about giving people an opportunity to do whatever . . . they want while they're out there [at Burning Man]."[49] In a 1996 memo, Stuart Mangrum confessed his misplaced belief in the importance of the budgetary and business aspects of organizing: "I fell prey to the lure of Big Numbers. I did my job without enough regard to its consequences, [I was] too tightly focused on the bottom line. In short, I treated it too much like a business. Burning Man is in fact a business, but it's a poorly-run one and probably the better for it."[50] In such instances, members accepted the trade-offs of mixing collectivist and bureaucratic practices under a particular legal form.

Citing the need to increase organizational accountability to their interests, members used collectivist practices to ensure that organizing efforts encouraged flexibility, responsiveness, and meaning. This use of collectivist practices helped prevent bureaucratic practices from overrunning organizing efforts with efficiency concerns. Combining collectivist and bureaucratic practices thus helped curb possible under- and overorganizing tendencies. This combination enhanced organizational accountability beyond the standards associated with the kinds of legal forms and practices advocated by Burning Man critics. As scholars have cautioned, a nonprofit form in itself does not guarantee accountability (e.g., Frumkin 2002). Therefore, organizers in general should consider additional ways of improving accountability.

Clarifying Decision-making Areas

Members also raised questions about their participation, particularly in decision making. The collectivist practice of decision making by consensus allowed members to participate in organizing matters. However, members disagreed about how much input they could exercise, as some members claimed that they should have a say in all decisions. Organizers countered that they alone were responsible for decisions in matters such as finances. These countervailing interpretations illustrated one ill of underorganizing that immobilized and fractured other organizations: excessive ambiguity about who had the authority to do what.

Burning Man members and organizers navigated a tricky balance in specifying how members should participate in decision making. For example, some volunteers believed that given the organization's practice of decision making by consensus, the entire Burning Man community should function as a democracy of decision makers for all matters. In an e-mail to the Media Mecca listserv, volunteer Fiona Essa wondered whether recent organizing decisions represented event attendees' interests: "I'm somewhat curious as to how much of a democracy the temporary community of Black Rock City really is. It seems as though some of the ideals and philosophies of [the Burning Man organization] are in direct opposition to the desires of our participants."[51]

In response, organizer Marian Goodell rebutted this conflation of democracy and collectivist practice with the statement that not all issues were up for collective consideration:

> uh, [can] anyone find me anything that indicates Black Rock City is a democracy? any documentation, literature? i know of none. that's never been part of the structure. . . . it's an assumption made due to our size and dominant paradigm. . . . it's a democracy as far as it asks for people to contribute . . . if that even constitutes a democracy.
>
> LIKE I said the other day, we will have a public meeting in December, our email addresses are ALL OVER the internet. If people can't get their ideas to the organizers then they are daft. We will listen, but we don't have the resources to TRY all ideas, nor the inclination. You should see some of what we get. . . . one person suggested we get sponsorship to cover the increased BLM costs . . . duh![52]

Goodell clarified that organizers would take into account members' suggestions, but that the organizers held final authority in deciding the event's direction. Observations of meetings substantiated that members' views were incorporated into decision-making processes.

Organizers further noted that this chain of command did not prevent members from taking action. While organizers reinforced their authority to make decisions in certain matters, they still urged eventgoers to take action, particularly in initiating and carrying out projects and activities. Before a town hall meeting, organizers and staff rehearsed answering anticipated questions about participation:

ANDIE GRACE: Is Black Rock City a democracy, and are we citizens?

MARIAN GOODELL: It's a do-ocracy.

LARRY HARVEY: You can't buy decision making with a ticket. The Project is another thing, it's a do-ocracy, you come in and do.[53]

Here, organizers articulated a previously implicit understanding: members could participate by initiating grassroots action, not just by following top-down directives. Under a "do-ocracy," individuals could launch an activity or project that addressed a "civic need."[54] Participants planned and implemented several initiatives, including a message service and a recycling program, which eventually became part of the event's infrastructural services. In making these distinctions about participation, organizers made clear where they held decision-making authority, but they also demarcated areas for members to take action. These specifications enabled activities, thus avoiding both the confusion of underorganizing and the suppression of members' interests by overorganizing.

Besides determining where decision making by consensus applied, members debated how to carry out decision making. In part, these debates reflected growing consciousness about how to formalize a decision-making process that, according to organizer Harley Dubois, had arisen from "organic" ad hoc experimentation over the years. Dubois speculated that with his "success" and "perspective," organizer Larry Harvey could have imposed a more bureaucratic top-down approach to decision making. Instead, organizers made an explicit policy that explained how to carry out existing practices: "He [Larry Harvey] realized the beauty in what had been created organically, and we formalized it. . . . We just didn't really realize that we were . . . operating by consensus, and we started calling it that." Dubois explained that they realized that they were practicing decision making by consensus when they began teaching newcomers: "We had new people coming in, and we had to explain to them why we were doing things the way that we were doing it."[55] Interestingly, this post hoc realization differed from other organizations that specified from the outset their process of decision making by consensus.

The Burning Man organizers subsequently wrote documents that specified how to implement decision making by consensus. One of these documents, which cited a guide to consensus available on a university Web site, emphasized creating agreement among all participants, rather than relying on a majority vote:

> Consensus is a decision making process which equalizes power over a group of people. Instead of simply voting for an item, and having the majority of the group get their way, the group has to sit down and get a solution to a problem that EVERYONE is ok with. . . . The solution that the group thinks is the most positive gets chosen, unless a member of the group finds the solution totally unacceptable. Consensus is based on compromise, and the ability to find common ground.[56]

Another description, which appeared in an annual report, underscored the collective aspects of agreement:

> Consensus means that that everyone who is party to a discussion agrees to a course of action. For a decision to be adopted, everyone must give his or her consent. This doesn't mean that everyone agrees that a particular decision is the best decision. It simply means that everyone will go along with what the group decides.[57]

These folksy descriptions belied the difficulties of creating consensus.

Observations of meetings revealed that organizers struggled to work out the particulars of decision making by consensus, including whether to practice it on a selective basis. Ironically, not everyone agreed on what constituted consensus. For example, at a senior staff meeting, two organizers disagreed about whether decision making by consensus applied to a particular issue. In this instance, Harley Dubois questioned Marian Goodell's decision to allow *Evening Magazine,* a local television program, to cover the 2000 event. When Dubois suggested discussing this decision at the meeting, she and Goodell started to argue about whether they had reached consensus on the matter in a previous meeting:

GOODELL: It could have been discussed last week; I didn't know.
DUBOIS: We did not—
GOODELL [*interrupts*]: I think the group reached a consensus; you're the only person who had a question.
DUBOIS: You've done all the research I need. This is not consensus.

As Dubois and Goodell aired their disagreement, Larry Harvey questioned whether Dubois had authority over Goodell's responsibilities as head of communications. In response, Dubois claimed that they had not yet established consensus on the matter:

LARRY HARVEY [*to Dubois*]: Do you have veto over this department?
DUBOIS: No, but we have not reached consensus. We have consistently done that.

Dubois's questions upset Goodell, who had not anticipated this interaction. Goodell defended her decision to allow the news crew into the event as warranted, supported by other organizers, and within the domain of her responsibilities. Harvey backed Goodell's claim that her decision should not be held up for consensus:

GOODELL: I'm not going to bring all of the major media [proposals up for debate at senior staff meetings]. I got a lot of feedback; I'm not having them debated ad nauseam.
DUBOIS: You did bring one [here]. . . .
HARVEY [*defends Goodell*]: I don't bring art [proposals] and have people chew on that, for what's acceptable. There are things you don't want to bring [to meetings for discussion]; you don't want people looking over your shoulder.

Dubois argued that this issue was appropriate for collective discussion, while Goodell disagreed and said that she would not raise other matters for consideration at meetings:

DUBOIS: It [the *Evening Magazine* coverage] affects all of us in a huge way; every once in a while [proposals] really [should be] discussed by all of us.
GOODELL: No, I learned my lesson; I'm not going to bring any others [proposals for discussion].

Despite the tension between Goodell and Dubois, members continued to discuss the issue at length. Dubois and other meeting attendees expressed reservations about the impact that such media coverage might have upon the event's present and future attendance. Dubois eventually acquiesced, but she restated her concerns: "I will make a comment and then hold and go with consensus. It [the *Evening Magazine* coverage] will hurt us because it will offend people in the organization who are beloved to us. . . . We could lose another level of folk; this is not a wise decision. I will fold to consensus and move on."[58] Even after reaching this agreement, Dubois and Goodell were visibly distressed by their confrontation. Other research has reported similar reactions to the intense interactions and emotions generated by decision making by consensus (Mansbridge 1983).

Dubois later reported that after such difficult meetings, organizers learned to informally communicate with one another before meetings. This ensured that they were familiar with issues before the official discussion began:

> Mostly because I don't want to get shot down in flames in the first two minutes, I will talk to somebody ahead of [the meeting]. . . . I'll try to talk to them outside of our staff meeting so that they can be more educated as to where I'm coming from. So when we get [to the meeting], . . . we're not having knee-jerk reactions. . . . Larry will frequently call me now and say, "OK, this is what's coming up at the next meeting, and I want to give you some background before you get to the meeting so that you're up to speed on it."[59]

Dubois elaborated that in the past, they had not engaged in such premeeting communication. An underorganized process subjected decision making to wild swings: "We learned the hard way, that that's a really stupid way to go. We've had a lot of hurt feelings. We've had a lot of swinging of the pendulum, way back and forth, before we settle someplace."[60] In contrast, premeeting discussions widened decision making beyond official meetings. This extended phase allowed members more time to assimilate and integrate other perspectives, steps deemed critical by decision-making experts such as Follett ([1925] 1995).

Other researchers identify how the consensus-creating process enhances members' solidarity, understanding of collective interests, and commitment (Polletta 2002; Rothschild and Whitt 1986). However, they rarely mention how members cultivate stronger analytic and collective decision-making skills.[61] For Burning Man members, decision making by consensus facilitated deeper reflection and honed analyses. While others seemed inclined to accept matters without much discussion, Dubois identified these as opportunities to examine facts, pose pointed questions, and evaluate procedures. Dubois reported that she conducted research before meetings, for instance, to learn how other organizations coped with similar challenges. Such preparation allowed for a better understanding of decisions up for discussion. Dubois also used decision-making moments to evaluate whether proposed or current services supported the organizational mission. In critiquing the unmindful routinization of activities, she advocated for more conscious consideration of otherwise taken-for-granted practices: "People would just start doing things, and they would turn into the way it is, but we never really asked, is that really what we want to do?"[62] By explicitly considering activities' relations to goals, such contemplation can curtail overorganizing. It can also validate diverse viewpoints, thus staving off the suboptimal, conformist decision making generated by groupthink (Janis 1982).

On the other hand, decision-making processes can unnerve and alienate participants with conflict, emotional stress, unsatisfactory decision outcomes, and excessive time expenditure (Mansbridge 1983; Rothschild and Whitt 1986; Sirianni 1984). Interviews and observations revealed that the Burning Man organization was not immune to these consequences. Observations indicated that meeting participants occasionally reached consensus when dissenters wearied of arguing and abstained or agreed rather than continue the discussion.[63] Such outcomes exacerbated members' perceptions that meetings wasted their time. Member Joegh Bullock described the conundrum of balancing the countervailing desires for timeliness and expressiveness:

> You get people to the point that they're saying, "Ohmigod, another four or five hour meeting." . . . It's mostly the discussion that takes a long time, and the discussion is important. . . . People have to rant and rave about their things. . . . When you get a lot of opinionated people together, that's bound to happen.[64]

Observations also indicated that emotional stress accompanied decision making by consensus. For instance, when individuals proposed unpopular views, other visibly agitated organizers questioned these individuals' loyalty to the organization. Given such reactions, members might hesitate to present material or views.[65] After a particularly grueling meeting, one organizer admitted that she had to borrow deodorant to retard sweat,[66] and another organizer cried on the sympathetic shoulder of an assistant.[67] These reactions demonstrated the toll inflicted as members struggled to carry out practices that valued and encouraged participation.

A few members questioned the appropriateness of emotional displays during decision-making discussions. In one meeting, Duane Hoover, a former academic who advocated decision making by consensus, objected to the tearful manner in which fellow organizer Marian Goodell advocated event safety. He argued that although he, too, might have strong feelings about an issue, he was not accustomed to displaying such emotion, and he worried that others might dismiss his points if he did not emote.[68] Indeed, other organizations' employees have expressed discomfort with emoting on demand (Martin et al. 1998). In a similar vein, volunteer Dana Harrison, a.k.a. BizBabe, criticized organizers' emotional expression and interpersonal conduct at meetings as "unacceptable." At the same time, she recognized how a collectivist commitment to Burning Man elevated members' emotions in ways that a bureaucratized workplace could not:

The level of personalization and personal attacks, childish tantrums, storming out of the room . . . I worked for eighteen years [in a corporation]; I never had to put up with that kind of thing. . . . But on the other hand, part of the reason that you don't get that level of emotion in a corporate setting is that most people don't care that much. It's a job. In this situation, I can appreciate that stuff gets personal because for people, it is personal.[69]

Burning Man members seemed willing to engage in conflict and discussion, but this sometimes incurred emotional costs that some would prefer not to bear. In calling for more "professional" meeting conduct, Harrison drew upon bureaucratic practices to dampen what she considered to be excessive emotionality. Such reminders cooled the hegemony that could arise from a culty collective's tendency toward conformity.

Members also complained about having to revisit unclear decision outcomes, evidencing how underorganized decision making by consensus can misdirect activities (Mansbridge 1983; Schwartzman 1989). During one meeting, a participant reminded others: "We did discuss this about three months ago, this exact topic."[70] Harrison similarly described how fellow organizers revisited ambiguous decisions:

Something hot comes up, it's either discussed or not. . . . Variously conflicting opinions are offered, and in many cases, we move on without . . . any resolution at all. And then people aren't clear whether or not there was a decision, and this stuff festers, and then it comes up later, and people are trying to act based on something, and they're not clear what the answer is, and then it blows two months later, and then we spend another two hours or whatever it is arguing about the same stuff. It's dumb.

Harrison further explained that they relied on both members' input and hierarchical authority to make decisions. She thus advocated calling their practice "modified" decision making by consensus:

It [Burning Man] is not a consensus organization. Larry is the leader, and Marian is his second. And consensus is only used in a situation in which Larry or Marian agree with the apparent consensus of the organization. If they do not agree, then we go to . . . these other . . . informal processes where they more or less decide or guide. . . . It's a perfectly legitimate decision-making mechanism; it's probably the most typical decision-making mechanism. If that's going to be true, let's say that! And then let's operate in the . . . modified consensus mode where people get to offer an opinion, people get to advocate on one side or the other, and then the leader decides, based on the arguments. I don't at all have a problem with that. I have a problem with saying one and doing the other.[71]

Such complaints that organizers misapplied the term *consensus* elicited clarifications of how they made decisions. At a public talk, organizer Larry Harvey explained that decision-making practices relied upon consensus, but also benefited from hierarchy: "You have to have hierarchy, because someone always has to get up and look down at the big picture."[72] Organizers identified certain issues, such as determining financial allocations, as more appropriate for top-down decision making by leaders rather than decision making involving all interested members.[73] Coordinators like Molly Tirpak reported that several departments selectively implemented decision making by consensus, depending on the issue under consideration.[74]

Observations revealed that members introduced bureaucratic practices to facilitate meetings and support the collectivist practice of decision making by consensus. Meeting attendees rotated responsibilities such as timekeeping among themselves and set agendas in advance of meetings. These practices allowed meeting participants to focus their attention on discussing issues, rather than coping with underorganizing. For instance, in past meetings, organizers interrupted discussion for small but crucial tasks, such as setting up conference calls and faxing materials to out-of-town attendees. These delays heightened frustration among waiting members until the administrative staff took responsibility for these tasks.

Observations also showed uneven adherence to these newly formalized procedures, demonstrating that some members had difficulties adapting to the changes. To help streamline meetings and provide more time for discussion, organizers asked attendees to submit written reports that could be read in advance of meetings. Several staff members struggled to file their reports before meetings and extended apologies for delays that cited time management or computer problems. As the event's opening drew closer, nerves frayed over perceived infractions. Organizers complained when others violated new rules by failing to announce guests before meetings, proposing agenda items after the submission deadline, or arriving late to meetings, as demonstrated by this exchange:[75]

HARLEY DUBOIS [*sighs*]: We make the rules, and we always break them.

MARIAN GOODELL: What rules? [*looks unhappy*]

DUBOIS [*addresses Larry Harvey*]: Your staff report was six minutes. It wasn't a staff report.

LARRY HARVEY [*disagrees*]: We agreed to go over.[76]

Such confrontations reminded members to respect new procedures and clarified permissible actions.

As people gained experience with working together, issues still emerged, but how meeting attendees approached these issues mellowed with time.[77] Routinization helped meeting attendees exchange information, focus on the subject matter, and make decisions. Bureaucratic practices thus supported collectivist practices while curbing both under- and overorganizing. Even so, members still struggled to replace old habits with formalized practices, and they continued to debate the extent to which they should apply collectivist practices.

Conclusion

Burning Man members' concerns about formalization could have fed what Weeks (2004) termed an "unpopular culture" where members bond by bemoaning their organization's practices. With ritualistic commiseration, members could distance themselves from taking responsibility for possible organizing improvements and even accelerate declining conditions. But unlike the British bank that Weeks studied, concerns about the consequences of under- and overorganizing did not go unheeded in the Burning Man organization. In fact, skepticism about the effects of organizing practices promoted reflection, leading to reevaluation and change.

The Burning Man organization combined collectivist and bureaucratic practices to both avoid the disabling chaos of underorganizing and to keep the iron cage of overorganizing at bay. In specifying collectivist practices, Burning Man organizers encouraged members to act on their bugaboos, rather than wallow in the status quo. At the same time, organizers reinforced their authority to make decisions in certain areas such as finances. Such clarified boundaries helped shift the organization away from disabling chaos, allowing the organization to carry out activities such as allocating resources and encouraging members to act on their interests.

Burning Man organizers also used criticisms and suggestions to tailor conventional organizing practices. In particular, criticisms about the Burning Man's legal form and decision-making processes pushed the organization toward demonstrating greater accountability. For example, members' demands for accountability encouraged organizers to modify the organization's for-profit form, increase financial transparency, and add a nonprofit arm. These critiques thus helped check excessive rationalization and oligarchy. Moreover, they revitalized organizing by substantiating members' interests.

The Burning Man members were not unique in asserting their opinions about desired organizing practices. Organizations that depend heavily upon members' commitment and input, such as nonprofits and voluntary associations, face similar challenges of coordinating large-scale production and organizing. Like the Burning Man organization, they may lose members' support over disagreements about the organization's direction, or they may become embroiled in debates about appropriate ways to organize. For instance, volunteers may become disillusioned and quit if they believe that participatory practices have diminished and organizational objectives have been co-opted by funders and other external supporters (Kelley, Lune, and Murphy 2005). Even for-profit corporations, particularly those with participatory practices, must consider their employees' demands for flextime, benefits for same-sex partners, and other policies, lest they risk alienating their workforce (Creed, Scully, and Austin 2002; Jacobs and Gerson 2004). If organizations do not address such demands, they will lose highly skilled and experienced personnel (Hewlett and Luce 2005; Stone 2007).

Certain practices can help tighten otherwise diffuse links between organizational efforts and members' interests. For example, rather than depending upon governmental funding or corporate sponsorship, collecting revenues directly from members can help tie organizing activities to members' interests (Dees and Anderson 2004). Burning Man cultivated such ties by drawing revenues from event ticket sales and individual donations and eschewing corporate sponsorship. In addition, training, norms, and routines that groom future leadership and that encourage the constant questioning of authority and taking action can ensure that members' interests are incorporated rather than suppressed (Nyden 1985; Osterman 2006). In that vein, Burning Man's concept of "do-ocracy" encouraged individuals to take charge of issues overlooked by organizers. Moreover, if members are willing to examine organizing processes and engage in periodic conflict over possible actions, they are more likely to substantiate their interests (Disney and Gelb 2000; Rothschild and Leach 2006). Instead of avoiding conflict, Burning Man members grappled with contentious issues and reevaluated the efficacy of practices. Furthermore, an ideological commitment to a mission may help members resist pressures to alter practices (Minkoff and Powell 2006). With the mission of producing an arts community in mind, Burning Man members could contemplate the possible effects of changing practices. In these ways, suggestions and criticisms about how to organize can help curb under- and overorganizing as organizations expand.

"Radical Inclusion"

Attracting and Placing Members

AS WE SIPPED drinks in a coffee shop, volunteer Scott Shaner talked about his decision to attend his first Burning Man event. Shaner explained that he became interested after hearing about "this crazy art festival" on a radio talk show. However, he did not become a Burner until after his life had changed:

> I didn't know exactly what it [Burning Man] was, but it sounded like fun. But at the time, I was married. . . . Eventually I got divorced, and I thought, well, I've lived a pretty drab life. . . . I thought well, if I'm going to do something, I want to do something big and . . . really crazy. . . . I'll go [to Burning Man] . . . and I'll see what it's all about.

Shaner recounted his initial reactions to the event and his conversion from a fearful attendee into an active volunteer:

> I was scared to death. . . . It says on the [event] ticket that you could die. . . . You're taking your life in your own hands going into the desert . . . and so you better be prepared. And I thought well, if I'm going to die, I might as well die with my best friend, so I drove him down, and I absolutely hated it. I hated it

because there were . . . weird, freaky people walking around, and I just didn't get it. I thought, why am I here? There's nothing about me that relates to this.

Over the next year, I kept getting cards in the mail. . . . I got a [card] that said that they were having a volunteer party, so I went. . . . I made a bunch of signs for [the Center Camp Café]. . . . [The Café manager] said, "Well, I need somebody to manage ice." . . . I said, "Sure, I'll do whatever I can," and before I knew it, I was managing the ice.[1]

As a volunteer manager, Shaner oversaw ice sales and its subsequent transformation into Camp Arctica, where he and fellow volunteers sold bags of ice to eventgoers, with the profits benefiting local community service groups in Nevada.

As Shaner's story intimated, people flock to the annual Burning Man event for a variety of reasons. Some want to vacation in the desert during the Labor Day holiday; others seek to satiate curiosity piqued by media coverage; some strive to build and share art; some look forward to spending time with friends; others aim to meet like-minded people. But for some individuals, their original reasons for attending the event no longer sufficed as reasons to return. They thus sought out more fulfilling experiences that engaged their skills and interests.[2] Like Shaner, some joined the volunteer force that powered the Burning Man event and organization.

This chapter examines how the Burning Man organization attracted and placed volunteers. To accommodate growing organizational needs and individuals' interest in volunteerism, organizers revamped recruitment practices, which were previously based on network ties, to include routinized procedures. They also formalized collectivist practices to reinforce an ethic of "radical inclusion," which emphasized incorporating rather than excluding persons. With collectivist practices, volunteers could also create roles based on their interests, rather than be placed solely on identified organizational needs. These changes transformed a small, insular group into an expansive community with an estimated 1,300 to 2,000 volunteers.[3] This mixture of bureaucratic and collectivist practices forestalled tendencies toward under- and overorganizing in member recruitment and placement.

Recruitment: Allowing Multiple Entry Paths into the Organization

Some workplace, voluntary, and religious organizations solicit new members through ties with acquaintances, friends, and family (Biggart 1989; Chambré 1991; Granovetter 1995; Stark and Bainbridge 1980). Some communes and worker cooperatives require referrals for new members—a prospective member could gain membership only if an existing member sponsored this proposed entry with other members' agreement (Jackall 1984; Jackall and Crain 1984; Kanter 1972). For organizations, recruitment by such ties is a low-cost, minimal-effort way of identifying qualified potential recruits (Marsden 1994; Mayhew 1968). Those who are recruited by network ties are more likely to join (McAdam 1986) and initially produce (Castilla 2005) than those who are not referred by ties.[4] On the other hand, since people tend to be friends or associate with those who are "like" themselves, such recruitment can homogenize organizational membership by race, age, gender, or other characteristics (Kanter 1977) or reinforce inequality by stratifying positions along racial and gender lines (Reskin and McBrier 2000).

Like other small, less formalized organizations (Marsden 1994), Burning Man originally relied upon recruitment through ties. During the organization's earlier years, recruitment efforts were underorganized and ad hoc, restricting the intake of volunteers. Organizers invited their close friends (those connected by relations that sociologists call "strong" ties)[5] and those who demonstrated expertise and commitment to the event's cause. Organizers eventually realized that these recruitment practices could not accommodate growing organizational needs and stymied would-be volunteers' efforts to participate. A specialized staff subsequently introduced standardized recruitment procedures and formalized collectivist practices under the principle of "radical inclusion." These changes relieved the bottleneck on recruitment and diversified an otherwise homogenous and insular membership.

Underorganized recruitment by network ties and demonstrated expertise

During the mid-1990s, prospective volunteers had to repeatedly approach those who controlled entry into the organization and gain their confidence.[6] At the time, a small circle of founding members and their close associates ran the event. As volunteer Jennifer Vermut described, "It was almost like if you weren't one of the original members that started [the Burning Man event], it was very difficult to break in." According to Vermut, this emphasis on informal relations shifted during difficulties with the 1997 event: "Things started to change, and the organization started to realize that it needed more help and . . . more volunteers." County sheriffs had confiscated ticket receipts, which comprised the event's sole source of revenues. The ensuing financial crisis persuaded the Burning Man organizers to seek and accept help on a wider basis.[7]

However, the organization lacked the infrastructure to handle large-scale recruitment and placement. Overworked organizers were too focused on other logistics to accept offers of help in a timely manner. Prospective volunteers thus waited for a response or in some cases, a frustrating nonresponse, about possible volunteer opportunities. Organizer Marian Goodell admitted that some prospective volunteers still undergo a drawn-out entry process that she herself experienced in the mid-1990s:[8]

> Nearly almost every person that I know that has volunteered for Burning Man had to pound on the door more than once. . . . That's the way it was for me. I'd send an e-mail, I'd get a response back for a job that was bigger than I wanted to handle, and then I'd leave messages, and I'd get either no answer or a weird answer of what's available, and that's totally what we still experience now.
>
> We offer things to people that may not be the right size for them or [tap] the right interests. Then sometimes we don't have time to call people back, and then you see the person again, and they show up at another party, and they remind you [that] they want to do this thing . . .[9]

Interested persons had to be persistent in pursuing volunteer opportunities, as demonstrated by the experiences of Jim Graham, a.k.a. RonJon. Several months passed before Graham, who repeatedly approached organizers, could volunteer his professional public relations skills.[10] Such delays in placement discouraged less motivated individuals and escalated the commitment of those who did join.[11]

To fill positions of greater responsibility, organizers recruited individuals with demonstrated organizing skills and ties.[12] For example, Dana Harrison became acquainted with organizers while helping with the 1998 event site cleanup and commissary. She explained how this familiarity led to an invitation to manage other operations and volunteers: "A lot of the organization is based on trust [and] personal relationships. They [the organizers] felt like I was serious about working with the organization and . . . willing to do the dirty work and could be trusted."[13] Likewise, individuals who had organized local Burning Man fundraisers in 1998 were asked to join or lead various groups within the organization.[14]

Such recruitment methods required little effort for organizers but limited the number of volunteers accepted. Such selective recruitment practices did not harness the talents and capacity associated with a larger, more diverse membership pool. Moreover, tasks were uncompleted because organizers did not delegate these to individuals who were eager to help. During the mid-to-late 1990s, organizer Marian Goodell recalled, "There was lots of stuff that no one could do anything about. It would just sit there. There was only so much time."[15]

Routinizing recruitment

To address these issues, organizers added bureaucratic practices that helped recruit volunteers in a more standardized and timely fashion. These changes included designating more coordinators to process volunteers and formalizing recruitment policies. After the 1996 event, volunteer coordinator John Nettle single-handedly responded to prospective volunteers' inquiries and placed volunteers before and during the event. Citing burnout from the overwhelming amount of work, he took a break from his position in 2000. Based on his experience, Nettle's successor Molly Tirpak realized that one individual could not handle all of the volunteer recruitment and placement. She and organizer Harley Dubois assembled a team of volunteer coordinators and designated an additional coordinator for each department. By converting a single centralized position into several specialized positions, Tirpak distributed the responsibility for recruiting and placing new volunteers across the growing organization. Tirpak and Dubois also formalized organizational guidelines for cultivating volunteerism and identifying departmental needs. They provided coordinators and departmental leaders with management tools, including a "how-to" handbook and training sessions.[16] These efforts were intended to increase responsiveness in matching volunteers with responsibilities.

In addition, the organization standardized and centralized the collection and dissemination of information about prospective volunteers. Previously, prospective volunteers had phoned or e-mailed their information in an unstandardized format. Their information was forwarded to relevant departmental managers, who then constructed and maintained their own databases of prospective volunteers. This process duplicated efforts across departments. To improve the efficiency of this process, IT volunteers developed a Web interface and computerized database to collect prospective members' information for organization-wide use.[17] Prospective volunteers completed a lengthy questionnaire about their experiences, talents, and interests on the Burning Man Web site. Volunteer coordinators then accessed this database to construct their own department-specific databases or to conduct searches for particular skills or interests. By 2000, this database contained information on an estimated 1,000 persons.[18]

Continuing networked recruitment

In addition to rationalized recruitment processes, members continued to draw upon their personal networks to recruit and vouch for new members.[19] Interviewed members reported that they became "Burning Man evangelists" by convincing their friends to attend the event and, in some cases, volunteer for their respective teams.[20] Jess Bobier, a.k.a. Nurse, who herself joined the organization because of a friend's involvement,[21] explained the kinds of persons she approached about the Burning Man event:

> The people that I feel need to go to Burning Man are people . . . that want to share, they want to share with strangers, they have something to give, they're upbeat and positive and really have an enthusiasm for living in general, approaching life in a new way, being fresh, keeping things exciting, sometimes mixing things up . . . people that are aware of other people, people that have a sense of community.[22]

In selecting those who might benefit Burning Man, members screened prospective members for commitment and skills.[23]

However, critics complained of cliquishness in departments that drew upon friendship networks.[24] Such privileging of informal relations suggested possible underorganizing issues. Differential treatment can intimidate newcomers and prevent members from cohering as a collective (Polletta 2002). While network ties can facilitate routinization and coordination among those who have previously worked together in other organizations (Beckman 2006), they may also inadvertently reproduce undesired practices drawn from other experiences (Becker 1999; Conell and Voss 1990). Burning Man members counterbalanced these underorganizing tendencies with a collectivist mandate to include all newcomers.

Formalizing a collectivist recruitment policy

In revamping recruitment practices, Burning Man implemented a subtle but powerful volunteering policy, one that formalized a collectivist emphasis on cultivating flexibility, responsiveness, and meaning for volunteers. This policy explicitly sought to facilitate the participation of all interested persons. As the mission for Burning Man's Community Services division stated, "It is our goal to find a place for every person that wants to get involved."[25] In addition, Burning Man's principle of "radical inclusion" emphasized welcoming rather than excluding individuals.[26] Under this collectivist policy, organizers and coordinators accommodated individuals' desires to work toward Burning Man's mission, rather than restricting volunteer opportunities to identified organizational needs.[27] For example, volunteer coordinators were instructed to "allow as many people to participate as possible. If you get a big group, divide jobs up to maximize the resources at hand."[28]

At a meeting of volunteers, organizer Harley Dubois explained that including people trumped efficiency concerns: "When people say they only need 6 [volunteers], I say could you use thirty—it's not about being efficient, it's about making people a part of something."[29] In an interview, volunteer coordinator Molly Tirpak described how the Burning Man organization expanded volunteer opportunities so that more individuals could participate, even though this required more effort:

> Burning Man has devoted itself to volunteering so that even though . . . you could bite the bullet and pay somebody, more often than not, Burning Man says "no, let's create this opportunity for volunteers." . . . It's a much bigger deal to give ten [people] something to do than it is to give five. . . . They're all happy then. . . . It just gets infectious.[30]

Tirpak claimed, "There is a job for everyone—kids, too. I'll find something [for each person]."[31] Jim Lamb's experiences with the Lamplighters demonstrated Burning Man's policy of inclusion: "They [Lamplighters] want to try to get as many people to help out as they can, so there aren't heavy restrictions. . . . They take most people who come along."[32] Even departments that relied upon highly specialized skills welcomed people with a range of experiences. At a meeting, Joseph Pred explained how the Black Rock Ranger recruitment followed Burning Man's policy: "Part of Burning Man is trying to be as inclusive as possible and not elitist." He explained that rather than turning away less skilled and experienced volunteers, "we defaulted to [being] more inclusive."[33]

To help manage the growing influx of Burning Man volunteers, Dubois, Tirpak, and organizer Marian Goodell developed and disseminated a twenty-two-page, single-spaced "Successful Volunteerism with Burningman" packet concerning volunteer recruitment, training, and retention. Dubois estimated that 120 manuals had been distributed to organizers and their staff, volunteer coordinators, and regional contacts as of 2000.[34] While this guide offered bureaucratized routines for managing volunteers, it also stressed relaxing bureaucratized expectations of stability and efficiency. For example, the manual cautioned against applying "standard business criteria" to volunteers' productivity: "Productivity will rarely be where you would like and this should be expected."[35]

Instead, the manual reminded readers to adhere to collectivist concerns: "Personal and community growth is held as a higher premium."[36] In this vein, the manual advocated letting volunteers experiment with responsibilities: "Allow volunteers to try jobs that they have not done before." At the same time, the manual clarified that managers should be prepared to intervene and support volunteers' efforts:

Remember this as [*sic*] a primarily volunteer organization[;] it is understood that perfection is difficult to expect. . . . This is not to say that successful completion of a task is not expected, however it's up to you to put back up plans into place when experimenting with a new idea, task, process or volunteer.[37]

Departments held trainings to reinforce such policies, acknowledging that some members needed to learn otherwise unfamiliar ways of organizing. As organizer Larry Harvey observed, "We're growing and getting people from different worlds; many are used to really hierarchical systems."[38] At a volunteer meeting, members discussed topics such as how changing a top-down directive into an inclusive *we* could elicit unanticipated results. After volunteer Joe Fenton, a.k.a. Boggmann, stated that, "semantics are very important," Tirpak explained how to invite individuals to more fully participate:

Someone gave an example of when they were building something. Instead of saying [to volunteers], "you need to do this"—it's "how are we going to build this?" A lot of times you don't know what kind of resources they're [volunteers are] going to bring to it [the work]. It's just amazing to see how people respond to that call. . . . They [volunteers] will impress you.[39]

With this explicit policy of "radical inclusion," the Burning Man organization formalized openness to a wider range of possibilities.

Placement: Shaping Roles for People

While formalized recruitment practices aimed to widen member involvement, revamped placement practices considered members' interests in determining appropriate roles. But organizers did not subsume their organization's sustainability to individuals, an imbalance that can threaten the survival of cooperatives, communes, free schools, and voluntary associations (Kanter 1972; Polletta 2002; Rothschild and Whitt 1986; Schwartzman 1989; Swidler 1979). Rather than privileging one set of needs over others, Burning Man's flexible placement policy negotiated between organizational and individual needs by introducing bureaucratic routines to help place volunteers. They also formalized the collectivist practice of role creation, in which individuals could tailor roles to tap their talents and interests. Members could explore and train for chosen areas of responsibility even if they did not have appropriate qualifications. Although researchers have described the presence of such practices in organizations and lauded their benefits (e.g., Aldrich and Ruef 2006), not much is known about how members enact these practices (Miner 1987, 1990).

Creating and supporting roles

During the years preceding formal organizing efforts, members could create roles based on personal interest or perceived event needs. As Black Rock Ranger Joe Fenton, a.k.a. Boggmann, recalled, prior experience or expertise were not required:

> In the old days, '91, '92, we used to call [Burning Man] "the Make the Wish Foundation" because you could make a wish: "I wish I was in charge of the Gate. Ok. I'll do the Gate." And you can do it. "Have you ever done the Gate?" "No." "Have you ever collected money before?" "No." "Have you ever torn tickets before?" "No." "Have you ever been to the desert before?" "No." . . . Whatever it was that you wanted to do, you could do that kind of thing.[40]

Naomi Pearce similarly recounted how organizing was "organic," as in "things didn't pop up until they were really needed. . . . If people were overheating, you need a medical person, so the medical camp . . . cropped up."[41] Members did not wait for top-down orders to take action.

Individuals continued to create roles based on their interests and organizational needs during the 1990s. Rather than waiting for more senior organizers to assign their areas, Marian Goodell and Harley Dubois took charge of projects that they identified as relevant. Goodell recalled how she "would grab [a task] if it related to communications," which was not yet developed.[42] While volunteering for the Black Rock Rangers, Jennifer Vermut realized that she preferred a different kind of responsibility, one that could address an emerging need. She recalled:

> I wanted to be more of an informational type of Ranger rather than going around and doing the typical things that Rangers do. . . . A lot of the people were coming up to the Rangers and saying, "Hey . . . what's happening with that?" Do we [the Rangers] do this? . . . It was really distracting for the Rangers. They needed somebody there to answer those questions.[43]

At a desk set under a shade structure, Vermut staffed a new question-and-answer service that later became Playa Info.[44]

However, as the organization grew, prospective volunteers needed help with finding their niches. To facilitate volunteer placement, organizers formalized a bureaucratic routine for matching people to roles. At a training meeting, volunteer coordinator Molly Tirpak described a routine that other volunteer coordinators were expected to follow when interacting with prospective volunteers. Referring to a list of screening questions (i.e., "Have they been to Burningman before?"), Tirpak read aloud questions and shared tips that were intended to help place persons:

- "Have they volunteered before?"
- "Have they a particular skill that you know we need?"
- "Are they local if they don't need to be?" [*Comments to audience*] I don't recommend anyone for Tech team if they're not local [to the Bay area], because they [Tech team] work here.
- "Have they filled out the questionnaire for fun, for a free ticket, or because they genuinely want to help?"[45]

In addition, Tirpak discussed a handout about different departments and their volunteer opportunities. She suggested potential matches by volunteers' interests, skills, and desired work intensity. When asked by a new volunteer coordinator what to do with less dependable volunteers, Tirpak contrasted departments that were happy to accept "warm bodies" with those that demanded extensive training and hours:

CAROLINE: If [the prospective volunteers are] flaky, what do we do?
MOLLY: Do we have people who are ultraflaky to ultraserious? In the words of Brien Burroughs, "You can never let us down at the Lamplighters." Whereas with the Rangers, you come to the ROM [Ranger Orientation Meeting], and you're going to work eight hours a day during the event. We have everything in-between.[46]

The Burning Man organization also recognized that some placements took time, as roles were not readily apparent. Volunteer coordinators and departments were expected to enact collectivist practices for their flexibility and responsiveness to members' interests, rather than turn prospective help away. The "Successful Volunteerism with Burningman" guide answered the question of "What to do when you're not sure WHAT a volunteer can do" with a recommendation of allowing volunteers to explore possibilities:

Well, if they have the basic skills, but not a defined role, and you think you'd like to work with them eventually, put them on your team anyway. They'll eventually show their stuff, or they'll leave the team. Not many who volunteer know exactly how they want to help. Often it becomes more clear as the group dynamics and needs reveal themselves.[47]

In addition, the guide suggested developing new roles for individuals as they appeared: "In some cases[,] you won't really realize you need a particular role until the right person walks up to you with a certain set of skills. . . . In this case[,] the role will define itself."[48]

With such a flexible placement process, volunteers who wanted to apply particular skills or technical expertise, such as business management or computer programming, could invent new positions and responsibilities.[49] For instance, a college student proposed an arts management internship and became the first of several summer interns.[50] Other volunteers initiated new projects or even new departments. Organizers supported these volunteers, even if their initial efforts went awry. With a laugh, organizer Harley Dubois stated, "My philosophy with volunteers is to kind of let them hang themselves." She viewed her role as enabling volunteers, even when they experienced setbacks or failures:

> Let them get out there and try it. Empower them. Give them all the information they need so that they can make educated decisions. And empower them to feel confident to go out and do it. And if they do something stupid, . . . they themselves will realize that they did something stupid, and they will themselves correct what they've done, or when it's pointed out to them, they'll want to, or they'll say, "I'm not willing to do that," and they'll leave.[51]

Organizers and volunteer coordinators were prepared to support a wide range of outcomes, including failure.

Given such possible setbacks, organizers recommended that they and other members should exercise patience and tolerate inefficiency as volunteers discovered their roles. This formalized collectivist policy reminded members to support participation and to resist the temptation to adopt a strictly bureaucratic approach to placing people. Volunteer coordinators and organizers explained how accepting more volunteer help than needed not only compensated for likely no-shows (Chen 2005), but also allowed individuals to "feel valued."[52] Furthermore, organizer Larry Harvey advised that rather than taking over lagging projects, coordinators should either give volunteers more time or redirect them to new tasks: "People constantly need to be repurposed [given more appropriate conditions and tasks]—give them enough time to do the job or repurpose. The least effective thing is to say 'oh fuck it, I'll do it.'"[53] At a volunteer meeting, Harley Dubois noted the importance of giving volunteers ample opportunities to realize their potential: "You don't want volunteers walking away feeling like they've failed."[54]

Organizers supported members' efforts even if proposed projects and responsibilities did not efficiently allocate resources. For example, Dan Miller established a department that solidified and disseminated environmental conservation policies across other departments, even though organizer Harley

Dubois did not view this as a best use of resources.[55] Similarly, skeptics initially viewed proposals for new departments, such as Dubois's proposal to establish Greeters, as unnecessary, but they still supported development efforts. Such departments often flourished, assuaging initial skepticism.[56]

Members, however, did not develop responsibilities without input from others. On occasions, others interceded if they thought fellow members had overestimated their abilities, or if they indulged in "power-tripping" over others.[57] Jesse Jones reported that the Café staff collectively discussed whether individuals had the capacity to fulfill their tasks. Members rejected his own proposal to decorate the football-field-sized Café, given his already considerable managerial duties. As Jones ruefully admitted, "In hindsight . . . there's no way that I could have done it," and another individual carried out the decorating project.[58] Through such informal "checks and balances," coordinators persuaded overextended members to accept help, thus increasing the chances of success and decreasing potential burnout.[59]

Placing difficult or outdated members

With the ethic of "radical inclusion," organizers and coordinators helped even the most difficult-to-place individuals find fulfilling roles. Organizer Larry Harvey explained that Burning Man's expansion allowed him to develop roles for more individuals: "As the scope of what we're doing gradually increases, those people with odd little constellations of talent that had no place [before] now have a place because [Burning Man]'s a bigger canvas." This included individuals "like Gerald Parsons, we could never figure out what to do with Gerald [before], a writer with no talent for writing. . . . He had made a little niche in the world [writing for the Web site] that worked for him and where it worked for us."[60]

Organizers and members recognized that flexibility in determining roles could satisfy both individual and collective interests. Harvey, for instance, enjoyed matching organizational needs and individual interests: "I love finding roles for people or finding venues for artists, finding ways to make the world consonant with their powers. . . . I look at what they are, what we need to do, and how you could possibly match those two things together."[61] Organizer Harley Dubois similarly regarded tailoring placements as one of the more rewarding and "beautiful" aspects of her work:

> If you can . . . give them an opportunity to use these skills that they don't get
> to use otherwise, that aren't something that they realize that are skills that are
> really valuable . . . , it can just do everything for them, change their self-esteem.

They come back and quit their job, and start on a new path, go back to school, whatever it is.[62]

Both the organization and individuals benefited from the unleashing of otherwise untapped potential.

However, tailoring roles to individuals could provoke tension with other members, as critics complained about "deadwood" or seemingly unproductive individuals. Larry Harvey illustrated the problems of "radical inclusion" by discussing the changing roles of a fellow organizer. In the past, Michael Mikel had played a critical role in organizing the event and establishing the organization's first legal form, but his place was unclear in the revamped organization. Rather than pushing him to retire, as other organizations do with former leaders (Greiner 1972), Harvey encouraged Mikel to become a symbolic leader for the Black Rock Rangers. However, according to Harvey, others voiced complaints about Mikel's new responsibilities: "There was tension about Michael with the [middle management of the Rangers] because they said, 'He's not managing . . . he's just sopping up the gravy, what's he doing?'"[63] Harvey expressed his relief about being able to tailor another role for Mikel. As a traveling ambassador for the Burning Man organization, Mikel could use his storytelling skills to help regionals form and organize local activities.[64]

Some Burning Man members worried whether collectivist retention and placement practices could undercut the organization's performance. Although some members retooled for new tasks, others opined that such individuals were not the best candidates for their responsibilities. Critics worried, for example, whether administrators were skilled enough to handle multimillion-dollar revenues.[65] In addition, Burning Man members did not take an efficient, bottom-line approach to organizing, a common issue in organizations with collectivist practices (Greenberg 1984). However, critics like Dana Harrison recognized that their colleagues did not aim to uphold bureaucratic standards of efficiency and effectiveness:

> One of the things that I have to remind myself often is that the people who are associated with Burning Man were not traditionally structured, organized, analytic thinkers who . . . worked well within established structures, gave reliable responses, etc., that . . . probably would have been sitting in the next office over from me at [Charles] Schwab. . . . They don't show up on time, they don't do what they're supposed to do when they're supposed to do it, the work product response is often of fairly dubious quality. . . . They don't have the skills to do what they're doing, they don't have the resources to get the skills. . . . A lot of the work is being done by people who have backgrounds as artists and fire

dancers. They've never worked in an office, so no wonder they don't have any idea of how to behave themselves in an office. Not only did they never work in an office, they never wanted to. . . . It's this whole different motivation, whole different personality styles and behaviors.[66]

Members did not view bureaucratic practices, such as hiring qualified personnel, as appropriate solutions for redressing such issues. Like other volunteer-based organizations, Burning Man members feared that paid personnel would undercut the normative basis for contributing and thus detract from the Burning Man mission. For example, Steve Mobia opined that "[the] problem is that probably there could be people that could do that work much better, but then they would have to be paid, and then it would become a job for them."[67] Furthermore, members argued that Burning Man would lose its distinctiveness if produced by professionals. Dana Harrison, whose concerns about efficiency were quoted earlier, stated the caveat: "The event is very much informed by the quirky sensibilities of the people who are running it, and I don't . . . believe that we could replace the LLC with a bunch of talented event organizers and managers . . . and have Burning Man at all."[68] Eric Pouyoul hoped that nonprofessionals would continue to run the event and accepted that their output could vary from "chaotic" to the "best": "If you put professional people, [or] people who do know what they're doing [in control], then it tends towards borders and limits about how to do things. If it's kind of chaotic, where anything can happen, [then] the worst can happen, but as well as the best."[69] According to this reasoning, individuals' idiosyncrasies and impassioned beliefs were crucial to creating Burning Man, but people had to be willing to tolerate unpredictability and variability.

Thus, members took chances with finding responsibilities for individuals who seemed difficult to place or even unwilling to volunteer. With the right conditions, these individuals could become "stars." For instance, organizer Harley Dubois shared how she converted two individuals who were caught trying to enter the 1996 event without tickets or supplies. Since the failed gate-crashers did not have enough money to pay for tickets, Dubois arranged a work assignment so that they could attend the event:

The two chicks had no money, no water, no food, nothing. They were getting more sassy. . . . I said, "Ok, you're going to work for your tickets." One whined, "You're going to make me scrub toilets." I said, "Listen, bitch, I'm going to get you the best job," and got on the radio and called around for people needing volunteers. Finally [I find out that] Plundertown [a theme camp] was doing a life-size game of Mousetrap, I send them over, and I never see these people again [at Burning Man].

When she later ran into the reluctant volunteers at a San Francisco arts event, one woman admitted, "You were right, that was the coolest job ever," vindicating Dubois's efforts.[70]

Volunteer coordinators and organizers preached persistence in placing persons, particularly in "repurposing" or reassigning underperforming volunteers. Volunteer coordinator Molly Tirpak described how she removed a mischievous volunteer from his position at Playa Info because he intentionally provided incorrect answers to inquiries. That same volunteer later became a "star" by bringing a friend who could perform the rigging work needed to secure the Café shelter. Not only that, "That same guy who was a total nightmare at [Playa Info], days later, him and his loud voice were at Recycle Camp. . . . He's now the volunteer coordinator of the Recycle Camp."[71] Such accounts demonstrated how a change in work conditions unleashed the talents and initiative of those who might otherwise have been dismissed as useless, annoying, or marginal within more bureaucratic organizations. Rather than reassigning problematic individuals to worse positions as punishment, as employers clandestinely do (Morrill 1995), or foisting them onto other unsuspecting departments, the Burning Man organization allowed individuals to uncover their potential through experimentation.

Volunteers valued being able to try different departments and roles, especially as their interests and skills changed. For instance, Brien Burroughs volunteered for several projects before finding his "home" with the Lamplighters.[72] Alice Freedman appreciated the fluid and meaningful volunteer opportunities available in the Burning Man organization, which she contrasted with previous volunteer experiences:

> [The other volunteer organizations] are organizations that are very much more institutionalized and corporate and have a very developed and defined volunteer program. . . . They have certain jobs . . . that they reserve for their volunteers. . . . [At Burning Man], it's a very different kind of experience— you feel that you're doing something that's much more vital to the organization and that if you want to take on any kind of a project, that [the organizers are] probably willing to go along with it. . . . I feel like whatever volunteer experience that I have, it can evolve, whereas in the other kind of volunteer experiences that I had, you never had a sense that it would evolve into anything.[73]

Freedman's experimentation with various departments within the Burning Man organization led to "finding [her] people" at the *Black Rock Gazette* newspaper, where she engaged her writing interests.[74] As Freedman pointed out, such opportunities would not be available if bureaucratic practices restricted volunteers' activities. Collectivist practices elevated Burning Man's responsiveness to the interests of members like Freedman.

Sustaining Bureaucratic and Collectivist Practices

At times, members wrestled over the appropriate mixture of collectivist and bureaucratic practices. In particular, organizers debated whether they should specify responsibilities for members, particularly when the work was paid, rather than allowing members to propose their own responsibilities. During an LLC meeting in 2002, organizers discussed whether to accept a volunteer's proposal to perform a highly technical task for pay. Organizer Harley Dubois objected to the proposal and suggested a more bureaucratic practice in which organizers, rather than members, had the responsibility of creating jobs and matching individuals' skills to possible roles. Other organizers disagreed and opined that they did not have the technical expertise to specify a job description for this case:

> HARLEY DUBOIS: We [should] have not people create the jobs, but we create the jobs and have people slotted into them. We have a combination of both here.
>
> MICHAEL MIKEL: [The volunteer] hasn't had the time; I think if Burning Man supported him, he would give more of his time, and I think he's good enough that he could [work] in any direction. I don't think that we necessarily have to pigeonhole him, but he has enough skills and awareness, I see the value.
>
> . . .
>
> MARIAN GOODELL: I think, Harley, in some cases when we have a new morphing job . . . I don't feel comfortable creating a job description and putting it out there.[75]

Despite Dubois's objections, other board members did not find sufficient reason to rely upon a more bureaucratic placement practice.

Similar debates indicated that members preferred having some control over their responsibilities. In one instance, members resisted a volunteer coordinator's top-down attempt to design and assign roles. Monica Senter tried to staff the newly formed Tech team by first evaluating the organization's needs and then assigning volunteers to specified roles based on their skill level. Organizer Marian Goodell, who supervised the team, endorsed a less bureaucratic way of assigning tasks, arguing that members should "organically" self-determine roles. Members apparently also questioned the proposal by emphasizing that they were volunteers, not paid employees. After Senter withdrew her proposal, members collectively allocated responsibilities among themselves. While this process may have increased members' commitment to their self-designed roles, it consumed a year of sometimes heated and acrimonious group negotiations over who should lead.[76] Although Burning Man organizers wished volunteers would undertake certain needed tasks, they also respected volunteers' selectivity about their working conditions. Volunteers could exercise their preferences for fun or challenging projects,[77] working with specific organizers, and learning new skills (Chen 2005).[78] Constant discussions about how to carry out practices helped prevent under- or overorganizing.

Conclusion

By mixing bureaucratic and collectivist practices, the Burning Man organizers expanded recruitment efforts that were previously limited to connected individuals. Standardized recruitment procedures, a specialized volunteer staff, and a mandate of "radical inclusion" helped expand a small, tightly constrained group into a more diverse membership body. With the collectivist practice of role creation, organizers and coordinators fostered conditions that matched individual interests and collective needs without sacrificing one to the other. Members' ongoing debates about how to apply bureaucratic and collectivist practices demonstrated the reflection that helped keep under- and overorganizing at bay.

As organizations promote more member participation, such blending of collectivist and bureaucratic practices could spread across organizations. For example, Miner (1987) estimated that between 7 percent to 12 percent of all new jobs at a large research university, exclusive of faculty and student positions, were tailored to the individual job holders' interests.[79] In self-managing teams, members propose their responsibilities (Hackman 2002). With corporate America's shift toward a service economy and a growing population of "high-caliber," adaptable individuals, some predict that corporations will stop slotting people into predetermined, static positions (Snow and Snell 1993: 449). Instead, corporations' staffing practices will capitalize upon market needs and individuals' strengths, allowing for more flexibility (Snow and Snell 1993). Staffing thus will be emergent rather than predetermined (Stewart and Carson 1997).

W. L. Gore & Associates, the manufacturer of Gore-Tex fabric and other cutting-edge products, is a contemporary exemplar of such placement practices. With the guidance of a chosen "sponsor," newcomers explore possible roles and design their own "commitments," which are not fixed. Such practices have been credited with fostering innovation and strengthening members' devotion (Shipper and Manz 1992).[80]

The Burning Man case shows how "radical inclusion" and role creation can elicit performance. However, these strategies of accepting all interested individuals and then tailoring and adjusting roles to individuals' strengths and interests require time, experimentation, and patience, which some organizations will not or cannot invest. These strategies also call for a skilled, powerful human resources staff that many organizations lack (Snow and Snell 1993).[81] The Mondragón worker cooperative provides an example of how to establish a strong personnel board. Members help design and implement strategy, and they also emphasize the balance between individual interests with collective interests (Whyte and Whyte 1988). Implementing this strategy requires resources and recognition of possible trade-offs. However, blended collectivist and bureaucratic practices can harness individuals' interests and initiative for collective purposes, as the next chapter demonstrates.

: : :

"No Spectators"

Motivating Members to Contribute

VOLUNTEER DANA HARRISON, a.k.a. BizBabe, sat, with a slightly preoccupied look, in the sun-filled living room of her home in Berkeley, California. As she recounted how she had been invited to share her professional expertise with the predominantly self-taught senior staff, she jokingly described her role as a "gadfly." When asked about her motivations for contributing, Harrison singled out the amusing and fun aspects of her Burning Man work:

> The three-ring circus element of it [organizing Burning Man] is damn fun. . . . Here we are doing something that we believe in, and my role in it is a bunch of tasks that are pretty easy for me to perform, and I get to be part of the three-ring circus. Sometimes I do get pissed about the way we're using time and people being late and other stuff. But most of the time, it's kind of through-the-looking-glass of my old life in a way that cracks me up. . . . There are times that are just so absurd, you just have to laugh.

Harrison's tone turned serious as she speculated about her future involvement with Burning Man. She talked about how her decision to contribute today could change tomorrow: "I can't always maintain finding it funny. . . . I think I can also cultivate a certain detachment because I'm not dependent on Burning Man for my livelihood. On the day it is no longer amusing, bye-bye."[1] If volunteering no longer meets her needs, Harrison might walk away from her managerial position at Burning Man, just as she did from her vice president position at an investment firm.[2]

As Harrison's ongoing evaluation of her involvement demonstrates, organizational conditions can impact members' desire to contribute. In particular, too little or too much organizing can undermine members' involvement. Members may overextend themselves to compensate for underorganized conditions, which lack the structure and coordination to retain and use resources effectively. On the other hand, members may become constrained and alienated by overorganizing's excessive structure and coordination. Organizations thus face a delicate balance: develop sufficient structure and coordination to guide, but not overwhelm, members' efforts.

Establishing this balance is especially difficult when managing members who are volunteers. Volunteers provide labor and expertise without demanding a commensurate salary or wage, but their availability and productivity may vary. Bureaucratic practices such as standardizing policies or tying financial compensation to tasks can decrease this uncertainty. However, these practices can also undercut collectivist practices, such as members' commitment to a mission or ethic and taking responsibilities based on their interests. While collectivist practices can amplify members' commitment to a collective mission, practices enforced with coercive control can induce a culty or feel-good collective.

In this chapter, we shall see how Burning Man's volunteerism policy and practices formalized a collectivist approach to motivating volunteers by catering to a variety of volunteers' motivations and incorporating members' interests without veering into overorganizing. I will then examine how the organizers used perks, including financial compensation, to heighten members' accountability to certain tasks.

Linking Motivations with Volunteer Opportunities

At a volunteer training session, organizer Harley Dubois stood before a crowd of volunteer managers seated in ragged rows of folding chairs. The session concerned an issue common to all organizations: how to create conditions that continuously tap members' motivations to contribute. Dubois exhorted the managers to first find out each volunteer's motivation:

> Find out why the volunteer is here. Find out what motivates them. If you do that, then you have done fifty percent of the work already. Find out who the

person is, and how they're going to learn from you, how to keep them coming back. They're not here for money, because they're motivated [by other things].

When asked "What are some reasons why people might volunteer for Burning Man?" volunteer managers suggested possible motivations. Using a whiteboard, Dubois recorded their answers as the following list:

fun
structure, purpose
community
perspective
part of something
desire to educate
meet new people
chance to interact
learn new skills[3]

Interviews of eighty-one past and present volunteers and organizers substantiated this list. Some volunteers sought fun while others wanted structured activities and direction at an otherwise chaotic and overwhelming event. Some volunteers also yearned for connections with other people and a sense of belonging; others desired opportunities to practice skills. According to psychology researchers who study volunteerism, such motivations comprise distinct categories. These categories explain how volunteers are motivated by the chance to (1) enact and affirm values, (2) facilitate self-understanding through learning experiences and opportunities to exercise knowledge, skills, and abilities, (3) access social networks and relations, and (4) elevate positive mood through personal growth and esteem (Clary and Snyder 1991, 1999; Clary, Snyder, and Stukas 1996; Snyder and Omoto 2001).[4] Individuals can have more than one type of motivation for volunteering (Clary et al. 1998; Knoke 1988; Pearce 1993). However, in managing volunteers, organizations tend to cater to one type of motivation and ignore others (Pearce 1993), which can affect member retention.

Particular societal and organizational conditions can encourage individuals to volunteer (e.g., Eckstein 2001; Ostrower 1995; Skocpol, Ganz, and Munson 2000). For instance, institutionalized cultural frames (rules, institutions, and ideas) delineate what forms of volunteer activities are possible and appropriate. These frames account for national differences in voluntary associations' membership numbers (Schofer and Fourcade-Gourinchas 2001) and differences in voluntary association activities among cities within the same nation (Barman 2006). Formal organizations also cultivate volunteerism by channeling activities and reshaping conceptions of possible actions such as donating time, money, and even blood or organs (Bacharach et al. 2001; Healy 2004, 2006).

In addition, organizations use incentives and other means to convince their members to contribute. Solidary incentives involve intangible rewards, such as fraternizing with other members, accruing status from a group affiliation, and deriving a sense of belonging or fun. Purposive incentives concern the intangible rewards associated with pursuing organizational goals. Material incentives consist of tangible rewards such as pay, increased value, or benefits (Clark and Wilson 1961). In the workplace, members comply because of the pay and the control embedded in bureaucratic practices, such as hierarchy, rules, job descriptions, and career ladder (Edwards 1979; Etzioni [1961] 1975; Weber [1946] 1958). In some organizations, a leader's charisma or exemplary qualities can push members to obey and produce (Boltanski and Chiapello 2005; Pearce 1993; Weber [1946] 1958).

Collective activities also build members' commitment.[5] Some organizations steer members with rituals, symbolic rewards that confer esteem or prestige, and negative or positive reinforcement such as ostracism or praise (Etzioni [1961] 1975). Religious organizations and communes promote rituals that bind members together by renouncing other relations and activities, engaging in regular self-criticisms and confessions, or emphasizing a group identity through distinctive attire and activities (Kanter 1968, 1972). Such practices strengthen members' commitment, especially since they often preclude other activities or responsibilities (Iannaccone 1994; Kanter 1972). Within this context of curtailed choice, some organizational members cannot conceive of alternative venues for expending their efforts (Lalich 2004).

Workplace organizations use similar forms of normative control to solidify members' commitment. Some firms cultivate a sense of family or kinship among employees; this transference of familial roles encourages employees to cooperate and obey their superiors (Biggart 1989; Kondo 1990; Lee 1998). Other firms develop a corporate culture with a "unique" organizational identity, norms, rituals, and values that exhort members to contribute their utmost (Biggart 1989; Kunda 1992; Martin 1992; Schein 1992; Sherman 2007; Van Maanen 1991). In such workplaces, a selection process weeds out the least committed and able individuals, while training and indoctrination aim to forge bonds among selected members (Graham 1995; Griswold 1994; Milkman 1997). Teamwork adds peer pressure to not let fellow teammates down (Barker 1993, 1999; Graham 1995; Sewell 1998).

These practices intensify commitment and control beyond bureaucratic practices' obedience to position and rules (Barker 1993, 1999; Kunda 1992).

Bureaucratic rules, direct supervision, and normative control all push members to contribute (Van Maanen 1991). When used coercively, these mixtures of practices can create total or "greedy" institutions that engulf their members (Coser 1974; Goffman 1961; Lalich 2004). The ensuing totalitarianism, in which overorganized bureaucratic and participatory practices combine with coercive control, can neglect or suppress members' interests.

How can bureaucratic and collectivist practices be used to enable, as opposed to engulf, members? That is, how can an organization convince members to contribute in a balanced way, accommodating members' interests without devolving into coercive control?

Sustaining Volunteerism with Bureaucratic and Collectivist Practices

For years, the slogans "Participate" and "No spectators" prodded event attendees into activities including volunteerism. However, members worried that as the Burning Man organization formalized, volunteers' enthusiasm might wane. As Larry Harvey warned fellow organizers, "'Bigger is better' is not a good idea. We're all aware that people see [us] as bigger and are less willing to volunteer without compensation." Harley Dubois seconded Harvey's cautionary statement with a concern about bureaucratization: "It makes us less accessible."[6] An e-mailed meeting agenda for one department made a humorous announcement acknowledging increased organization: "Socializing begins at 7. Bureaucracy and red tape start at 7:30. Sharp."[7]

Given such concerns, organizers reinforced the formalization of collectivist practices alongside bureaucratic practices. This combination of practices supported members' interests without instigating overorganizing. Volunteer coordinators were expected to follow bureaucratic routines that facilitated interactions with departments and volunteers.[8] However, these routines incorporated collectivist practices' emphasis upon flexibility, responsiveness, and meaning. For instance, a volunteerism manual advised getting acquainted with new volunteers to better ascertain their motivations, aims, and interests: "Take the time to hear what their interests are."[9] The manual also specified a meeting routine, which included asking volunteers to introduce themselves, recount their past experiences with the Burning Man event, and share their reasons for volunteering.[10] This self-described "ritual" was intended to prime motivations: "This reminds everyone of why they're there. . . . For many[,] it's to connect with others who've experienced Burning Man as deeply as they have."[11]

Formalized collectivist practices constantly reminded members that adopting a purely bureaucratic approach was not appropriate. Through trainings, meetings, and documents, organizers and volunteer coordinators highlighted collectivist ways of organizing. For instance, the volunteerism manual stressed participation as crucial to the Burning Man mission: "The organization will always encourage participation as the foundation for creating a connective community."[12] Likewise, volunteer coordinator Molly Tirpak explained how she invited volunteers to contribute by depicting their participation as an integral and fulfilling way of accomplishing Burning Man's goals: "I said to people, 'Come help us build the city, so that your family, friends, and loved ones could enjoy it. You should feel proud that you helped build part of the city.'"[13] Observations revealed that volunteer trainings attempted to create such connections by immersing volunteers in the history and lore of departments, as well as recent developments and challenges.

In discussing ways to motivate volunteers, the volunteerism manual explained the importance of reflecting members' interests. Collectivist practices such as role creation were portrayed as heightening members' commitment: "Giving someone room to define their role and take ownership usually results in a longer-term commitment to the task/job/role at hand."[14] The manual also advocated including volunteers in planning and decision making, rather than directing them with a strictly top-down approach: "Allow as much input from the volunteers as possible. Remain flexible in your thinking. Your way, although proven to work, may not serve the needs of your team best."[15] In addition, the manual counseled volunteer coordinators to thank volunteers, regardless of their effectualness, especially since these volunteers might metamorphose and return:

> Thank everyone twice as much as you believe is necessary. . . . If they did it for free, they deserve the praise. Since we are operating outside of the box and effecting change in people through our event, you never know what changes that person may go through and what may come back to you at a later date.[16]

Similarly, a short section on tactics for dealing with "less successful volunteers" reminded readers of the variable, transformational possibilities of volunteerism: "Some of our best volunteers have turned into problems. Often though, our worst problem folks turn into great believers and volunteers. Time will tell."[17] However, coordinators understood that not all individuals were willing or able to contribute. Some members used "code 48," a shorthand for "useless hippie," to refer to those who did not respond to motivational efforts.[18] Nevertheless, coordinators were expected to give all interested individuals the opportunity to either self-select into or out of volunteerism: "Let people screen themselves out."[19]

Volunteer coordinators set conditions to encourage wider participation among those who had not otherwise considered volunteering, converting event attendees into on-the-spot volunteers. John Nettle approached event attendees with a direct request for help:

> The most effective way of asking people and getting people to help on-site is just going up to them and asking them to help. I would go up to people and say, "Excuse me, but can you help me?" They would look at one another, or they would look at me and say, "Sure, what do you need?" . . . It [Burning Man] really is about participation. . . . People are generally receptive to helping out.[20]

Similarly, Molly Tirpak discussed how she used the collectivist norm of participation to prod early arrivals to the event into helping build the event and art:

> I remember walking up to a couple lying in the back of a truck. . . . They were totally fried from traveling. I said to them, "You really need to be working." I go back a couple days later, totally expecting them to not have left their van. It turns out that night they walked in the Café and helped [artist] David Best, who built the Asian-style portal to the Café. . . . They had a great time.

She elaborated on how she encouraged individuals with some direction and tips:

> When they first arrived, they were confused. I told them to help at night with the Café, explaining that it was easier to work at night. . . . The point is to nudge them [prospective volunteers], give them a little bit of structure—"come to Check Point, I'll find something for you." . . . I walk up to people, greet them, and then I'll stumble upon them later working elsewhere. You just never know.[21]

When provided with a context for volunteering, some individuals contribute, as demonstrated by these accounts and other studies.[22]

Even seemingly onerous or undesirable tasks could attract volunteers when work conditions were tweaked. To "hook" event attendees on recycling, Recycle Camp founders Simon Hagger and Diane Whitman transformed the tedious tasks of collecting and crushing aluminum cans into a fun, meaningful activity. Volunteers, including children, biked around the city with special carts to collect cans. At Recycle Camp, volunteers could either whack the cans with oversized mallets or pedal a modified bicycle with oversized tires to flatten the cans.[23] Hagger recounted his philosophy of transforming work conditions:

If you give [people] an option of doing it [recycling], they want to do it. If you give them a good way of doing it and you don't make it a smelly nasty thing, then people really want to do it. And if you make it fun, then they REALLY want to do it. . . . If you give someone a good experience, they take that with them . . . and they pass it on.[24]

Earth Guardians Karina O'Connor and Antony "Shona" Guerra reported that theme camps took a similar tactic in transforming dirty work. Camps enlivened cleanups with competitions and awards to the fastest person to fill a bag with litter collected from the ground.[25] Such experiences not only helped reduce waste, but also convinced some event attendees to practice recycling in their everyday lives, an outcome that managers like Hagger found especially gratifying.[26]

Coordinators believed that enticing work conditions also ensured greater volunteer turnout. After only 10 out of the 130 scheduled volunteers showed up to sell ice during the 1999 event, manager Scott Shaner reevaluated his four months of preparation and decided to redesign the volunteer experience for the 2000 event:

I said, "You know, people don't want to come and hang out behind hay bales and sit around for four hours, five hours a day, while the party's going on around them, and schlep ice back and forth. We've got to make this fun, we got to make it happen, we got to have costumes, we got to have fun music going to be a part of this giant circus. . . . " So we got to be a theme camp.[27]

The nondescript ice sales became Camp Arctica, an impressive igloo-shaped structure with costumes, communal activities, and customized counters for handling ice bags. Shaner attributed higher volunteer commitment to this makeover, based on how eagerly Camp Arctica volunteers began planning months in advance of the next year's event.[28]

Observations and interviews revealed that for the most part Burning Man members responded positively to these practices and work conditions. In explaining why they contributed, volunteers expressed their appreciation of how Burning Man's practices incorporated their interests. First, members valued how they could contribute toward fulfilling a mission and enacting values. Members also lauded the organization's support for experimentation and skills development. In addition, members enjoyed the networks and solidarity catalyzed by the organization. Finally, members were energized by feedback that affirmed meaning and fulfillment.

Opportunities to contribute toward fulfilling a mission and enacting values

In discussing why they contributed, interviewed members referred to the Burning Man mission of developing a temporary arts community. With this collectivist guide to action, they could enact, or carry out, values of importance to them. For instance, volunteers reported that they enjoyed enabling transformational experiences via the Burning Man event. Volunteer Fiona Essa liked helping others gain new perspectives: "I'm a sucker for utopian visions, and I think that [Burning Man] will shake people's reality from their foundations in a way that few things do. . . . Being able to give that to other people is highly satisfying."[29] Interviewees reported that involvement with Burning Man inspired new activities and exploration of careers and interests.[30] For instance, Burning Man convinced Holly Kreuter to pursue her interests in performing in a band and publishing a book of her photographs. She sought to share the transformative aspects of Burning Man with others:

> [Burning Man] changed my life so tremendously that I want to see it continue, and I want to see it affect people's lives. I think it's really important that people learn what their potential can be. . . . When I came my first year or two, I knew I could take pictures; I had done it on and off my whole life. I knew I was interested in music; I had been in choir in high school. But once I saw the people at Burning Man just doing it, I . . . got it then. . . . It's one of the reasons . . . that makes me feel that I can actually start something and finish it. And Burning Man shows you that that's very possible and that there's a lot of other like minds that will collaborate with you and help to . . . get [it] done.[31]

Other members singled out specific aspects of the Burning Man mission, such as expanding participation in the arts. Burning Man art curator Christine Kristen, a.k.a. Lady Bee, explained how Burning Man's efforts to make the arts more inclusive and accessible coincided with her democratic, community-oriented conception of art: "I was so taken with [Burning Man] because . . . I had very traditional ideas about art-making, which is that it should be for the community. People should relate to it. It shouldn't be detached and removed and rarefied; it should be available."[32]

Interviewed volunteers drew satisfaction from carrying out the goals and values associated with the Burning Man mission.[33] As P. Segal noted, "The great pleasure of Burning Man is making it happen. Not being an attendee, [but] being a worker. The joy . . . from knowing that the fourteen hours a day that you worked made a difference is extraordinary."[34] Similarly, volunteer Ray Bruman quoted philosophers to explain the attraction of volunteer work:

> Happiness consists of using the skills that you have to do work that you believe is valuable or important. That is the way that human beings become happy. . . . The peak experience that people have is usually not recreational experience, it's usually a working experience, where people say, "Wow! That was cool." So the work itself to an extent is its own reward.[35]

Such quotes indicated that Burning Man provided the chance to experience intrinsic motivation, in which individuals derive rewards from the work itself (Lette 2006).

Furthermore, members appreciated how collectivist practices ensured their input in work. As Department of Public Works volunteer Kat De-Lurgio explained:

> Everyone's opinion is heard; . . . it's not run solely by rank, you know: "I'm the line manager, and what I say goes." It's like, "Hey, let's talk about this—what does everyone think about the best way to do this?" So there's a lot more . . . round table discussions about how something is going to be done.[36]

While such discussions may have slowed the work process, they also ensured that the organization adhered to the participatory emphasis of collectivist practices. If members can participate in decision making, they are more committed to their organizations (Knoke 1981), and they are more likely to spend extra time and effort on their work (Hodson and Roscigno 2004).

Support for experimenting and developing skills

Members reported that they appreciated how Burning Man supported the development of skills that were underutilized in their other organizational experiences. For instance, Karina O'Connor taught conservation practices at Burning Man. She relished this hands-on educational interaction, as her environmental engineer position at the Environmental Protection Agency did not include such outreach activities.[37] Likewise, two volunteers on the Tech and Web teams described how they enjoyed learning how to collaboratively use new tools and develop programs, as their work as consultants did not involve such opportunities.[38] Jim Lamb said that he learned "how to manage larger projects and larger groups of people" through his volunteer position at Burning Man, an opportunity that his small workplace did not provide.[39] Volunteers also appreciated the chance to do physical labor, design, and other work that was not part of their regular jobs.[40]

When expressing what they liked about Burning Man's volunteer conditions, some members identified how Burning Man supported experimentation. Individuals could initiate activities with organizers' support and make mistakes without fearing punishment. Members contrasted Burning Man's openness with the curtailed opportunities and coercive control of over-organized groups. As Jess Bobier, a Burning Man volunteer-turned-employee, explained, "You have the opportunity to screw up, and you're not docked your pay, or it's not something that goes on your record."[41] Burning Man volunteers liked how they could take risks, such as spearheading a new project, and fail without being penalized. Volunteer Rob Oliver praised Burning Man's capacity for making learning fun and enjoyable: "Burning Man has so much fun . . . it makes you want to learn. It's like when you go to school, the best teacher was the one who made you enjoy what you were learning. . . . You made a mistake, oh, [*laugh*] you crack up about it, and you fix it in a positive . . . fashion."[42] With such conditions, Burning Man members could savor experimentation, irrespective of whether it generated a successful outcome. Volunteer Jim Lamb cherished Burning Man's openness to the uncertain outcomes of new projects: "You just sort of throw it out and see what happens. Sometimes it flies and sometimes it doesn't. That's another thing that I like about the event—it's just a huge experiment."[43]

Given the uncertainties of the desert environment and the limits of human abilities, volunteers and attendees alike realized that even the best plans could not prevent spectacular failures and disappointments.[44] Volunteer Eric Pouyoul explained how innumerable contingencies forced people to adapt plans:

> Nothing you planned is going to happen the way you planned. Things are going to be changed because either the land [site] you're going to get is not the same, or because it rained, maybe the people you were counting on are not coming up, maybe because a piece of equipment you need is going to be broken. . . . If you try to make it happen the way you want, you're going to fail, and that's not the goal.[45]

To remind members to take such challenges in stride, a volunteer training agenda included an oft-repeated mantra in its list of bullet points: "Remember—it is only a camping trip!"[46] Disruptions and complications highlighted the limits of rational planning for cultivating efficiency and stability,[47] forcing people to relax expectations of newly implemented projects and organizing practices. Organizers recognized that members would undergo various setbacks and that complex endeavors involved an incremental learning process that could span several years. Organizers therefore supported the long-term development of projects with resources and time, rather than forcing predictability with procedures that could lead to overorganizing.[48]

With such support, Burning Man volunteers and workers could practice what Langer (1989) calls "mindfulness" in experimenting with how they did their work and what they produced. Such conditions have been shown to encourage trail-and-error learning and proficiency (Lee et al. 2004). As Burning Man members gained experience, they challenged themselves to improve on previous efforts.[49] Such instances demonstrate how involvement can build skills and self-confidence and spur individuals to achieve more (Kleinman 1996; Warren 2001).

Catalyst for networks and solidarity

In addition, Burning Man volunteer opportunities catalyzed connections among individuals, cultivating a sense of solidarity. For example, after attending a Burning Man event in which he metaphorically "went crazy [from] not talking to people," Mike Warner volunteered for the Greeters. By welcoming newcomers to the event, Warner could "talk to people without having to be like, 'I have to talk to you now.'"[50] Because volunteers could choose responsibilities based on their interests, rather than based on experience or expertise, members mixed across networks that might not otherwise overlap in overly bureaucratized groups.[51] For instance, art school students, punk circus clowns, former NASA employees, mechanics, riggers, architects, engineers, and other professionals worked together on the Department of Public Works (DPW) to build the event's infrastructure.[52] Members learned how to pool resources and ignore preconceptions that might have otherwise restricted contact and cooperation with others.[53] In working alongside others, individuals developed and pursued new interests and skills, such as fire spinning or managing small arts events.

Technology enhanced the connection and coordination of those who could not have face-to-face contact because of their distant locations. Members could dial a toll-free number to conference call meetings held at Burning Man's San Francisco headquarters or watch town hall meetings online and e-mail questions. Using discussion lists, members could exchange arguments, support, thanks, humor, gossip, and information around a virtual water cooler twenty-four hours a day. A member described one discussion list as "like a conference room full of hundreds of people talking."[54] Like other organizations (Sproull and Kiesler 1986), members also posted requests or information that did not concern Burning Man issues, such as job positions, available housing, and related events which others might find useful. This online communication helped ensure the constant renewal and maintenance of the Burning Man community.

The collegiality fostered by participating together reinforced some volunteers' decisions to continue contributing to Burning Man.[55] As volunteer Susan Strahan noted, "I'm motivated by the enthusiasm and commitment from the people who are involved. . . . I find myself being happy to be part of that."[56] Productivity only underscored the satisfaction of volunteering with others, as volunteer Mike Wright commented: "When things work well, there's this sense of satisfaction, but mostly it comes out of having people that are fun to work with."[57] The social ties fostered through participatory practices heightened members' commitment and involvement, supporting the findings of other studies (Jackall and Crain 1984; McAdam 1986).

Feedback to affirm meaning and fulfillment

In both under- and overorganized organizations, members may not know how their contributions affect the overall output. For instance, without specified goals or an agreed-upon means of reaching these goals, an underorganized group's members can neither coordinate their efforts nor determine whether their efforts have an impact. These conditions can lead to the group's premature dissolution (Polletta 2002). On the other hand, an extreme division of labor or centralized coordination can prevent members from knowing the effects of their contributions (Marx [1844] 1978). The ensuing alienation can strip away meaning, demoralizing and paralyzing members' efforts. For example, after a difficult experience with one developing department, a Burning Man volunteer chose not to return because he "felt that the lack of organization wasn't going to get any better."[58]

In contrast, if members are able to get feedback on the effects of their contributions, the resulting sense of meaningfulness and accomplishment can heighten motivations to contribute (Hackman and Oldham 1980; Pearce 1993). Sufficient structure and coordination allow members to participate and understand the impact of their contributions. Lamplighter Steve Mobia explained the effect of seeing the lamps he had placed on the spires along the city's walkways: "There's fulfillment knowing that you've put all of those up there."[59] Similarly, Playa Info volunteer Rob Oliver enjoyed responding to event attendees' queries: "By answering someone's questions and helping them have a better experience at Burning Man, that's kind of like a reward."[60] Participation and knowledge of results enabled volunteers to more fully experience their work as palpable and meaningful.[61]

Burning Man's emphasis on expression spurred the recognition of members' efforts. For example, at the end of each Burning Man event, the Department of Public Works members parade through Black Rock City and are greeted by applause and cheers of "We love you, DPW!"[62] Such Burning Man rituals and exchanges affirmed emotional feedback as a valid rather than extraneous need. When asked "What's the most enjoyable part about being a volunteer?" volunteer John Graham answered, "A feeling of love that you get back when you've helped somebody do something that is important to them."[63] Ranger Mary Ellen Burdwood, a.k.a. Dirtwitch, countered skepticism about whether affect could motivate self-interested individuals to contribute:

> [Volunteering is] really satisfying, I mean you hear that, they're always calling like the Peace Corps . . . [or] any volunteer organization, and they always say, "Oh, you get out of it more than what you put in," . . . and it always sounds like a bunch of hooey because a lot of people think "Well, I'm not going to spend all of my spare time working for other people." But you do.[64]

On the other hand, some members grumbled when their peers failed to express sufficient appreciation of their efforts. For instance, DPW operations director Flynn Mauthe predicted that the pursuit of appreciation could "kill" the organization. With a wave of a hand at the conference table where organizers held meetings, he claimed, "Burning Man will always be there except the day it's destroyed around this table. . . . Sometimes [the meeting is] a giant bitch session, and . . . everybody feels like they're not being appreciated."[65] Members and managers reported that they did not always have the technical skills or time to assess an individual's efforts and deliver the desired feedback, disappointing those who expected external affirmation.[66]

A few members tried to help others understand the limits of depending on appreciation as a motivation for volunteering. In describing an online discussion, Burdwood recounted her response to a fellow Ranger's complaint about not receiving thanks or appreciation from those he helped: "I just said, 'You guys, we don't do this to get thanks; we do this because we're Rangers. If we do this because we want the thanks, then you're doing it for the wrong reason. . . . That's not what it's about. It isn't about you.'"[67] Such caution was pragmatic, as those who received help sometimes forgot to express their thanks. Worse yet, they might even react in an aggressive or confrontational manner, as Rangers responding to domestic disputes discovered.[68] If volunteers developed a sense of service that did not depend on such kinds of feedback, they could better weather slights and rebuffs without doubting their efforts. Such an approach to volunteerism has helped sustain commitment in other groups (Colby and Damon 1992; Kaminer 1984).

Re-evaluating Commitment

Research has increasingly recognized the importance of understanding how members make decisions to continue contributing (Pearce 1993; Snow et al. 1986) and the kinds of organizing practices that can stoke commitment (Bacharach et al. 2001). Interviews revealed that Burning Man members monitored their motivations, interests, and commitments. For example, Steven Raspa's response to the question "What's the least enjoyable part about being a volunteer?" demonstrated one such assessment:

> Sometimes it does feel like work. . . . After doing it for five years, some of the novelty has worn off, and I don't need it . . . for friends anymore because if I didn't work with [Burning Man], these people would still be my friends. . . . I'm not being paid for it, so I have to ask myself, "Why am I doing this?" Then I remind myself, "Oh yeah, I do like it." It's just that every now and then, it does turn into an obligation.[69]

After fulfilling one motivation for volunteering, Raspa had to determine whether volunteering met other motivations.

Other members considered whether their volunteer responsibilities depleted their enjoyment of the event.[70] Some volunteers decided that they could continue volunteering if they made changes, such as requesting more help and increasing the division of labor. Such changes promoted the collectivist aim of wider participation while bureaucratization improved the organization's stability. During the 2000 event, Lissa Shoun realized that she needed to share the responsibilities of running the event's airport:

> This year, I was just so exhausted halfway through the event. . . . I can't go out during the day and just wander around and talk to people and go see the artwork . . . because I'm so busy working. Halfway through the event, I decided that was it, I wasn't going to do this next year. My first job the minute I got home was . . . to start looking for somebody else to take on the job of airport manager next year, but I felt better after a while, and I have some plans on how to relieve my workload during the event with some other volunteers.[71]

Coordinators validated such reflection and helped locate additional volunteers. Volunteer coordinator Molly Tirpak recounted how learning to delegate was an inevitable and positive experience of sharing organizing responsibilities:

> It's a little process that every volunteer manager has to go through at least once, where you don't really want to give something up because it's actually part of your job that you really like, but you know it's something that you can give up, and so you give it up to somebody, and then they take and do something with it that like is ten times better than you ever could have imagined. . . .

> You get re-energized by that . . . little process of delegating something and then watching [the person] blossom.[72]

At a meeting, Harley Dubois advised convincing a volunteer to share, rather than monopolize, responsibilities by using Burning Man's participatory ethic: "If somebody is hogging the ball, say 'give somebody else the opportunity.'"[73] With such encouragement, individuals not only learned their limits, but they also learned that asking for help was not a sign of weakness, but a chance for others to contribute and excel. In addition, such reevaluation moments provided the chance to recognize and correct for underorganizing by increasing structure and coordination.

Sometimes finding more help was not feasible, especially for projects that needed highly technical skills. In such cases, members assessed how much they could accomplish on limited resources, and they learned to scale down overly ambitious plans. Raines Cohen, who volunteered for IT projects, explained this process:

> It's challenging to come in knowing that . . . you're looking to devote only so much. . . . We can design a great plan, but then when people say, "Ok, I can do this much" . . . and that isn't enough to get it done . . . and we need to scale things back, then that can be disappointing. . . . I can't devote all of my time into doing this just because I'm already over-committed with my time.[74]

Among Burning Man members, such reevaluation did not reflect negatively upon an individual's capacity. Instead, it demonstrated that an individual could maturely handle responsibilities.[75]

Members also reevaluated their organizational involvement when faced with competing responsibilities and life changes. For instance, several avid Burning Man members who became parents reduced their involvement until their children were old enough to accompany them to the Burning Man office and event.[76] Since the event and organization accommodated virtually all ages of participants, such members could integrate their family and volunteer responsibilities. These differed from studies of organizations in which members viewed those responsibilities as incompatible (Delago 1986; Sager 1979).

For other Burning Man members, a reevaluation led to the decision to stop volunteering. Naomi Pearce described the factors that convinced her to quit:

> It's like a lot of energy over a long period of time, and then [when] you get done with it, you've been completely overstimulated. You can't work right after you get back [from the event], you just have to decompress from all of

this lights and sound and chaos and stress and everything like that, so it's much more than a vacation. . . . It's not trivial. . . . To me, the cost out to the benefit back was starting to get a little bit out of whack.[77]

Some volunteers took a hiatus to take care of other responsibilities,[78] while others, like Pearce, exited without plans to return. Such scenarios demonstrate how members' motivations for volunteering were not constant; they intensified or declined with circumstances.

Coping with burnout

Dealing with burnout presented a bigger challenge. When people suffered from burnout, they no longer had the physical, mental, or emotional resources to perform tasks. According to Jackall (1984: 129), an imbalance between responsibilities and resources can lead to burnout: "Burnout is the experience of feeling constantly overworked, of having too much responsibility and not enough organizational support to carry it out, of never having enough free time for personal pursuits, of constantly being hassled, of, in one worker's phrase, 'losing your soul.'" Burnout is particularly problematic for new or struggling organizations, as members may overwork to compensate for underorganizing. Burnout can also incapacitate members when they take heroic efforts to uphold a mission with insufficient resources (Barker 1999). Moreover, burnout can hasten organizational closure if too many members quit (Kanter 1972; Newman 1980; Parks Daloz et al. 1996; Pearce 1993; Riger 1984; Rothschild and Whitt 1986; Schwartzman 1989; Swidler 1979; Zwerdling [1978] 1980).

Demanding physical conditions and deadlines exacerbated burnout among Burning Man members. During the weeks leading up to and during the event, volunteers worked intensely on Burning Man activities, often to the exclusion of other responsibilities. Some labored in the Black Rock Desert, where they were depleted by sun exposure and temperatures exceeding 100 degrees Fahrenheit. To help members recover, coordinators acknowledged volunteers' distress, increased resources that might alleviate overload, and refrained from making requests or demands:

> [Volunteers] feel really good while they're at the event, but when they come home, and no one noticed [their contributions], . . . it really drained them more than they thought—they will go through all sorts of feelings of anger and feeling used. And they'll burn out, and sometimes it just takes a pat on the back; sometimes it takes leaving them alone; sometimes it takes restructuring . . . that particular organizational area, Greeters' station again maybe—I'll need to have

more people there. I'll go to them and say, "To avoid this kind of thing next year, we'll do this. Maybe you did do a good job and that things happen." So they may get over that kind of burnout.[79]

Nevertheless, whatever had sustained volunteers' commitment could change, leading volunteers to end their involvement, as Harley Dubois explained:

But then there is a long burnout that happens. . . . All those feelings that I've just described, that they've learned to recycle, that they've learned to get over all this—"It's just not worth it anymore, I've had it"— . . . over time, you might decide that that's not for you anymore.[80]

Coordinators provided safety valves to strengthen members' resilience against burnout. These included reminders to volunteers to take care of themselves and suggestions for less taxing work conditions. More importantly, coordinators encouraged individuals to request and accept assistance with recommendations like, "Don't try to be a hero on your own."[81] Megan Beachler, a.k.a. Sacred Flame, recounted how she split organizing duties with another volunteer who almost quit because of burnout:

[Harley Dubois] talked her into the idea of co-managing, so that she could still have some fun and still be managing and be involved with the organization, and that was perfect for me because that was what I wanted to do, be able to have a way of volunteering and helping, but also feel like I had some time to myself, where I could wander around and enjoy it and not be on all the time.[82]

The Greeters added transition shifts between regularly scheduled shifts, and the Café extended managers' shifts to ensure more comprehensive coverage.[83] In addition, the organization hosted regular social events to facilitate relaxation and connections among members. During the Burning Man event, fellow volunteers conspired to ensure that hard-working compatriots took time off.[84] Moreover, organizers recognized that they could not expect members to always contribute at a constant rate. They were willing to relax a bureaucratic assumption that productivity should be stable. With this understanding, overwhelmed volunteers could take a break or even walk away from a task to recuperate.

Easing transitions

When members stopped volunteering, their departures sometimes caused "a lack of continuity" and delays as remaining members and newcomers struggled to learn their responsibilities.[85] This was especially problematic if a departing individual did not leave sufficient records behind and his or her skills were difficult to replace. For example, Chris Lewis unexpectedly left after six years of managing the Gate's collection of event tickets, forcing others to reconstruct those procedures without records.[86]

Such departures highlighted how underorganized areas needed to transfer knowledge from experienced members to newcomers. Organizers increased bureaucratic practices and coordination, hoping to speed the acclimation of newcomers.[87] Organizers sponsored interdepartmental meetings where members swapped "best practices" and ideas and pushed members to record their activities. Keeping records became a regular task for groups like the Tech team, which started to document databases and other computer applications for future users.[88] Departments also produced and handed out manuals detailing their operations and practices, and representatives attended meetings with other departments to improve interdepartmental coordination.

To further smooth turnover and minimize burnout, organizers also distributed knowledge and responsibilities for crucial or complex tasks across teams, rather than giving one individual sole responsibility. Organizers emphasized teaching volunteers so that they could in turn teach others. For example, a formal mentoring system matched new recruits with experienced Black Rock Rangers. Likewise, the two most experienced leaders of the Gate planned to train a large team of members who could take over their responsibilities.[89] E-mail lists also enabled experienced and novice volunteers to regularly interact and build knowledge. Through virtual contact and occasional face-to-face meetings, novice members revitalized organizing efforts with fresh ideas, while experienced members shared their knowledge and expertise.

Reinforcing Contributions with Perks

Although some volunteers' contributions met or even exceeded organizers' expectations, other volunteers were savvy enough to realize that organizers would accept whatever they delivered.[90] Much to fellow members' chagrin, not all volunteers carried out tasks in an accountable, timely, or desired manner. Volunteer labor tapped greater creativity and enthusiasm but introduced uncertainty. Like artists and musicians, Molly Ditmore explained, volunteers are "very flaky people . . . big ideas, low execution rate, but it's great to be around all of these people that have all of these great huge ideas because you just feed off of it."[91] Some volunteer coordinators countered the "flake factor" of no-shows and attrition by scheduling more volunteer help than needed (Chen 2005).[92] Organizers also introduced incentives to encourage more consistency.

These incentives included thanking volunteers through public recognition, trinkets, social gatherings, and perks. By acknowledging volunteers' efforts on the organization's Web site and at gatherings, organizers extended the recognition and appreciation that some volunteers craved.[93] The organization also sponsored regular "thank-you" mixers where volunteers could socialize and form ties across departments. In addition, coordinators granted volunteers access to resources that were not available to most eventgoers, such as prime viewing spots of the bonfire of the Man or advance information of theme camp placements.[94] Organizers distributed "swag," or stickers, CDs, videos, and t-shirts emblazoned with the Burning Man or departmental insignias. After completing long, labor-intensive shifts at the Burning Man event, volunteers were offered passes for meals at the commissary.[95] In select cases, organizers reimbursed the cost of volunteers' event tickets, sold lower-priced tickets, or bestowed complimentary tickets.[96]

However, organizers struggled with the distribution of the limited meal passes and comp tickets. Organizers had neither the resources nor the desire to reward all volunteers with such incentives, and they also did not want volunteers who were attracted only by free items.[97] At a meeting, Marian Goodell worried, "It [volunteerism] has been misinterpreted as a way to get a [comp] ticket."[98] Volunteer coordinator Molly Tirpak tried to explain the different rationales for allocating meal passes within three departments:

> For example, . . . you can't feed 100 Lamplighters a day. . . . There's 100 people who work in the Café in a day; you can't feed those guys either. On the other hand, Rangers, maybe we can feed, why is that? I don't know. If you work an eight-hour shift with the Rangers, you usually get fed. . . . Is there any valid reason into that? Well, yes, Lamplighters is more like an artistic thing, more like an art performance piece. . . . But Rangers always got fed, so there's a lot of precedents, personalities, opinions, and stuff.[99]

Tirpak detailed another difficulty of distributing such perks: "It's this weird thing—it's the only way to say "thank you" to people; it's like a small token of our affection and appreciation. But on the other hand, sometimes it becomes less of a thank-you and more of a right."[100] While a few members opined that they should not offer such incentives but instead encourage volunteers to exercise self-sufficiency per event norms, these discretionary practices continued.[101] To help volunteer coordinators cope with e-mail inquiries about getting free event tickets, Tirpak provided a detailed script explaining that volunteers were expected to purchase their tickets.[102]

Introducing and justifying financial compensation

When Burning Man's financial resources were scarce, members understood the futility of requesting compensation for their efforts. Only select individuals received limited compensation during the event's earlier years.[103] But as the organization's resources increased, organizers could proffer financial compensation on a wider basis. This changed some members' conceptions of their responsibilities, as monetary incentives carried symbolic and contractual significance. Stipends induced recipients to prioritize Burning Man over other commitments, allowing organizers to gain more control over the work process and outcome. Such control was important in establishing the organization's legitimacy to other actors (Milofsky 1988), such as governmental agencies and politicians. However, financial compensation also raised questions about its appropriateness in a voluntary organization. In the Burning Man organization, stipends were not just an exchange between an individual and an organization; members reported that stipends impacted how they related with the organization and other members.

Like other volunteer-based organizations, Burning Man stipends were below market rate and were not intended as a primary source of financial support for recipients.[104] Stipends functioned as, in the words of the staff and members, a "token" acknowledgment and a way of helping those of limited means.[105] In some cases, organizers surprised volunteers with small checks as thank-yous. In one observed instance, a staff member handed a summer intern a check for her three months of full-time work. The staff member warned the recipient, "Don't tell anyone about this. And don't expect any more!"[106] Unlike self-managed organizations such as worker cooperatives, Burning Man members did not control the determination or distribution of salaries and stipends, although they could request compensation for their expenses or labor. Coordinators advocated on individuals' behalf to convince the LLC board, which governed the organization's financial allocations, to approve compensation.

Not all members welcomed financial compensation. Like volunteers who resisted establishing paid positions in collectivist organizations (Taylor 1979), some Burning Man members disliked the expectations associated with receiving financial compensation. Stipends introduced aspects of bureaucratic control: the organization now derived authority from formal positions, and members became connected to the organization through compensated responsibilities, rather than just their beliefs. Some individuals preferred the autonomy of volunteering and refused to accept stipends. These persons wanted the freedom to choose or defer tasks, even though they carried out the same work. In such cases, organizers had to tolerate possible vagaries in these volunteers' work.[107]

Those who accepted stipends expressed mixed feelings about how compensation altered their outlook on work. For example, Erik Waterman described how his perception of his volunteer work changed when he received a stipend to launch an image gallery on the Burning Man Web site, a project that had previously languished: "I felt weird about the money issue. . . . I think it changes things. . . . It makes it more like a real job. . . . It also starts putting a monetary value on things that you're doing."[108] These comments pinpointed the symbolic distinctions between uncompensated and compensated work. Financial compensation pushed members to reexamine their motivations for contributing, leading to a complicated and perhaps even troubling calculus of assigning values to their activities. This calculation included notions of fairness, as illustrated by a compensated member's expressed guilt that others were doing the same or similar work without pay.[109] Such ambivalence illustrated the difficulties of applying abstract calculations to volunteer involvement. These issues suggest that voluntary and collectivist organizations do not easily submit to rationalization by money.[110] The exchange of money, even small token amounts, can affect how people conceptualize relations with each other (Zelizer 1996).

For those who had become dissatisfied with their Burning Man experiences, financial remuneration enabled them to distance themselves by viewing their Burning Man work as a job. However, Kimric Smythe reported that financial compensation was not enough to sustain his flagging efforts: "I don't feel like I want to keep asking for more money. . . . This is like, 'why am I going to this thing anymore?' . . . it's just like a job that I don't really enjoy."[111] DPW volunteer Kat DeLurgio believed that pay was not a sufficient inducement for performance: "I think that . . . I do a better job than somebody who's just working for a buck because I actually care about the results, and I'm not just fulfilling a job requirement."[112] Such comments suggest that a financial incentive by itself may not be enough to foster a long-term commitment (Staw 1976). On the other hand, some members speculated that a stipend would help alleviate financial pressures that prevented them from volunteering more time. Matt Dineen explained how money prioritized his efforts: "If I got paid for [my volunteer work], then I could put more time into it. . . . Being a volunteer has to be a lower priority than other things because I need to pay the bills."[113]

Coordinators hoped that stipends eased such reprioritization of Burning Man responsibilities. At a meeting, organizer Marian Goodell worried that uncompensated volunteers would not be motivated enough to complete certain kinds of work: "I'm going to have trouble doing [the] Web site and tech without compensation. Some of this [work] is going to die on the vine without [us] paying people."[114] Highly technical, on-call services, such as IT work, became compensated because they demanded constant, round-the-clock accountability.[115] Joseph Pred, a Black Rock Ranger manager, explained the purpose of distributing stipends among the line managers in his department:

> My goal is to make [volunteering] painless. . . . A lot of people lose money go-ing to Burning Man. They take a vacation . . . usually it's time off without pay versus a vacation. . . . At the very least, [if] we can at the lowest level of man-agement, they get paid really a pittance. Really, what it is to cover the week that they're gone, that portion of their rent, their expenses, a few items . . . it makes it a little easier psychologically, and they feel like, "I'm being paid."[116]

Compensation enhanced managerial control over how volunteers carried out work. Organizer Crimson Rose explained, "By paying someone, there is an expectation and accountability versus waiting for the person to come in."[117] Moreover, Joseph Pred reported that "you can be more direct" with compensated volunteers.[118] Informants reported that work handling financial transactions, such as ticket sales at the box office and barista service in the Café, were compensated to forestall embezzling.[119] The Department of Public Works turned to financial compensation after repeated difficulties with unpaid volunteers. Organizer Will Roger described how some volunteers' expecta-tions of work clashed with those of the DPW: "What they want to do is take acid and go to the hot springs, well, they're not going to run my forklift after a day of doing that."[120] DPW operations director Flynn Mauthe explained that such volunteer labor drained, rather than enhanced, resources: "Some of the volunteers . . . just cost me money and cost me time." In comparing the DPW with other departments, Mauthe noted that the DPW's physically demanding and extensive work periods were less amenable to volunteerism, as workers camped and labored together for several weeks at a time with minimal ameni-ties.[121] The DPW eventually standardized a system of financial compensation that helped managers enforce professional conduct among DPW members. By elevating standards for conduct, managers could remove those who were involved in physical altercations, made verbal threats, and disrespected locals.[122]

At times, organizers had to publicly justify the use of financial compen-sation. For example, when an e-mail newsletter requested applicants for a newly created paid position, the notice included a caveat about Burning Man's dependence on volunteerism:

It is still necessary for Burning Man to be a primarily volunteer organization. However, there are paid jobs that require a high level of accountability and commitment. Positions may be administrative, technology based or mission critical [Dept. of Public Works] positions. For the most part, however, we still depend substantially on the 1500 individuals who offered some level of service/time to Burning Man at the event and throughout the year.[123]

Organizers acknowledged that they could not pay people what they were worth. For example, a document about DPW's operations stated that its "workers are asked to labor in . . . [physically challenging] conditions for 4 weeks to 4 months, for less than equitable compensation."[124] Over the years, financial compensation aroused contention about who got paid and whether the pay was sufficient. Critics accused organizers of exploiting gullible workers and going "corporate."[125]

Given such controversy and the dependence on volunteers, organizers preferred not to publicize the changing compensation practices. Interviewees indicated that an organizer had demanded that they not discuss compensation with others,[126] suggesting the potential for coercive control. At a meeting, organizer Harley Dubois addressed the issue of disclosing compensation:

The last point [on the agenda], "paid staff vs. volunteer staff." If you're paid staff, this is not a recommendation, this is part of your job. Never initiate conversations about compensation, it's not smart. Never evade the truth when directly asked. Have facts as to why some people are paid and why some are not. . . . It's a difficult conversation. If the conversation doesn't go well, let someone else do it [or else] it's going to fester. Those ideas will grow and grow and come back and haunt the organization; it's not something that you want to leave hanging.[127]

Dubois's recommendation acknowledged that financial compensation raised uncomfortable questions about equity and differential rewards. In one instance, a volunteer was told that fellow team members objected to his request for financial compensation. He received complimentary event tickets instead.[128] Secondhand reports indicated that several DPW members had expressed discontent with the different compensation brackets, indicating how incentives could introduce or exacerbate conflict. Burning Man organizers tried to minimize possible distinctions by calling both compensated and uncompensated members "staff." Other organizations have similarly handled potential divisions between paid and unpaid labor by smoothing over distinctions in status (Pearce 1993). Such issues illustrate how financial compensation was not just a private, one-time transaction between an individual and the organization. Rather, these exchanges provoked deeper introspection of members' involvement and relations.

Conclusion

Organizational work is never-ending. Once an organization recruits its members, it must encourage members to keep contributing, even as these members' motivations change over time. The Burning Man organization's collectivist practices, such as its mission and participatory emphasis, ensure that a variety of motivations are supported. Practices facilitate acknowledgment of individual efforts, positive feedback, and the ability to connect with others. Volunteer coordinators view their roles not as maximizing organizational efficiency, but as fulfilling people's desires to collectively contribute. With this philosophy, coordinators created conditions that drew in even those who had not intended to contribute.

However, members' motivations for contributing are not fixed. For some, life changes and experience reprioritize commitments. For others, burnout erodes their abilities to contribute. Organizers established safety valves that helped members manage their responsibilities and feelings and introduced bureaucratic practices to transfer knowledge from more experienced to new members in the event of members' departures. To reinforce members' commitment and accountability, organizers dispensed incentives, including memorabilia, privileges, and financial compensation. Although remuneration increased accountability from some individuals, this practice altered recipients' perspectives on their relations with the organization and each other. Compensation could also fan dissension and distinctions between those who received compensation and those who did not.

Although discussions about how multiple motivations drive members to contribute date back to Chester Barnard ([1938] 1968), organizations have usually focused on manipulating members' motivations through financial incentives. While financial compensation can bolster members' accountability, the Burning Man case reminds us that people respond to a variety of levers. As other studies have shown, volunteers value their involvement as a chance to engage in meaning making (Allahyari 2000; Bender 2003). Positive feedback and opportunities to experiment can inspire some individuals to contribute. Practitioners and researchers, particularly those in the work-redesign field, have claimed that organizers can more effectively design such practices to tap workers' motivations (Hackman and Oldham 1980).

However, organizers cannot presume that an enthusiastic member body and a compelling mission are enough to sustain an organization over the long term. In particular, organizations that depend upon volunteers may neglect organizing structures because of a lack of resources and time or because their ideology eschews certain organizing practices. This neglect can create a vicious cycle as disenchanted members quit. In addition, organizations that pursue goals that are diffuse or are difficult to measure, such as long-term social change like poverty reduction, may have difficulties giving desired feedback to their members. A lack of feedback can discourage members (Frumkin and Galaskiewicz 2004). Introducing practices such as policies to guide volunteers' efforts can provide desired stability and decrease member turnover (Pearce 1993). In addition, supportive learning opportunities can encourage members to explore possibilities that might enhance their performance, rather than getting stuck in a rut (Hackman 2002). On the other hand, motivating people to contribute need not involve the coercive control of an oppressive organizational culture. Numerous studies have depicted how organizations push members to contribute to the point of burnout (Graham 1995; Kunda 1992). If collectivist practices are used to reinforce respect for members' interests and variable abilities, as done in Burning Man, organizers can avoid creating disempowered teams or culty collectives.

Burning Man members used both bureaucratic and collectivist practices to bolster opportunities for participation without depleting members. Given some imagination, members transformed even unattractive tasks of carrying five-pound bags of ice or crushing aluminum cans into satisfying, desirable experiences for volunteers. Such considerations can create mutually beneficial outcomes in the workplace, voluntary associations, and other organizations, as demonstrated by collectivist ventures like the Mondragón cooperatives (Whyte and Whyte 1988). As individuals engage in such collective work, they forge networks that are crucial to advancing and sustaining ideas and practices (e.g., Turner 2006). Indeed, over the years, Burning Man volunteers have mobilized to address non–Burning Man endeavors, such as voter registration, environmental conservation, and disaster relief.[129] This spread of volunteerism beyond the Burning Man organization suggests that the conditions that help convince individuals to contribute in one organization might precipitate collective contributions to larger society. Therefore, it is important to understand how to establish conditions that enhance and sustain participation.

Burning Man supplies available for sale at a camping supply store in Reno, Nevada, in 2007. Burning Man participants are expected to bring their own food, water, shelter, and supplies, since vending is prohibited at the event, with the exception of coffee and ice sales. All photos courtesy of the author unless stated otherwise.

A Gate staff member checks a vehicle for stowaways and prohibited items at the entrance to the Burning Man event, 2007. Some Burning Man participants use rental trailers and trucks to transport their camping supplies and artwork (in this case, a polar bear).

Burning Man participants line up at the Black Rock City Post Office (BRCPO) in Center Camp, where they can request a special postmark and delivery of stamped postcards and letters to a U.S. Post Office, 2007. The BRCPO is notorious for lampooning governmental bureaucracy with its often surly, demanding service. Past services have included strip-o-grams and the Immigration, Naturalizations, and Socialization Services (INSS).

(opposite top)
A Burning Man participant runs after an impromptu shower as volunteer Black Rock Rangers (to the right) take a break on their bikes, 2005. Water trucks regularly spray the Black Rock City streets to reduce dust.

(opposite bottom)
Burning Man participants park their bicycles in front of Playa Info (previously known as Check Point Salon), 2007. At this Center Camp service, participants can request a volunteer assignment, inquire about found items, locate a registered theme camp and friends, or ask questions.

The Dreamer, by artist Pepe Ozan, 2005. Participants could enter the installation and relax inside. Note the used cotton swab to the left.

Koilos, by artist Michael Christian, 2007. Burning Man emphasizes interactive art that must be completed by participation by the audience—here, a visitor climbs the sculpture.

Twilight Anima Rising, by Mardi Storm, 2005. The sculpture is composed of mud and dirt.

Trainspotting, by Sasha Malchik and Ami Katz with Marat Garagutdinov, 2005. Burning Man participants relax at a train station installation. During one visit, a woman attired in a rail conductor's outfit punched London Underground tickets for those waiting on the platform.

Temple of Forgiveness, by David Best and Tim Dawson, 2007. This intricate installation was composed of wooden puzzle negatives, exemplifying the reuse of materials. Participants were invited to leave messages and mementos to honor departed loved ones. Toward the end of the event, the installation was set afire, emphasizing the ephemeral nature of art.

La Contessa, by the La Contessa Crew, 2005. This school bus turned Spanish galleon transported its crew and participants across the Black Rock City. Art cars licensed by the Black Rock City Department of Mutant Vehicles (DMV) may roam the playa.

The day after the Burn, participants inspect the Burn site, 2005. Because of environmental concerns, partici-pants started using burn blankets and elevated platforms to protect the desert surface from direct fire.

(opposite)
The Man burns as fireworks shoot overhead at the end
of the Burning Man event, 2007.

A fire-spinner performs before an audience at a regional Decompression, a post-Burning Man event, at the Queens Museum of Art, New York, 2007.

A volunteer helps direct participants to the New York City Decompression from a subway stop in Queens, NYC, 2007.

"Immerse Yourself"

Managing Relations in the Pursuit of Legitimacy

IN 1997, the Burning Man event took place for the first and only time on privately managed land in Washoe County, Nevada. In describing the Burning Man organization's new relations and obligations, organizer Larry Harvey contrasted the relative difficulties of working with Washoe County versus the Bureau of Land Management, a federal agency:

> We went from the frying pan and went straight into the fire. In other words, the BLM was a federal agency, although not always trustworthy—they were governed and bound by federal rules meant to ensure fairness. Whereas the county wasn't bound by any rules, it seemed.[1]

County officials imposed onerous fees and restrictive stipulations that Harvey and others believed were intended to drive the event out of the county's jurisdiction.[2] While officials "lacked the political nerve to outright ban us," they made demands that could, in effect, cripple or end the event.[3]

However, county officials had not anticipated how Burning Man's relations with the media allowed organizers to fend off their demands. As Harvey recalled with grim satisfaction, "That was the year we got a tremendous amount of media, and the party prepared to tell the media the story was us."

Harvey entreated reporters with a plea for the event's future: "We're fight-ing for lives here; we need a story that makes us look responsible." Given a compelling story, media such as the *Nightline* evening television news show produced coverage that celebrated the event's endeavors and criticized the county's efforts. Harvey averred:

> The principal lesson is that if you deal with the media, you should have a story ready, that's what they're looking for. Not merely the facts, but something that will interpret those facts. . . . They [*Nightline*] did a story that made us look like art saints and made them [county officials] look like thugs. . . . They [the county] never had been subjected to that level of national scrutiny before.

In what Harvey described as an ensuing "sea change," the county refunded a portion of collected fees, hoping that this reversal would end the bad public-ity. Even so, Burning Man faced "hundreds of thousands" of dollars in debt that threatened to curtail the event's future.[4]

In addition, other parties wanted to use the Burning Man name, symbol, and imagery to advertise products and services, ranging from pornography to parties, for their own commercial gain. Burning Man members worried that these activities would detract from the event's activities and meaning, particularly since the event preached participation, "radical self-reliance," and a gift economy. In an e-mail sent to the staff listserv, a concerned member sought guidance on how to protect the event from commodification:

> I would like to be better educated on the issue of how people rip us off, specific incidents (i.e., an image from BM ending up in a Nike commercial or what-ever that was), and how to be more alert to it before it gets out of hand. . . .
> So my question on ownership of BM culture leads to: how closely must it be "guarded" from rip-offs and incursions from "outsiders"?[5]

Organizers formalized policies that designated some activities as acceptable, such as the posting of the Burning Man name or imagery on personal Web sites and references to Burning Man in the descriptions of listings on the online auction eBay. For activities deemed unacceptable, such as the use of the Burning Man name or imagery on commercial Web sites and the titles of eBay listings, members pursued violators.

These issues highlight a point relevant to all organizations. Organizations must engage in activities and relations with their surrounding environment or field, which includes competitors, resource providers, interest groups, regulatory agencies, and the state. Some of these entities control access to resources such as funds, supplies, and permits that organizations need to function and produce; other entities impact organizations' abilities to operate through regulations or competition (DiMaggio and Powell 1983; Scott 2008). Thus, managing relations with these entities is crucial to an organization's survival (Pfeffer and Salancik 1978). However, if groups are underorganized, they lack the structures or coordination to effectively engage in such relations. By formally organizing, groups can develop these relations and weather changes in their environments (Staggenborg 1988).

While relations help secure resources, they can also affect how organizations develop and operate. To facilitate exchanges, entities such as resource providers, regulatory agencies, and the state may pressure organizations to adopt certain practices, particularly bureaucratic ones. Given such pressures, some organizations will favor commonly accepted practices over unconventional practices.[6] By adopting the demanded practices, organizations are more likely to secure needed resources.[7] For instance, women's groups initially endorsed collectivist practices such as flexible rules and rotating positions; they believed that these practices were crucial to ensuring goal attainment and egalitarianism among members. But funding agencies expected these groups to rely upon bureaucratic practices such as a division of labor, rules, and routines such as record-keeping. To secure funds, women's groups adopted standard practices rather than collectivist practices, eroding these organizations' original intent for forming (Matthews 1994; Wharton 1987). While these changes may improve operations, they can also alter goals and displace collectivist practices that embody members' values and beliefs, allowing oligarchy to take root (Kanter 1972; Markowitz and Tice 2002; Newman 1980; Zwerdling [1978] 1980). By providing resources such as funds and personnel, external entities can also steer or co-opt an organization into serving their own purposes, thus displacing an organization's original mission (Selznick 1949). These conditions can alienate even the most loyal members, who may quit as a result (Hoffman 2006). Thus, organizations must consider the impact of their practices upon both external entities and organizational members (Jasper 2006). To avoid such overorganizing outcomes, some organizations try to retain their practices despite pressures to change by various parties.

To show how an organization can manage relations while avoiding organizing excesses, this chapter examines how the Burning Man organization handled relations with the three types of entities introduced at the beginning of this chapter: (1) governmental agencies, (2) the media, and (3) commodifiers of the Burning Man name and imagery.[8] These entities demanded that the Burning Man organization adopt standard practices and activities, and they also attempted to expropriate aspects of Burning Man for their own purposes. Had Burning Man accepted these entities' demands and adopted their activities, the organization could have lost the support of its members and relinquished control of its outputs, inviting overorganizing and perhaps forsaking its mission. I focus on Burning Man members' attempts to legitimize their organizing practices and efforts, which allowed them to evade and in some instances, shape these external pressures. By analyzing how organizations can steer such relations, we can identify the conditions under which an organization can interact with other actors without overorganizing or undercutting its mission. This chapter thus provides insight into how organizations can use collectivist and bureaucratic practices to deal with external pressures.

Organizational Responses to External Pressures

Theories predict that if organizations do not adopt commonly accepted practices, they will have difficulties getting the resources needed to expand, produce, and survive (DiMaggio and Powell 1991; Pfeffer and Salancik 1978). While these theories suggest that organizations can innovate (Clemens and Cook 1999; DiMaggio and Powell 1991; Zucker 1977), much research has focused on how organizations acquiesce to standards. Some organizations adopt practices out of habit, while others comply with accepted standards or imitate other successful organizations' practices (Oliver 1991). These studies suggest that organizations lack agency beyond conforming to taken-for-granted, standard practices (DiMaggio 1988). Moreover, studies have documented how external pressures can decimate organizational development by hastening closure (e.g., Simons and Ingram 2003).

More recent research (Alexander 1998; Barman 2002; Oliver 1991) has called for further study of how organizations respond to external pressures with strategies and tactics besides conformity. According to Oliver (1991), organizations can either comply with standards or attempt to reshape them. Organizations may compromise by balancing the expectations of multiple constituents, pacifying constituents through accommodations, or bargaining through negotiations with stakeholders. Organizations practice avoidance when they conceal their nonconformity, buffer problematic activities by "complying" without internalizing expected values and practices, or escape by altering or eliminating offensive features. Under the strategy of defiance, organizations dismiss standards as inappropriate, challenge standards, or publicly attack those who pose standards. Organizations engage in manipulation when they attempt to alter standards or how they are applied through co-optation, or bringing in influential constituents. Alternatively, some organizations attempt to influence the shaping of values and criteria, while others exert control by dominating constituents and processes (Oliver 1991). Organizations can also cooperate or form associations to influence existing standards (Aldrich and

Ruef 2006; Disney and Gelb 2000; Galaskiewicz 1985; Hoffman 1999; Kaplan and Harrison 1993; Miles 1982; Murmann 2003).

Researchers have further argued that organizations and their fields can influence each other, coevolving or changing in tandem (Djelic and Ainamo 1999; Haveman and Rao 1997; Hoffman 1999, 2001; Lewin, Long, and Carroll 1999; Minkoff 2002). Changes in general societal conditions, such as the development of new technologies, economic upswings or downturns, or the strengthening or weakening of the state, can alter opportunities and constraints on possible organizational actions. With such shifts, once inconceivable practices may become internalized as organizational strategy and treated as a source of competitive advantage. For example, petroleum and chemical companies initially dismissed pollution concerns as peripheral; they now proactively address environmental issues, viewing these practices as central to their mission and market competitiveness (Hoffman 2001).

Pressures to conform can also highlight contradictions or incompatibilities between desired and accepted practices, spurring organizations to challenge existing beliefs about how to organize (Seo and Creed 2002). By challenging standards and promoting shifts in beliefs and activities, organizations can facilitate large-scale change. For example, social movement groups and voluntary associations have promoted new organizations, practices, and changes that have since become taken for granted in the United States. Recent examples include nonprofit consumer watchdog organizations (Rao 1998), civil rights (McAdam 1996; Morris 1986), recycling (Lounsbury, Ventresca, and Hirsch 2003), services for victims of sexual assault (Matthews 1994; Martin 2005), and programs for those living with HIV/AIDS (Chambré 2006; Lune 2007).

Scholars claim that we need to learn more about how organizations grow or transform, particularly as they interact with other actors and influence their field (Campbell 2005; Hoffman 2001; Troast et al. 2002; Zald, Morrill, and Rao 2005). This suggests that we should examine not only how an organization's members learn to accommodate the surrounding environment, but also how members attempt to shape the environment. In particular, we should pay attention to how organizations like Burning Man try to legitimize outputs, activities, and practices that do not conform to prevailing standards. Such organizations seek legitimacy, or "a generalized perception or assumption that the actions of an entity are desirable, proper, or appropriate within some socially constructed system of norms, values, beliefs, and definitions" (Suchman 1995: 574).[9]

If an organization does not have sufficient legitimacy, it may be pressured to adopt existing standards or practices that are inapplicable or incongruent with its enterprise (Rothschild and Whitt 1986). Prospective members and external parties may also withhold their support. Without the support of members and other parties, organizations may decline and close (Hsu and Hannan 2005; Pólos, Hannan, and Carroll 2002; Zuckerman 1999). In short, if organizations do not have enough legitimacy in their field, they may not be able to sustain themselves (Hannan and Carroll 1992; Stinchcombe 1965). Therefore, securing legitimacy is especially salient for organizations that produce a novel product or service and organizations that use unconventional organizing practices.

In seeking legitimacy, organizations try to convince constituents and external parties to recognize their organizations, outputs, and practices as appropriate (Ashforth and Gibbs 1990; Dowling and Pfeffer 1975). Previous research has shown that members mobilize support with social movement-like activism. Within an organization, members try to convince their colleagues to support particular practices over other approaches (Espeland 1998). Organizations also develop specialized departments and personnel to advocate and codify new practices, especially when working with other organizations (Colyvas and Powell 2006; Hoffman 2001). In addition, organizational members lobby the government to accept their activities and propose new standards in the courts or via professional associations (Aldrich and Fiol 1994; Greenwood and Suddaby 2006; Murmann 2003; Rao 1998; Rao, Morril, and Zald 2000; Scott et al. 2000).

Moreover, organizations engage in organizational perception management or impression management. Members share explanations that either enhance their organization's legitimacy or discount possible detractions from their legitimacy (Elsbach 1994, 2003; Staw, McKechnie, and Puffer 1983). Using annual reports, press releases, and verbally recounted stories, members depict their organizations and activities as legitimate for potential investors, customers, and supporters (Arndt and Bigelow 2000; Caronna 2007; Elsbach 1994; Elsbach and Sutton 1992; Fiss and Zajac 2006; Lounsbury and Glynn 2001; Schmitt and Martin 1999). For example, when new firms disseminate press releases that reference similar organizations, such categorical associations can help establish their legitimacy in emerging markets (Kennedy 2008).

In examining how organizations advocate their legitimacy, recent research has typically analyzed print media, such as newspaper articles, press releases, court records, annual reports, and other archival material (Deephouse and Suchman 2008).[10] Regular behind-the-scenes activities, however, are rarely recorded in publicly available print media (Barley 2008). Analyzing such activities within the Burning Man organization can therefore add to our understanding of how organizations manage relations, particularly as they pursue legitimacy for their organizing practices and outputs.

Managing Relations with Governmental Agencies, the Media, and Commodifiers

The Burning Man organization provides an opportunity to examine in depth how members gain acceptance for their organizing practices and outputs while deflecting external entities' attempts to impose conventional standards and practices and expropriate resources or outputs. Relations with governmental agencies, the media, and commodifiers of the Burning Man name and imagery each affected the Burning Man enterprise (see table 6.1).[11] At crucial junctures, governmental agencies refused to cooperate. Or they demanded that the Burning Man organization pay large fees and adopt regulations and procedures that were either impractical or incongruent with the Burning Man endeavor. Since the Burning Man organization depended upon governmental agencies for access to the event site and to provide related services, these demands presented legal and political obstacles to the event's continuation.

Producers of media such as television news and shows, newspapers, and documentaries expected Burning Man members to follow quid pro quo public relations conventions by accommodating their requests in exchange for publicity. Unlike other organizations, the Burning Man organization was not dependent upon media-generated publicity to advertise its products or services. Nevertheless, the media affected the Burning Man organization's representation to the general public. In turn, this representation impacted the organization's abilities to operate and its relations with other entities. For example, media coverage that emphasized the event's deviant activities could invite critical scrutiny, which organizers worried would push law enforcement and governmental agencies into exercising coercive control over the event.

As the Burning Man event became better known, both individuals and organizations attempted to expropriate its name and imagery for their own purposes. These groups transgressed Burning Man norms by commodifying the event to pitch unrelated goods and services, thereby enmeshing the event in exchanges in the economic market. Even though the Burning Man organization did not depend upon these parties for resources, members worried that their activities could detract from Burning Man's growing legitimacy, erode its meaningfulness, and invite further commodification and its perceived ills.

If governmental agencies, the media, and commodifiers imposed their standards and activities upon Burning Man, the resulting overorganizing could transform the event and its organization, displacing members' interests. Rather than acquiesce to these pressures, Burning Man members deflected demands with bureaucratic and collectivist practices that supported the Burning Man enterprise. In working with these three sets of actors, Burning Man

Table 6.1 Relations between the Burning Man organization and governmental agencies, the media, and commodifiers

Type of entity	Areas affected	Pressures posed	Bureaucratic responses	Collectivist responses
Governmental agencies	Political and legal	• Refused to cooperate • Imposed inapplicable regulations and onerous fees	• Mobilized supporters • Supported agencies by forming departments • Questioned imposed standards and set new standards	• Mobilized supporters • Supported agencies by forming departments • Questioned imposed standards and set new standards
Media	Representational	• Posed demands in exchange for publicity • Produced press that inflamed relations with agencies	• Professionalized volunteer ranks and introduced routines • Banned problematic activities	• Immersed media • Promoted selected frames • Banned problematic activities
Commodifiers	Economic	• Expropriated the Burning Man name and imagery to sell unrelated goods and services	• Introduced routines to identify and notify commodifiers • Threatened legal action against commodifiers	• Made moral appeals to end expropriation

members sought to institutionalize these practices as acceptable and appropriate ways of organizing.[12]

Pushing Back Governmental Agencies

At a "Cooperators" meeting in 2000, representatives from the Burning Man organization, law enforcement, and other agencies assembled at the Bureau of Land Management's office in Reno, Nevada, where they discussed how to handle the Burning Man event. For instance, Pershing County sheriff Ron Skinner raised the issue of upholding laws while under public scrutiny: "No one in this country wants to be known as a drug-infested city; certainly you don't want to be labeled as that. Our job is to turn around those things."[13] This meeting reflected a shift in relations among the Burning Man organization and governmental agencies. These parties now recognized that each had a stake in the event's use of federally managed land and local services. They regularly coordinated efforts, rather than maintaining a wary, arm's-length distance.

During the event's first few years in the desert, Burning Man organizers had avoided contact with such agencies, lacking sufficient structure or coordination. Fortunately for the event, governmental officials did not intervene often during these years. But as governmental oversight and local opposition to the event's presence increased, organizers realized that they had to either work on these relations or risk Burning Man's survival. For example, during the mid-to-late 1990s, agencies imposed regulations and fees that Burning Man members argued were either inapplicable or unduly harsh. Organizers struggled to comply with these demands—by November 1996, the Burning Man event owed an estimated $28,000 in unpaid fees to a federal agency.[14]

Agency officials also complained that the growing event strained their limited resources. In 1996, a Nevada newspaper quoted Sheriff Skinner's suggestion that the event move to another site: "If [the Burning Man event is] going to continue with the steady growth without too many controls, I'll have to say I don't want it in my county. . . . [The event] needs to be where local government has the resources to deal with it."[15] Conflicts over the event's location and activities marred relations between governmental agencies and the Burning Man organization.

With effort, the Burning Man organization was able to reshape relations with three governmental entities: the federal Bureau of Land Management, local law enforcement, and other state and local governmental agencies.[16] The BLM oversaw the event's use of the Black Rock Desert, issued permits before the event's start, monitored bonfires and other activities at the event, and inspected cleanup efforts after the event's end. A small rural law enforcement force, which included the county sheriffs and BLM personnel, patrolled the event for legal violations and emergencies. Other state and local governmental agencies such as the county health department monitored the event for compliance with regulations.

Interviewees reported that relations with each of these groups were erratic and at times adversarial during the event's earlier years in the desert. After adding departments and formalizing procedures to coordinate cross-agency efforts, Burning Man members were able to work with agencies and balance their demands. Using the strategies of manipulation and defiance, members fended off threats to Burning Man's interests with bureaucratic and collectivist practices that supported their endeavor.

Three factors helped organizers strengthen relations with these governmental agencies in Burning Man's favor. First, agencies had to demonstrate accountability to multiple audiences, including local communities, the general public, and Congress. Mobilized Burning Man supporters used this accountability to demand actions that benefited their event. Second, strapped agencies needed funds and other resources, including manpower, to serve both their rural communities and the Burning Man event. By supplying resources, the Burning Man organization could encourage agencies to support the event. Third, agencies lacked precedents for managing a large-scale desert event. By coordinating with agencies, Burning Man developed applicable standards, which prevented overorganizing with inappropriate standards.

Coordinating mobilization for accountability

During the late 1990s, agencies tried to avoid cooperating with the Burning Man event. For instance, the BLM claimed that due to backlogged work, it did not have enough personnel to process the permit application needed for the 1998 event site.[17] Based on the previous year's difficulties with an alternative, privately managed site, organizers concluded that the BLM-managed site in the Black Rock Desert was the event's only feasible option. Organizers therefore wanted an official permit for the site.[18] They used e-mail lists to mobilize constituents and coordinate letter-writing campaigns urging the BLM to reconsider the permit application. In particular, organizers relied upon the *Jack Rabbit Speaks,* the Burning Man organization's official e-mail newsletter. This electronically disseminated newsletter provides regular updates about event preparations and related activities. An August 1998 *Jack Rabbit Speaks* reported reaching "over 4,200 happy campers,"[19] a number equivalent to about one-third of the 15,000 who attended the 1998 event.[20]

Through such outlets, organizers mobilized supporters to work bureaucratic channels by tapping a collectivist commitment to Burning Man. By providing context about the challenges confronting the event, templates for writing letters, and contact information for politicians, organizers demonstrated how members could demand accountability from governmental agencies. For example, in one newsletter, organizer Marian Goodell compared the BLM's refusal to process permits with a hypothetical scenario in which post office workers claimed that they were "too tired to deliver the mail."[21] She urged Burning Man supporters to contact the BLM and congresspersons about the permit. As a federal agency, the BLM had to respond to correspondence and congressional inquiries. After the ensuing deluge of letters and media coverage, the BLM reversed its position and approved the permit, allowing the event to take place.

Burning Man organizers applied similar tactics to oppose proposed legislation that threatened Burning Man's access to the event site. After the *Jack Rabbit Speaks* call for help, Burning Man supporters sent the BLM at least two hundred letters, the largest number of letters about the proposed legislation. Supporters also attended public meetings about the legislation, thus ensuring the representation of Burning Man interests.[22] In addition, Goodell used the *Jack Rabbit Speaks* to recruit volunteers who had the expertise or contacts to assist with legislation and legal matters.[23] Organizers also searched a centralized database of Burning Man volunteers to identify persons, including a Washington, D.C., contact with lobbying access to senators, who could help influence legislation.[24] By mobilizing such support, organizers were able to reinforce agencies' accountability toward Burning Man efforts.

Supporting agencies

Agencies had difficulties cooperating with the Burning Man event because they lacked the experience, personnel, equipment, and funds to serve both the growing event and surrounding local communities.[25] Burning Man organizers realized that they had to support these agencies with funds and assistance, as well as acclimate agencies to Burning Man's unique attributes. For instance, organizer Larry Harvey explained how BLM officials needed Burning Man's help in learning how to manage large-scale events:

> [The BLM] were failing deadlines. They were not delivering on promises. . . . They're a small agency, and they weren't accustomed with dealing with things in such a public way or at such a scale. We forced them up a steep, steep learning curve. . . . If you go to their office in Winnemucca, you'll see that they have a large office with storage areas, they fight fires. . . . They're pretty sophisticated and able and professional in doing those things. But in the realm of large-scale public events and public exposure, they're not. They're very much our juniors in that. . . . They're not used to . . . recreational events like this.[26]

BLM official Barb Keleher explained that the BLM usually worked with smaller recreational events that attracted between one and two hundred persons. Although "the sheer numbers" of the Burning Man event posed the daunting challenge of "managing a city," Keleher opined that Burning Man organizers were easier to work with given their expertise and experience, whereas other smaller events were run "as a hobby" by individuals who "don't understand all of our [the BLM's] needs."[27] Governmental agencies like the BLM could better fulfill responsibilities to groups that were more rather than less formally organized.

Burning Man members worried that relations with agencies would introduce unreasonable demands and coercive control. For example, Burning Man members accused agencies of treating the event as a "cash cow" and posing excessive fees and demands that did not fairly assess the event's needs.[28] Harvey indignantly recounted that for the 1999 event, a Pershing County sheriff demanded that Burning Man provide his force with riot gear and tear gas: "If his men were attacked [by participants], he wanted his men to be protected. Well, that's a far cry. They would use force to move the crowd to go where? Home? There's no place to move them."[29] Organizers understood that law enforcement feared being overwhelmed by the large number of event attendees and being blamed for not fulfilling duties. But organizers and event attendees questioned whether Black Rock City needed constant surveillance by flak-jacketed law enforcement in Hummers and helicopters, which were rumored to have been funded by fees charged to Burning Man.[30]

Burning Man provided funds and resources that could potentially strengthen agencies' capacities to exercise coercive control against the event. To prevent such an outcome, the Burning Man organization attempted to align agencies' interests with Burning Man's interests. In particular, members developed two departments to build and support relations across organizations. While these departments drew upon bureaucratic practices to coordinate activities, they also reinforced a collectivist mission of producing the Burning Man event. The Earth Guardians, a new department, cooperated with the BLM to focus on concerns raised about the event's impact on the Black Rock Desert. Similarly, the Black Rock Rangers worked with law enforcement and medical and fire services, buffering event activities against external coercive control.

Forming a collaborative department. Several interest groups, the BLM, and Burning Man members raised concerns that Burning Man eventgoers polluted the Black Rock Desert with trash and toxic bonfires. Organizers realized that such criticisms could delegitimize the event's activities and fuel prohibitions that would curtail or end the event. At a meeting, organizer Marian Goodell recalled how Burning Man initially addressed conservation as a public relations matter in 1998: "We only became committed to it [environmental conservation] when it became a PR issue."[31] With this impetus, members from the Burning Man organization and the BLM synergized conservation efforts via the Earth Guardians, a Burning Man department established in 1998. This collaborative department aims to conserve the Black Rock Desert for all of its recreational visitors, not just the Burning Man community.[32] But organizer Harley Dubois clarified that the Earth Guardians' activities did not include advocating for the Burning Man event in political matters, such as proposed legislation to designate the Black Rock Desert as a National Conservation Area (NCA):

> Whenever talk comes up on the [Earth Guardians' e-mail] list about the NCA or something, I say, "You guys are welcome to talk about the NCA, I can give you information on the NCA, but this list is nonpolitical, and we are not a political organization, so can you talk about that privately." So our first priority is always to the Black Rock Desert itself.[33]

To fulfill this priority, Earth Guardian volunteers and seven "Leave No Trace" (LNT) master trainers, including a BLM official, adopted and disseminated environmental conservation principles developed by the national LNT nonprofit organization. Before and during the event, the Earth Guardians taught eventgoers how to minimize their environmental impact by, for instance, packing out their garbage for proper disposal elsewhere. The Earth Guardians also conducted experiments to decrease the environmental effects of bonfires. By advising eventgoers on how to protect the desert from direct contact and discoloration from fire, the Earth Guardians promulgated practices that exceeded the BLM's requirements.[34] Throughout the year, Earth Guardian members also built bird roosts and bathrooms, preserved the local hot springs, conducted cleanups, and held training sessions.

In cooperating with the BLM and other environmental groups, the Earth Guardians could focus on addressing each group's concerns about protecting the Black Rock Desert. This helped the Burning Man organization to comply with governmental requirements about, for example, the postevent cleanup. According to BLM official Mike Bilbo, the new department also eased coordination efforts with the BLM agency, transforming "coexisting" actors into cooperative "teams."[35] By using such bureaucratic and collectivist practices, the Burning Man organization converted a once external threat to the event's viability into a taken-for-granted, collaborative activity.

Buffering activities. In a similar manner, the Burning Man organization developed the Black Rock Rangers. This department simultaneously supported agencies' efforts and buffered event activities from agencies' intervention. Once a small search-and-rescue party, the Rangers transformed into a trained, uniformed force that patrolled Black Rock City, mingling with participants and checking for emergencies and possible problems. As volunteers with experience in the medical, fire fighting, and related professions joined these ranks, the Rangers adopted standard bureaucratic practices, such as a chain of command, division of labor, and rules and regulations. These practices enabled the Rangers to coordinate with governmental agencies and hired services, particularly when responding to emergencies.

At the same time, the Rangers upheld a collectivist mission of protecting the Burning Man endeavor, thus preventing the Rangers from becoming a civilian extension of law enforcement. Trainings and other activities reinforced how the Rangers held responsibilities and ethics that differed from those of the governmental agencies and hired services. As Mary Ellen Burdwood, a.k.a. Dirtwitch, explained to new recruits at a Ranger training, "Your work is to establish community." In the ensuing discussion, Joseph Pred corrected possible misconceptions about the volunteers' roles by identifying equipment that they should refrain from carrying: "No big flashlights. No apparent utility knives, because that adds the additional intimidation factor." He explained, "This is not a wannabe cop fantasy."[36] Michael Mikel, founder of the Rangers, highlighted the department's boundary-spanning role between participants and law enforcement: "Often the freedom of the city is in contrast with the existing standards or even laws of local authority and local counties, so we often are an intermediary between our citizens and . . . law enforcement. We . . . form a buffer."[37] Unlike other departments, the Black Rock Rangers constantly balanced serving the event's interests and working with laws, regulations, and agencies.

The Rangers deflected external pressures that could have triggered over-organizing with increasing regulations and coercive control. These efforts often involved creatively mediating conflicts among event attendees.[38] In some cases, the Rangers defused problems before legal authorities could intervene. In one instance, they disabled an art installation, a ten-foot-long pipe that could be used by passersby to smoke substances. While this intervention upset the installation's artists, Rangers contended that it preempted possible arrests and public controversy.[39] The Black Rock Rangers also assisted authorities in ways that were consistent with Burning Man norms. For example, the Rangers cooperated with authorities in the arrest of individuals who sold illegal drugs during the event. However, the Rangers helped on the grounds that the sales violated the event's prohibition against vending, not because the individuals broke the law.[40] In other instances, the Rangers emphasized creatively resolving issues. For example, rather than depending upon law enforcement to arrest drunk drivers, the Rangers confiscated car keys from offenders and even deflated tires to immobilize their vehicles. Such actions prevented accidents and helped agencies conserve their limited resources for other emergencies.[41] In addition, the Rangers' intervention shielded participants from coercive control by authorities.

Questioning standards

While the Burning Man organization supported agencies with departments of trained specialists, organizers also contested the legitimacy of agencies' requests as irrelevant or counter to the event's ethos. For example, before the 2000 event, the BLM requested an advance list of fire performances. Although Burning Man organizers viewed this request as impractical for an event famed for its spontaneous fire performances, they deferred to the BLM and provided a list of planned installations and performances. However, at a postevent meeting of Burning Man organizers, Black Rock Ranger director Duane Hoover reported that he had had to prevent a BLM official from stopping fires that did not appear on this schedule.[42] Organizer Marian Goodell later challenged this official about the monitoring of fires, questioning the usefulness of this activity.[43]

In a similarly memorable way, Burning Man organizers dissuaded an agency's attempt to tax exchanges at the 2000 event. While breakfasting in the town of Gerlach, Black Rock Ranger Joe Fenton encountered a state tax representative. The tax representative revealed that he was investigating whether the Burning Man organization was liable for taxes from barter exchanges made during the event. Fenton sped back to the event site and alerted the Burning Man organizers, who quickly met to strategize about how to receive this unexpected visitor.[44] One organizer then took the tax representative on a guided tour of Black Rock City, during which he contemplated several examples of Burning Man barter. As Fenton described, the tax representative soon realized the futility of assessing the value of these exchanges and abandoned the idea of taxing such exchanges for Nevada's coffers that year:

> They took him [the tax representative] out for a ride in a golf cart to see the city, and they took him to the Naked Miniature golf course and said, " . . . The only requirement for you to play it is that you get naked while you play. What's that barter worth?" And the guy sat there, watched some naked people play golf, and said, "Oh, never mind!" . . . He just realized that it was so absurd to try to put a valuation on something like that.[45]

Through such interactions, organizers deflected governmental agencies' regulatory attempts by emphasizing their inapplicability to the event's practices.

Cooperating to develop new standards

To dissuade officials from imposing irrelevant standards, Burning Man organizers developed and proposed policies that both incorporated agencies' concerns and supported the event.[46] But as Michael Mikel noted, "It took some time for us to convince the people in authority that some things were just not practical." To resolve a city councilperson's misconception that event-goers would cut down nonexistent trees in the Black Rock Desert, "Burning Man developed the guidelines and gave them to the county."[47] Harley Dubois recounted how she and other organizers resisted the Health Department's attempts to apply campground regulations that were ill-suited for a desert site:

> I remember the first year that the Health Department came along, they wanted us to show them a map where we had every single . . . lot for a person blocked out, . . . with numbers for each camp site. And they wanted lighting, so they wanted us to put up power poles for the whole city. What are they thinking? . . . KOA [Kampgrounds of America] campgrounds was the only standard that they had, so they tried to take that and apply it to us. Ok, let's be realistic here. And so we had to educate them and bring them up to speed. With every agency, we have to work with them to teach them what is it that we can do, what's going to work.[48]

Together, organizers and agencies such as the BLM sought applicable models in similar events, such as the Rainbow Gathering, the defunct San Francisco Renaissance Fair, and the Oregon Country Fair. For instance, BLM official Mike Bilbo reported researching large events like the Renaissance Fair, but ruefully concluded, "We looked at all of the examples to see what applied to this [Burning Man], and we didn't find much."[49] The Burning Man event's unusual aspects, such as its use of public land in a remote desert, its temporary camping community, and its no-vending concept, required that organizers and agencies work together to develop useful standards and practices.[50] For instance, BLM official Mike Bilbo described "brainstorming" with Burning Man organizers to develop policies about vehicles at the event. He characterized the resulting policies, such as the cleanup inspection procedures, as "unique to Burning Man."[51]

Interviewed agency personnel praised Burning Man's practices as helping agencies fulfill their duties and setting standards that extended beyond the event. For instance, Bilbo noted how Burning Man members went beyond the requested minimum in addressing issues: "The thing that I hope never changes [about Burning Man] is their ability to take an issue and solve it and make it better, improve it, take it beyond its minimum requirement—that's really also one of the things that has caused Burning Man to survive."[52] He cited members' thorough integration of "Leave No Trace" conservation practices with Burning Man event activities and norms as an example.

Participants implemented LNT practices not just at the Burning Man event; they also applied these practices to their everyday lives and smaller-scale local events.[53] These activities evidenced the increasing institutionalization and dissemination of Burning Man's organizing and event practices.

In working with governmental agencies, Burning Man organizers applied several strategies that helped ensure the event's survival without risking over-organizing. These strategies recognized overlapping stakes: members wanted the Burning Man event to thrive, while governmental agencies needed to demonstrate that they had responsibly performed their duties. In contrast with younger, resource-poor organizations, the Burning Man organization could deploy resources to exert greater control and influence in relations with agencies. When agencies balked at cooperating, the Burning Man organization mobilized its networks to demand accountability. Burning Man also provided funds and other support, established a department to promote environmental conservation, and buffered activities with a department that mediated between agencies and participants. In addition, organizers worked with agencies to replace inapplicable standards with ones that supported the event, facilitating the legitimization of new standards.

Reframing Media Coverage

Concerned that lurid media portrayals could detract from Burning Man's legitimacy and invite public censure, Burning Man members managed relations with the media in the hopes of influencing more flattering coverage. At a meeting, organizers discussed a fictional pornographic story in *Playboy* magazine that ended with a rock star character performing naked at the climatic Burning Man bonfire. One organizer asked another, a practicing lawyer, whether they could take legal action against the publication:

> LARRY HARVEY: The article in *Playboy* . . . it's just vile. Can we do anything about it?
>
> CAROLE MORRELL: No. It's not a product because it's fiction.
>
> HARVEY: It's written for middle-aged men on Viagra!
>
> MARIAN GOODELL: And it assumes that we're all nubile. [*She looks pointedly around the room at other organizers, whose ages span the mid-thirties through fifties.*]
>
> HARVEY: It does us no credit. It looks like he has never been [to the Burning Man event].[54]

Like other organizations with a public image to protect,[55] the Burning Man organization recognized that media coverage impacted their organizing activities and relations. At a meeting of volunteers, organizer Marian Goodell articulated the importance of working with media, particularly in the political realm: "These are people who will affect the way in which we are perceived and the politics in which we have to navigate."[56] Volunteers for Media Mecca, Burning Man's public relations department, specialized in trying to influence, or "spin," the media's output to support Burning Man. These volunteers worked with Web, radio, television, and print news reporters and documentary makers who covered the event for local, national, and international audiences.[57]

Based on analyses of media coverage, such as counts of media mentions of a particular organization or portrayals of an organization's activities,[58] researchers and practitioners posit that the media impacts how organizations pursue their goals. From this perspective, social movement organizations and the state view the media as a venue for reshaping discourse about issues, disseminating views and strategies, and recruiting support for their endeavors.[59] Similarly, commercial organizations use the media to publicize products and services, advance their goals of profit and stability, and recruit prospective employees.[60] While studies have underscored how media coverage benefits organizations, scholars have called for more empirical research into how organizations carry out relationships to elicit these benefits, including managing interactions with the media.[61]

Observations of Burning Man activities allow insight into how an organization can formalize relations with the media. Unlike social movement organizations, the Burning Man organization did not view the media as a primary means of achieving its mission and attracting recruits. Unlike commercial organizations, the Burning Man organization did not pursue the media to boost its reputation or secure free advertising. Although the Burning Man organization did not depend on the media for recruitment or publicity, its members, like those of other organizations, were concerned about how the media's coverage impacted Burning Man's legitimacy and relations with other organizations. At best, media coverage can enhance an organization's legitimacy (Balser 1997); at worst, it can incite public criticism and repression by the state (Gitlin 2003). Burning Man's handling of the media offers insight into how organizations can manipulate or fend off the media more generally.

At first, like other underorganized groups, Burning Man lacked procedures and coordination for dealing with the press.[62] Nevertheless, during the earliest years of the event, local media coverage validated the fledgling event's existence and facilitated organizers' endeavors. For example, a three-paragraph article about the event in a small local publication, the *San Francisco*

Focus, helped persuade an organizer's work supervisor to lend Burning Man a work lot: "The article convinced the boss that Burning Man is a real enough thing."[63] Media affirmation of the event as a bona fide endeavor expedited the flow of material and labor resources.[64] As the event grew, the trickle of media snowballed into regular coverage from national media outlets such as the *New York Times, Time* magazine, CNN, and *Nightline* and specialized outlets like *Wired* magazine. Participants also recorded their Burning Man experiences with handheld video and digital cameras, with some aiming to distribute their recordings as films and videos.

During the mid-1990s through the 2000s, volunteers sought to control and influence media portrayals of the event, especially when reports recounted controversial activities such as drug use, public sex, and nudity. Members expressed concerns that media coverage could harm the event's development in four ways. First, members feared that the media's depictions and labeling of the event would create a self-fulfilling prophecy.[65] For example, leader Larry Harvey referred to the media's "potential to perpetuate lies and attract the wrong people."[66] Members worried that sensationalist coverage could attract persons who were interested only in certain activities, such as ogling naked persons or taking drugs. Members predicted that an influx of such eventgoers would dilute community-building and art efforts, as well as dampen the diversity of event activities.[67] Second, in contrast with earlier years when the event benefited from media coverage, members worried that too much media coverage right before or during the event would attract last-minute attendees. The event infrastructure could not absorb a deluge of newcomers who were unprepared for desert camping; the resulting disasters could end or curtail the event.[68] Third, media coverage of drug use and other illicit or deviant activities raised questions about the legitimacy of the event's endeavors among government officials and taxpayers. Interest groups might use such reports to curtail the event's access to federally managed lands, thus ending the event. Fourth, although some event attendees welcomed their fifteen minutes of fame, others complained that photographers and journalists intruded upon their Burning Man experiences, treating them "like freaks in a side show" and making demeaning requests "to take off more clothes."[69] These attendees criticized the media for "spectating" by repackaging the event for public consumption and commercial gain, rather than participating and contributing toward the event's collective ends.[70]

To circumvent such issues, comparable events such as the Oregon Country Fair banned the media. In contrast, Burning Man members recognized that they could co-opt the media into helping rather than harming the event. Members reasoned that if they could persuade the media to disseminate accurate information about the event's norms and practices, then prospective attendees could better prepare for the event. In addition, positive coverage could allay public fears and misperceptions and build support for Burning Man's endeavors. However, volunteers rejected conventional public relations practices that could have generated overorganizing. Members formalized the Media Mecca department with bureaucratic and collectivist practices intended to assimilate the media and influence their content.

Increasing professionalization and routinization

Media Mecca members added several bureaucratic practices to coordinate and influence the increasing number and variety of media outlets that sought to cover Burning Man.[71] These bureaucratic changes helped the media carry out their work and protected Burning Man's interests. First, the Media Mecca department professionalized its ranks with volunteers who had public relations and media experience. To help prepare the media for the event, these volunteers posted information about the event and the organization on the Burning Man Web site and compiled and distributed official press kits. In addition, volunteers routinized procedures that required media outlets to register their information and proposals for coverage before the event's start.

Using information gathered from advance registration, Media Mecca members initiated discussions with the media about their plans before the event. Volunteers thought that such contact not only eliminated last-minute preparation by forcing the media to plan ahead, but also helped refashion proposals toward producing more flattering and nuanced coverage of the event. Volunteers also used this planning period to match media outlets with contacts. For instance, some media outlets wanted to interview event attendees and artists from a particular state or country or visit artists' local studios. With Media Mecca's help, the media could locate such persons before and during the event. Volunteers reasoned that with such preparation, the media were less likely to produce superficial or negative coverage.

Media Mecca members also maintained relations with the media after the event, contacting reporters with questions or clarifications that could influence future coverage. For instance, several Associated Press (AP) wire reports claimed that Burning Man's infirmary had treated seventy or more drug-related medical cases per day during the 1999 event.[72] Organizers disputed this figure as incorrect and blamed these heavily reproduced reports for intensifying political pressure upon law enforcement to pursue violations at the following 2000 event.[73] To monitor the content of future AP reports, organizer Marian Goodell regularly corresponded with the journalist responsible.[74]

Enhancing participation and immersion

Using collectivist practices that emphasized participation, the Media Mecca department also attempted to immerse the media into the Burning Man community. In doing so, volunteers deflected the media's attempts to engage in standard public relations practices.[75] Press who were unfamiliar with the event often demanded free entry, free passes to leave and reenter, press badges, and special access to "behind the scenes" action. They assumed that Burning Man would exchange these perks for favorable publicity, per PR conventions. However, the media's demands contravened event norms about participation. If Burning Man members complied, the resulting nonessential organizing activities, which did not serve members' interests, could trigger overorganizing. Furthermore, the resulting media coverage could detrimentally impact participants' experiences.

Since Burning Man no longer needed publicity to grow the event, Media Mecca volunteers rejected the media's requests for privileges.[76] They did so in tongue-in-cheek ways that subverted PR conventions and highlighted Burning Man's collectivist norms of participation. For example, volunteers distributed a so-called press pass to registered media. The illustrated badge stated, "This pass entitles you to absolutely nothing. Have a beautiful experience."[77] Media Mecca also used playful rituals to encourage participation. Former volunteer Naomi Pearce recalled that in 1995, the press had to take an oath: "We had a sign-in pledge. . . . The media had to put their hand on a picture of Elvis and repeat: 'I will not spectate,' . . . 'I will participate,' . . . 'I will take at least one picture of a non-naked person.'"[78] This ritual emphasized that participants' experiences superseded the media's aim of getting the perfect shot or footage: "That was their pledge just to . . . drive the point home to them that they are not allowed to just take, that they had to participate in some form."[79] Similarly, bumper stickers distributed in the press kits exhorted the media to plunge into the event: "The best coverage of Burning Man has and always will be that which is profoundly personal. Immerse yourself."[80]

Media Mecca volunteers helped the media with this immersion. They encouraged the media to camp at the event, rather than reside in off-site hotels, and located theme camps which were willing to host reporters and their crews. During several events, Media Mecca stocked costumes that the media could borrow during the event. Media Mecca also provided a shaded area for the press to mingle, relax, or meet with interviewees, and volunteers threw mixers for artists, press, and volunteers. Although volunteers encouraged the press to be self-sufficient, they helped the press with equipment and tasks, such as recharging equipment, locating supplies, and filing news reports, that were otherwise difficult in the desert. Such efforts helped members and the media establish longer-term relationships.

To ensure that the media abided by event norms, the Burning Man organization educated participants on their authority to regulate the media's actions. Through information disseminated via print and the Web, event attendees learned that all cameras used by the media and all video recorders should display tags indicating their registration with Media Mecca. Participants could also request that individuals stop filming or photographing their activities, and volunteers would investigate reports of noncompliance. Self-policing by the event population was effective enough to convince law enforcement to comply with these guidelines. During the 2000 event, a visibly flustered sheriff visited Media Mecca to register his video camera. He reported that several eventgoers had pointed out that his camera lacked a registration tag.[81]

Promoting selected frames

The Burning Man organization implemented guidelines to encourage the media to produce coverage that could benefit, rather than detract from, the event. By examining how Burning Man members developed and enforced these guidelines, we can understand, in particular, how members conceptualize, select, and reinforce a certain frame, or "schemata" (Benford 1997; Goffman 1974), for representing Burning Man activities among themselves and to a larger public.[82] Using selected frames, organizations try to assert and protect their legitimacy, especially when the media could delegitimize their activities with undesirable representations.

Observations revealed how members evaluated media accounts and attempted to reshape media coverage. Organizers and volunteers regularly examined and discussed articles and footage to identify coverage as either beneficial or detrimental to the Burning Man event's future.[83] The following list, which appeared on a dry erase board in a conference room at the Burning Man headquarters, contrasted possible portrayals:

Good words:
Gift economy
Community
Evolves/changes every year

Yucky:
Barter
Drugs

Rave
Party
Nudity[84]

As the list indicates, members disliked media coverage that emphasized nudity and sexuality, drug and alcohol consumption, and lawlessness; they also detested media stereotyping of the event as a party, rave, Woodstock, or pagan ritual. While members understood that such portrayals served the media's interest in attracting audiences, they worried that such representations marginalized the Burning Man enterprise as deviant. Members feared that these representations might antagonize the public into demanding that regulations or prohibitions be applied to the event.[85]

To counteract these potentially problematic frames, Media Mecca members drew on Burning Man's collectivist practices and mission, emphasizing how these exemplified larger society's values. Members portrayed Burning Man's aims and activities using the discourse of rights, such as freedom of expression, and collective interests, such as the arts and community.[86] Members also encouraged the media to focus on the event's distinctive practices, such as its noncommercialism and gift economy, support of art and community development, environmentally friendly practices, and constant experimentation to improve the event's operations. However, given the relative unfamiliarity of practices such as the gift economy, Burning Man members had to educate the media on how to represent these practices to the wider public.[87]

Burning Man organizers and volunteers rejected proposals that might generate unfavorable coverage, demanded edits from filmmakers, threatened legal action against recalcitrant media, and steered the media toward desired portrayals of the event. Organizers also warned event attendees that their indiscreet statements and actions threatened the event's survival. In addition, organizers banned certain problematic activities such as shooting guns.

To head off unfavorable coverage, Media Mecca members required the media to submit proposals in advance of the event. Volunteers scrutinized proposals and rejected those that did not evidence adequate preparation or focused on unflattering aspects of the event. In deciding whether to allow proposed media coverage of the event, members speculated about how it might impact the event. Decision makers considered the demographics of a media outlet's audience, as well as the coverage's anticipated angle. However, meetings and discussion lists revealed that members did not always agree on whether they had sufficient reasons for excluding particular media outlets from covering the event. At a Media Mecca meeting in San Francisco before the 1999 event, volunteers discussed whether they should reject a proposal sent by Music Television (MTV), a popular music video and entertainment cable station. Candace Locklear, a.k.a. Pippi, started the discussion by describing her interaction with MTV's representatives:

> We were approached Monday by MTV. . . . They said, "What do we have to do to get press passes?" I said that they would get run off the playa [by participants]. . . . I said, "It's not what you're filming but what you represent, the commodification of culture; it's what people are trying to escape from at Burning Man. . . . Why don't you come and do it next year? . . . There's only two weeks left [before the event's start]; I've been working with others [in the media] year-round. . . . You're going to risk bodily harm. . . . You should research [the event]."

Locklear pointed out that not only was MTV unprepared, but Burning Man attendees were hostile to this media outlet.

Other meeting attendees argued over whether coverage by MTV violated the event's emphasis on participation:

> JESS BOBIER, A.K.A. NURSE: It's letting people spectate. It's just that the framework flies in the face of what Burning Man is.
> ADAM ARONSON: They produce prepackaged consumption.
> JIM GRAHAM, A.K.A. RONJON: What media doesn't?
> ARONSON: . . . The vast majority [of eventgoers] don't want their image on MTV. This is different.

Although some agreed that the proposed coverage contravened the event's ethos of participation, one volunteer questioned the rationale for rejecting MTV's proposal:

> REBECCA PITT: Why are we treating them differently?
> LOCKLEAR: Their demographic, . . . especially with the rave scene that will drive them. They are so ill prepared—they will not be the type who reads the *Survival Guide* [a publication on how to prepare for desert camping and community living].

Locklear's reasons for rejecting MTV assumed that MTV's audience would not abide by Burning Man's tenets of preparation and self-sufficiency.

Despite these misgivings, some members wanted to give MTV a chance, albeit for the next year's event. One such member suggested that the coverage could contrast Burning Man's efforts with those of Woodstock '99, a commercial event that had ended with a fiery riot:[88]

GRAHAM: Let's bring him [the MTV documentary maker] around and then consider [a proposal] for next year.

MARIAN GOODELL: I can't say "no" just because it's MTV.

PITT: It's a chance to show how to do it right—in contrast to Woodstock '99.

GOODELL: Larry [Harvey] and I agree. The [*San Jose*] *Mercury News* reporter was asking about community—he understood it, his one question—at what point does growth, do the numbers become too much. . . . It's a really good reason not to have [the MTV documentary maker], he could have the door opened too wide. *Wired* did the article with the right demographic.[89]

Goodell cited concerns that MTV's coverage would attract a surge of event attendees who would overwhelm organizing efforts. In identifying *Wired* magazine as the "right demographic," she assumed that the magazine's older and more educated readers would responsibly contribute to the event.

However, MTV's subsequent subterfuge destroyed future prospects for cooperation with Burning Man. A MTV insider tipped off volunteers that the cable station had hired an undercover team to collect footage that would be aired without Burning Man's authorization.[90] The Burning Man organization took legal action that prevented the airing of the footage. Media Mecca members celebrated this as both a precedent-setting victory and as a warning to other media about obtaining coverage through such means. Rather than resort to undercover reporting as MTV had tried, other outlets that could not agree to Burning Man's terms decided not to cover the event.[91]

Media Mecca members also rejected proposals for coverage that could incense law enforcement or the public. For instance, the *Paramedics* reality television show proposed shadowing the Black Rock Rangers and medical crews during the event. This coverage could have highlighted the event's emergency preparedness expertise and enhanced the event's legitimacy. But Burning Man organizers rejected the proposal because the producers refused to guarantee that the coverage would not overrepresent the number of drug-related medical cases.[92] Likewise, members usually barred proposals that focused upon nudity or sexuality for commercial purposes, such as a pornographic magazine's plan to profile attendees on a commercial Web site. Members viewed such representations as undercutting the event's legitimacy.

Finally, the organization tried to discourage the media from portraying the Burning Man event as part of a party or rave circuit. Several theme camps regularly hosted "raves," or all-night dance parties where DJs spun electronically synthesized music, such as house, techno, or jungle. Burning Man members viewed these raves as part of, rather than representative of, a wide range of event activities and therefore rejected the labeling of the event as a rave.

Accordingly, organizer Marian Goodell tried to stop a music magazine editor from covering Burning Man in an article that described top raves around the world. Although Goodell could not prevent the editor from including Burning Man in the article, she convinced the editor to exclude photos of the Man and to include information about buying tickets in advance. Nevertheless, when Goodell displayed this magazine at a meeting, fellow organizers were vexed by the magazine's implication that the event welcomed massive sound systems:

> MARIAN GOODELL: We're in *URB* magazine. Now, don't fall all over yourselves getting over to read this. The editor said that she was going to write it up regardless. . . . [*Goodell reads aloud from the article*] "Create your own sound system."
>
> CRIMSON ROSE: Fucking slut!
>
> GOODELL: I was so mad that she put it in. It's like the *Wired* magazine for the rave community. It has the venues listed for other events. . . . We're the last one, . . . with no image of the Man. The goal is: have a little bit of control and no image of the Man.
>
> DANA HARRISON: We're probably the only ones who say, "Please hide us."[93]

Organizers worried that such coverage encouraged newcomers to bring more sound systems, aggravating conflicts with sleep-deprived participants.[94] Organizers also feared that depictions of Burning Man as a party or rave provided interest groups and authorities with the grounds to curtail the event's use of federal land.[95]

Much to Media Mecca members' irritation, other publications, such as the men's magazines *Stuff, Details,* and *Playboy,* similarly listed the event as a "must-attend" party akin to Mardi Gras or Rio de Janeiro's Carnival.[96] One morning television talk show even depicted the Burning Man event as an ideal marriage proposal and wedding destination. In an e-mail to the Media Mecca list, a volunteer complained, "'The View' mischaracterized the event horribly. It made it sound like we're a tourist destination similar to an all-inclusive romance resort."[97] Members worried that such coverage omitted important information, such as the need to purchase advance tickets and prepare food, water, and shelter, and misrepresented the event's purpose.

Although organizers were not always successful in reshaping press coverage, they were able to wield more editorial power over those who sought Burning Man's help with endorsing and distributing their works. In exchange for their official endorsement of films, organizers demanded that documentary makers edit out certain material. For example, at a Media Mecca meeting, Marian Goodell explained why she and other organizers did not want documentaries to depict public sex and drug use:

> The only content [that we at Burning Man are concerned about] is public sex and drugs. Like the documentary *Burning Man: Where's the Fire?*—we made them [the documentary makers Fernando Valasquez and his team from Peyote Pictures] take out the mushroom tea. That's what we care about—it's a great film, but our issue is how [viewers might be inclined] to take [that depiction] out of context.[98]

Second-hand reports indicated that, not unsurprisingly, filmmakers found such requests restrictive. To these persons, the organizers' requests smacked of censorship.[99]

To others, these requests reflected a deeper issue about collective responsibility for the event's survival. Members understood that the media's focus upon the more sensationalist aspects of the event conformed to industry standards. However, such portrayals could harm the collective's survival and demean the event's value. Members like Black Rock Ranger Mary Ellen Burdwood worried that media coverage reduced the Burning Man event to a "spectacle":

> It almost feels like when they [the media] take all of the bizarre pictures of the "Gay Day" ["Gay Pride"] parade, and all they do is show like the drag queens and the dykes on bikes, and they don't show the parents and friends of lesbians marching, they don't show all of the volunteers . . . who work really hard. . . . They want to just show . . . what they consider to be freaks and weirdoes. . . . I just don't want it to turn into a show, a spectacle for other people; I just want people to come there and do their art.[100]

Members wanted the media to cover the event in a more representative manner, rather than showing extreme images. Observations revealed that organizers, who had screened hundreds of hours of documentary and news footage, gave the highest accolades to an amateur documentary. This simple and short documentary profiled the event's art and community for a local cable access channel. As organizer Harley Dubois noted, she felt comfortable showing this documentary to her mother, as it presented the event's art and activities without slick voyeurism.[101]

To encourage the media to develop similar coverage, organizers challenged the media to cover topics without resorting to stereotypes.[102] In the "Media Myths" section of the Burning Man Web site, Larry Harvey outlined several overlooked topics, including the event's community-building efforts and alternatives to consumerism. Organizers also offered more help, including publicity, to those who covered desired topics. For example, organizers encouraged a documentary maker who was exploring possible subjects to focus on the gift economy. She subsequently filmed and released the documentary, which the Burning Man Web site helped publicize.

While organizers attempted to steer and influence media coverage, they also targeted activities that generated undesired coverage. Organizers warned eventgoers that their self-reports about illicit activities could damage the event's future, as they fueled critics' contentions that the event was too permissive and placed additional pressure upon law enforcement to act. As organizer Marian Goodell cautioned readers of the *Jack Rabbit Speaks* newsletter, "You do NOT help the situation when you tell members of the media that you're experiencing the 'best drug trip of your life' at Burning Man."[103] At an annual town hall meeting, she explained, "It's your responsibility to watch what you say to the media."[104] Goodell also negotiated with theme camps to skirt topics that could damage the event's credibility. For instance, the Ministry of Statistics theme camp surveyed passersby about their characteristics, views, and activities; the camp then calculated and released statistics, including the frequency of drug use. Media such as the *San Francisco Examiner* newspaper reproduced these statistics in a front-page article about the Burning Man event. Citing a collectivist responsibility to protect the event's interests, Goodell approached an organizer of the Ministry of Statistics theme camp with the request that the camp stop publicizing the statistic about drug use; Goodell reported that the organizer "reluctantly complied."[105]

For similar reasons, the organization banned loaded guns, shooting, and driving cars other than approved art vehicles during the event. As Naomi Pearce recalled, organizers feared the consequences of mixing guns with a growing population. Organizers also anticipated that media coverage of such activities would adversely affect the event's reputation:

> Communication with the media was [a] very tricky business because the potential for somebody to come in and exploit and not get what was going on, was really high. . . . If somebody just came in and filmed, it would be so easy for them to misunderstand what was actually happening, and to spin it and interpret in several really destructive directions.[106]

An interviewee recalled that Burning Man was "plugged in the media as . . . the most dangerous art festival."[107] After years of heated deliberations, organizers decided to prohibit the possession and use of loaded guns. To enforce this prohibition, the Gate staff search vehicles entering the event for such items.[108] By introducing and enforcing such rules, the event gradually shed its anarchist, Wild West image, allowing organizers to promote the event as an arts community.[109] Since art and community aligned with overarching societal values of expression and connection, organizers could more easily defend the event against criticisms.

Curbing Commodification

Over the years, the Burning Man event gained recognition in the arts and technology communities; organizers presented invited lectures at museums and academic conferences.[110] In addition, word-of-mouth and media coverage has propelled the Burning Man event to the iconic countercultural status associated with Woodstock. Moreover, increasing references to the event suggested that Burning Man had assumed cultural-cognitive legitimacy, or taken-for-grantedness, among some circles. As the event's reputation increased in cachet, individuals and organizations used Burning Man's imagery, name, and venue to promote their own goods and services.[111] To attract local residents to its speaker series, the nonprofit Commonwealth Club of California referred to Burning Man and one of its founders, who had been a featured speaker, in an ad that appeared on San Francisco buses and billboards.[112] The ad featured a young woman sneering beneath the statement, "I wanted to ask Larry Harvey if success is killing his original idea for Burning Man. So I did."[113]

By commodifying the Burning Man name, images, and experience, other organizations and individuals expropriated Burning Man for exchange in the economic market.[114] Such transgressions attested to Burning Man's growing legitimacy, but they also violated Burning Man policies and flouted event norms against vending and commercialism. Thus, members viewed commodification as detracting from Burning Man's meaning.[115] Given the collectivist mission of protecting the Burning Man community, members were on the alert for exploitative actions. Moreover, this collectivist mission and participatory practices enabled Burning Man members to challenge otherwise taken-for-granted practices of commodification.

Like other organizations, the Burning Man organization tried to guard against expropriation by other entities.[116] Volunteers turned down proposed product tie-ins and monitored the event, Web sites, advertisements, and other media for infringements. In confronting transgressors, members first explained how their activities were antithetical to Burning Man norms about supporting alternatives to commercialism. For actors who refused repeated appeals to desist, members resorted to legal action. When the offenders were members of the Burning Man community, members turned to moral appeals and censure, thus tapping collectivist commitment.

Several companies proposed using the Burning Man event as a site for giving away products, such as drinks and magazines. In an e-mail to the senior staff list, Candace Locklear recounted a discussion with a company representative who wanted to distribute free samples in exchange for a press release with the Burning Man name:

> Recently—a guy representing Nantucket Nectars . . . called to ask if they could "Airlift a couple hundred free cases to the site and set up a Juice Pavillion." . . . He instantly started in on me by explaining that he knew Burning Man was not commercial, and that this kind of thing might be frowned on. But when I asked him what they would want in return, he admitted that they would distribute a press release announcing the "gift" to Burning Man.
>
> I stopped him in his tracks, and explained the *Spin*/H20 debacle [a similar case of a commercial magazine that wanted to distribute free issues] . . . to illustrate that this is exactly the kind of activity we CANNOT and WILL NOT encourage, support or approve.
>
> He continued to ask if jets could land, as Tom & Tom (the owner guys) really wanted to fly in and get muddy, while STILL bringing in thousands of juice bottles. Surely your participants get thirsty? You can hand them out FOR FREE! he exclaimed.
>
> I again explained that any type of consumer items with corporate logos for distribution is what we DO NOT want on the desert, and that free juice was not welcome, but Tom & Tom were.
>
> . . . I explained that we encourage participants to bring EYNTS (everything you need to survive . . .) . . . and that providing free items like water and juice, altho useful, would create dis-incentives. . . .
>
> Just wanted to let you know that Corporate America is trying to beat down the Burning Man door.[117]

Locklear's e-mail clarified that under the collectivist ethic of inclusion, company personnel were welcome to attend the event, but their product endorsements, commercial sponsorship, and publicity were not.[118]

Likewise, members remonstrated commercial pitches that referenced the Burning Man event to promote unrelated products and services. For example, a press release advertised an event sponsored by personal data assistant device manufacturers with the tagline "First there was Woodstock, then came Burning Man and now. . . . SyncFest! (and you won't even have to camp out)." A tongue-in-cheek e-mail penned by Media Mecca volunteer Jim Graham protested this comparison:

> I'm sure it was creative fancy fueled by too much caffeine, but tell me you weren't serious in your email newsletter announcement for SyncFest when you compared it to Burning Man.

Granted, if SyncFest includes extreme temperature fluctuations, mobile living rooms blasting tinny techno music, lots of naked people and, at the conclusion, all the vendors burn their booths, then maybe this is something I need to check out.[119]

Advertisements of products and services with the Burning Man name and imagery raised even greater ire among Burning Man members. Media Mecca volunteers expressed anger when a software firm's Web site featured its products alongside an employee's personal account and photos of the 2000 Burning Man event. Volunteers pressed Burning Man organizers to stop the company from comingling advertisements for its products with portrayals of the Burning Man event.[120]

Like other organizations, the Burning Man organization turned to professionals to stop more serious infringements. A legal team targeted the unauthorized use of event images in commercial Web sites, print, and film. Information printed on the 2001 Burning Man event tickets warned that individuals might be photographed or videotaped and that the Burning Man organization might act on participants' behalf: "You appoint Burning Man as your representative to take actions necessary to protect your intellectual property or privacy rights, recognizing that Burning Man has no obligation to take any action whatsoever." In particular, organizers claimed that they had a moral responsibility to protect participants' privacy. They targeted pornographic Web sites and videos that used and sold images and footage of nude or partially clad participants without their consent.[121] The organization's legal counsel issued warning letters requesting that offenders either drop such images or obtain written consent from depicted individuals. Legal counsel also used aggressive legal means to shut down repeat offenders, like the producer of a series of unapproved pornographic videos.[122]

The organization also tried to ensure that published photographs or footage of artwork properly credited and compensated artists. For example, organizer Marian Goodell recounted her efforts to convince the television producers of *UFOs: Best Evidence Ever Caught on Tape 2* that an individual had sold them video footage of an artist's inflatable art installation, rather than a genuine UFO. In the *Jack Rabbit Speaks* newsletter, she wrote:

The producers of this show literally spammed [hundreds] of Burning Man participants, discussion lists and . . . organizers emails looking for verification of this UFO. I tried to convince them otherwise, and finally gave up. Let's just say we're allowing them to wallow in their own ignorance. Kudos to the artist!! [HOWEVER, Erik H., who sold the video to Kiviat Productions owes Burning Man AND the artist some Moola, and we're on our way to his door thanks to the fact that Lightning (our lawyer) is exactly that. Naughty, naughty selling footage taken at Burning Man without permission. . . . no one likes exploitation].[123]

Goodell used this instance to both educate readers about the Burning Man policy on selling footage of the event and publicly chastise the person who had violated this policy.

The organization also censured individuals who sold products under the Burning Man name. To identify offenses, volunteers scanned the offerings of music groups and eBay, a popular auction Web site. They sent personalized e-mails explaining why items could not be sold under the Burning Man name; they also asked that individuals either pull or revise their ads.[124] In most cases, the individuals apologized and removed the listings, but a few angrily responded with free speech or free capitalism arguments. For instance, when an individual posted a satirical ad on eBay for a street sign taken from the event, Media Mecca volunteer Jim Graham e-mailed him an admonishment asking him to pull the ad or be subject to legal action. The individual yielded, but with a stinging rebuke sent via e-mail, claiming that the ad was a prank, rather than a real ad: "Obviously a sense of humor is not allowed at burning man anymore. . . . next years theme: 'shut up & sit there where we can keep an eye on you.'"[125] Such individuals complained that members were too heavy-handed in protecting the event, which suggested a shift toward overorganizing's coercive control. On the other hand, members worried that even a joke about selling items with the Burning Man name could set a precedent for other, more serious cases of commodification.

Members also approached individuals who publicized their Burning Man ties while promoting their careers, artwork, and events. Rather than threatening legal action, Burning Man members made moral appeals based on collectivist norms and responsibility. They urged individuals to cease their activities, arguing against commercializing the event. For example, several volunteers scathingly criticized aspiring actress Jerri Manthey's references to Burning Man. While on the reality television program *Survivor II: The Australian Outback,* Manthey wore a necklace with a Burning Man pendant and made frequent references to her Burning Man experiences. She also appeared, adorned with a necklace that featured a Burning Man symbol, on the cover of *Playboy* magazine.[126] In the Media Mecca e-mail list, volunteers discussed whether it was feasible to request that Manthey stop mentioning the Burning Man event in the press. They worried that because of her effusive endorsements, unprepared viewers would attend Burning Man, expecting a *Survivor*-like set of participants. After talking with Manthey, organizer Marian Goodell reported in the *Jack Rabbit Speaks* newsletter that the actress showed sincere dedication to the event. This assuaged members' concerns, and the conflict passed.[127]

Likewise, members negotiated with individuals about how they associated the Burning Man name with artwork and events. For example, photographers wanted to publicize their art gallery shows with the Burning Man name. Organizers sought to control how the Burning Man name was used, especially in art sales, and sometimes negotiated a cut of the proceeds for authorized usage of the name. In one case, an event promoter tried to evade the prohibition against using the Burning Man name. He distributed ads that falsely claimed that Burning Man organizers Larry Harvey and Marian Goodell were sponsors of an art event that sold $100 tickets. Those who believed these sponsorship claims chastised Burning Man organizers for "selling out." Burning Man organizers then boycotted the promoter's event, and Goodell wrote an indignant blurb in the *Jack Rabbit Speaks* newsletter that denied Burning Man's links with that event. Goodell also explained the Burning Man organization's policy regarding the publication of associated events, and she educated readers about how to determine whether an event was sponsored or endorsed by the Burning Man organization.[128]

Members were less likely to censor struggling artists who promoted their Burning Man ties. However, pleading poverty did not always protect individuals from criticisms that they profited from the Burning Man name. Several Burning Man members rebuked performance artist Austin Richards, a.k.a. Dr. Megavolt, for appearing in a 1999 restaurant advertising campaign, even though the commercial did not mention Burning Man.[129] Critics also took offense to Richards's personal Web site, which implied that he held special status at Burning Man: "Tesla Coils featuring Dr. Megavolt a.k.a. Electrobot star[r]ing at Burning Man and available for Corporate parties, entertainment, raves, music festival, etc." This claim triggered an e-mail debate among Media Mecca volunteers about acceptable standards for self-promotion. The controversy ended with Candace Locklear's opinion that "like lots of other artists, the boy is just trying to make a living. As long as he does it with respect to [Burning Man], I think that is cool."[130]

Still, organizers expressed consternation when artists hawked art that had been funded by Burning Man.[131] At a meeting, organizer Larry Harvey fretted about an artist who had posted his Burning Man sculpture on eBay with a starting bid of $1,000:

> HARVEY: I've been dealing with cranky artist people for two days [about art
>   grants]! [This artist]'s selling neon Burning Man on eBay! I feel a certain
>   obligation to this person; I don't want to offend the man, but this is inap-

propriate. . . . They're out there bidding, so you've got to buy it at the market rate from him?

DANA HARRISON: So someone is offering art on Burning Man? That puts you in a bad situation.

Although Harvey found this situation distasteful, he decided he would rather maintain relations with this artist by purchasing the artwork for the Burning Man collection. As others privy to this exchange pointed out, Burning Man members would exert peer pressure to convince an artist to reconsider such advertisements.[132]

In dealing with those who commodified Burning Man, members appealed to their sensibilities and even threatened legal action. Although offenders did cease problematic activities, a few complained that these actions represented coercive control by dampening their free expression or undercutting their ability to make a living. In response, members pointed out that they had collective responsibility for the event's survival. If such commodification activities went unchecked, they could destroy what attendees valued about the event. As the event's reputation grows, more individuals and organizations are likely to try to capitalize upon the Burning Man cachet. Whether Burning Man members can prevent these activities from diluting Burning Man's reputation and experience remains to be seen.

Conclusion

Much research (e.g., Rothschild and Whitt 1986) has detailed how internal and external pressures spur organizations to either dissolve or replace unconventional practices with conventional ones. In comparison, the Burning Man organization has led a charmed life.[133] Its small local event not only survived initial pressures, but also transformed into a thriving, temporary city that now draws 47,000 from around the world. But given the obstacles, sheer luck cannot explain the Burning Man event's survival and growth during two decades.

Relations with several entities could have instigated overorganizing by introducing routines and procedures that were inapplicable or fostered coercive control. Governmental agencies sometimes refused to cooperate, and they claimed that the Burning Man organization had to adopt standards and practices in exchange for needed resources. However, the demanded practices did not address the event's unique conditions, such as its location in a remote desert with limited infrastructure. Similarly, the media expected that the Burning Man organization would grant their requests in exchange for publicity. If members accommodated the media's demands, they would not only have to routinize otherwise unnecessary practices but also deal with the possible consequences of the media's coverage, including incensed reactions by the public and governmental agencies. Moreover, other organizations and individuals tried to commodify the Burning Man name, imagery, or experience for their own purposes in the economic market. While this set of actors did not provide Burning Man with needed resources, their activities violated Burning Man's norms and threatened to detract from the event's meaning.

Rather than acquiesce by accepting imposed practices or activities, Burning Man members attempted to advance their organizing practices and outputs as appropriate or legitimate. While a few actions against individuals fostered accusations of self-inflicted overorganizing, other actions helped the Burning Man organization defy or manipulate relations without triggering organizing excesses.

A few practices occasionally drew accusations that the Burning Man organization had overextended its authority, thus feeding overorganizing. For example, when asked to desist from activities such as posting ads with the Burning Man name or publicizing deviant acts, a few individuals expressed resentment about having to defer to organizational concerns and questioned the legitimacy of the growing Burning Man organization. Moreover, critics questioned whether the Burning Man organization wielded too much influence over entities such as the media. Excessive influence would allow the Burning Man organizers to suppress rather than address issues such as the event's environmental effects and death and injury rates.[134] If organizations lack sufficient checks on their power or influence, they may skirt their obligations to members' interests (Perrow 1986).

While a few actions suggested possible overorganizing, Burning Man members took other actions that managed relations without triggering overorganizing. They formed new departments that coordinated activities with governmental agencies in ways that substantiated a collectivist ethic. Members also brainstormed with agencies to jointly develop applicable standards. When needed, Burning Man supporters goaded agencies into action and protested problematic legislation by writing letters to Congress and attending meetings.

Given that bureaucratic practices underpin the political and legal realms in the United States, organizations have to learn how to work bureaucratic levers or convince others to accept their alternative practices. Mainstream firms and radical social movement groups push for the acceptance of alternative, not yet legitimated structures or practices by associating them with conventional ones, typically bureaucratic practices (Elsbach and Sutton 1992; Hoffman 2001; Rojas 2007). As Burning Man members pointed out, governmental agencies respond to collaborations and lobbying, as they must demonstrate accountability to constituents. Governmental agencies are also more open to implementing changes if their ranks include professionals and if they are uncertain about how to carry out work (Espeland 1998).

To facilitate Burning Man's relations with the media, the specialized department of Media Mecca introduced both bureaucratic and collectivist practices. Using guidelines and procedures intended to influence the media's representation of the event, volunteers tried to discourage the media from depicting deviant activities or stereotypes that could delegitimize the Burning Man enterprise. Volunteers suggested topics that emphasized how Burning Man shared values with larger society. Moreover, volunteers encouraged the media to immerse themselves in the event, thereby familiarizing the media with the collectivist ethic. Previous research has documented the media's reliance upon bureaucratic routines (Fishman 1980) and proclivity for constructing reports with well-worn angles (Tuchman 1978). By mixing practices, the Burning Man organization simultaneously enabled the media to continue routines while breaking reporting conventions.

Such intensive public relations efforts can help organizations secure recognition and legitimacy for their practices and activities (Gamson and Wolfsfeld 1993; Kennedy 2008). For example, by immersing reporters in American military units, the Pentagon's embedded journalists program steered media coverage into supporting American foreign policy interests over other interests (Linder 2008).[135] Similarly, by codifying relations and procedures, a social movement organization increased media coverage that supported its goals (Ryan et al. 2005).

To dissuade commodifiers from expropriating Burning Man's name, imagery, or output for use in the economic market, the Burning Man organization resorted to legal threats and moral appeals, tapping both bureaucratic and collectivist practices. Members introduced routines for ferreting out and responding to transgressions with explanations of Burning Man's policies and mission. Members also took legal steps against recalcitrant offenders, such as pornography distributors. However, volunteers were willing to overlook minor cases of self-promotion, such as artists who were trying to make a living.

Like the Burning Man organization, new and established organizations are concerned about how actual or perceived ties with others might affect their legitimacy. New, innovative organizations carefully select which organizations to associate with, as the "wrong" ties might decrease their status and acceptability (Johnson 2007). Established, high-status firms may also shun ties with firms that might detract from their status, even if this means foregoing potential financial gain (Podolny 2005). On the flip side, lesser known organizations can enhance their legitimacy through ties with reputable organizations (Baum and Oliver 1991, 1992). Some organizations form symbolic ties for marketing purposes. In exchange for funds, a trusted organization such as a nonprofit professional association will license its name and logo for use in a for-profit organization's advertisement of products or services. In effect, this association implies that an organization endorses another organization's offerings (Galaskiewicz and Colman 2006). Organizations also cultivate ties by appointing representatives of other organizations to their board of directors or donating funds to philanthropies (Galaskiewicz 1985).

Not all organizations will be able to legitimize their distinctive practices (Murmann 2003). Therefore, identifying conditions that enhance legitimacy affords insight into how organizations can manage relations with their fields. The Burning Man organization cultivated several advantages that enhanced its abilities to weather challenging relations. Although Burning Man struggled to cover expenses during its earlier and middle years, its organizers were able to generate enough funds through ticket sales to sustain the organization and its output over the long term. Such self-sufficiency can protect against external influences. Otherwise, to obtain funds from banks, philanthropies, or the state, organizations may have to adopt undesired practices and forsake their constituents' interests (Oerton 1996; Powell and Friedkin 1987).

In addition, while the Burning Man organization had some conflicts with the state, relations with governmental agencies became more cooperative, although not without disputes.[136] Relations might have been more problematic had the Burning Man organization not refashioned its image and activities as an arts community. Had members or the media continued to glorify Burning Man's deviant aspects, governmental agencies could have treated Burning Man like a radical social movement, extremist political group, or a cult and systematically suppressed its activities in the way that, during the 1960s, the FBI mounted counterintelligence operations intended to sow dissent among members of leftist groups and the Ku Klux Klan (Cunningham 2004).

Moreover, Burning Man had the simultaneous disadvantage and advantage of being a "first" in its field.[137] On the one hand, the Burning Man organization lacked competitors that could have threatened its existence. Without competitors or comparable equivalents, the Burning Man organization had more room to experiment and a basis for rejecting externally imposed practices as inapplicable. On the other hand, the Burning Man organization had to expend considerable effort educating wary entities and the general public about its output and activities.

Survival concerns drove Burning Man's initial attempts to secure legitimacy for practices and outputs. Burning Man now evidences a new phase of that pursuit. A growing number of locally based events and voluntary associations, including nonprofits, have drawn on Burning Man's experiences to identify useful practices and avoid missteps.[138] This emulation of Burning Man's distinctive practices and output suggests that the Burning Man enterprise has acquired legitimacy (e.g., Aldrich and Fiol 1994). As other events and groups continue Burning Man's practices, the Burning Man legacy can endure even if its main event ends. For organizations such as Burning Man, the pursuit of legitimacy, rather than just accepting conventions, can involve a bumpy but worthwhile path.

:::

Conclusion

Sustaining Creative Chaos

IN AN INTERVIEW, former volunteer Naomi Pearce contemplated how the Burning Man organization had evaded under- and overorganizing extremes:

> If you get it too organized, it becomes a corporation . . . in the working sense. So, the fact that it's one step underorganized is good. It's not disorganized, it's not all the way over to that extreme. But it's not like so overstructured. . . . If you want to participate in the organization, there's probably some talents that they could use.[1]

Pearce's comment illustrates the difficulties of creating an enabling organization: how can members establish sufficient structure and coordination that support but do not constrain their activities? Without adequately specified organizing practices, underorganizing can result, hampering members' efforts. Insufficient coordination and organizing practices can embroil members in disputes about how to organize, curtailing productivity. The ensuing disabling chaos can discourage members from contributing time and effort, hastening their organization's closure. On the other extreme, practices that are mixed with coercive control, or overzealous or overly centralized control, can elicit overorganizing. Excessive rules, peer pressure, or top-down control can hamstring members' efforts. Rather than pursuing goals, leaders may redirect organizing efforts for their own benefit or focus on maintaining the organization. In the resulting feel-good collective, disempowered team, or totalitarianism, organizations lack accountability to members' interests.

Previous chapters examined how the Burning Man organization mediated between under- and overorganizing in producing its temporary arts community. After the 1996 event teetered "on the edge of total collapse and destruction,"[2] Burning Man organizers corrected for underorganizing by shifting from ad hoc to formal organizing. However, some members worried that this shift could introduce overorganizing. Critics like John Rinaldi, a.k.a. Chicken John, chafed at the increasing rules and longed for more chaos: "I hope that people get tired of the rules, [that] the organizers, [and] the people in the organizational body get tired of upholding the rules and allow more of the chaos to come in."[3] In contrast, other members emphasized how increasing organization enabled, rather than suppressed, efforts. On the staff listserv, Marian Goodell explained that she and other organizers had formalized a policy to guide volunteers' activities: "The [LLC] Board has tried to be responsive to the requests of the ever expanding staff, and one of those requests has been to better and more clearly define 'rules,' 'issues' and 'protocols' that may have been 'understood' over the years, but not defined."[4]

While a few interviewed members missed having a small, exclusive event that ran on minimal organizing,[5] most welcomed change as part of Burning Man's "creative chaos."[6] Members like volunteer Susan Strahan looked forward to expecting the unexpected: "I think that one of the exciting things about Burning Man is: what is going to happen next year? . . . I hope that the surprise never ends."[7] Follow-up observations indicate that the Burning Man organization and its event have continued to experiment with large and small changes.

During the time of my study, Burning Man members formalized practices that specified and coordinated activities but were flexible and responsive to changes in their interests and the organization's environment. They melded two kinds of organizing practices that traditionally have been viewed as incompatible. Bureaucratic practices such as a chain of authority, standardization, and specialization reinforced fairness, efficiency, and stability. Collectivist practices such as a mission, decision making by consensus, and role creation cultivated flexibility, responsiveness, and meaning. These two types of practices supported each other in checking under- and overorganizing; bureaucratic practices stabilized organizing efforts while collectivist practices ensured that members' interests remained a priority.

By specifying how to organize, formalized practices allowed Burning Man members to carry out their mission, rather than dissipating their efforts on unclear procedures. Disputes and discussions about the application of bureaucratic and collectivist practices helped clarify how to make decisions and elevate financial transparency. Moreover, such discussions spurred organizers to more closely align organizing efforts with members' interests. These actions helped elevate the organization's accountability to its members, correcting underorganizing and checking overorganizing.

Bureaucratic and collectivist practices worked synergistically in organizing members and external parties. For instance, organizers introduced both bureaucratic and collectivist practices to handle the recruitment, placement, and retention of members. Bureaucratic practices that created specialized volunteer coordinator positions and standardized procedures helped take in a larger number of volunteers, alleviating a bottleneck from earlier underorganized recruitment. Collectivist practices formalized under the principle of "radical inclusion" and a policy of role creation ensured that people could join and take responsibilities according to their interests, thus expanding recruitment and placement beyond identified organizational needs. Such combined bureaucratic and collectivist practices tapped diverse motivations for contributing; they also supported members' reevaluation of their commitment and helped ameliorate burnout by relaxing productivity expectations and encouraging members to share work.

In addition, collectivist and bureaucratic practices helped manage external perceptions of the Burning Man organization's activities and outputs as legitimate and appropriate. Familiar bureaucratic practices of rules, specialization, and a division of labor eased coordination with governmental agencies that provided needed resources and the media that covered the event. Collectivist practices helped immerse such external entities in the Burning Man milieu and strengthened the grounds for deflecting their attempts to impose unnecessary practices or expropriate Burning Man's name, imagery, and outputs.

The Burning Man organization is not unusual in its mixing of bureaucratic and collectivist practices. Recent research indicates that voluntary associations and business firms alike are adopting both kinds of practices (Bordt 1997; Cappelli and Neumark 2001; Hodson 2001). However, such research has criticized how organizations use these combined practices as a soft-gloved, coercive means to more thoroughly exploit members and suppress their interests (Barker 1993, 1999; Boltanski and Chiapello 2005; Perrow 1986; Rothschild and Ollilainen 1999; Sewell 1998). Do bureaucratic and collectivist practices inevitably trigger such overorganizing? When compared against other research, the Burning Man case suggests that an appropriate answer is a conditional "it depends." The more important question concerns how to set conditions that allow practices to create an enabling organization, rather than fostering under- or overorganizing.

Previous research has shown the general difficulties of combining practices of different types. For instance, introduced practices of one type can completely replace the practices of another type (Forssell and Jansson 1996; Thornton 2004). With such a thorough replacement, organizations risk discarding practices that reinforced members' commitment or facilitated their work. For example, when nonprofit organizations such as museums, theaters, and hospitals implemented business-oriented measures that promoted cost cutting and efficiency, these changes often displaced practices that members deemed integral to their work. Employees worried that the quality of their work suffered, and their organizational involvement decreased with such changes (Oakes, Townley, and Cooper 1998; Voss, Cable, and Voss 2000; Weinberg 2003). In addition, new practices can trigger "mission drift" or "mission creep" away from espoused goals (Frumkin 2002; Minkoff and Powell 2006). When organizations make dramatic changes to enhance their survival, they increase their risk of closure in comparison with organizations that keep original practices (Minkoff 1999).

When organizations combine practices, they may do so in ways that undercut the efficacy of their practices. This can happen, for instance, with participatory practices when upper management refuses to share control with line workers, resulting in disempowered teams. When tasked with greater responsibility but deprived of corresponding authority over the work process, workers expressed frustration and withdrew (Vallas 2003b). Such inauthentic participation widens rather than reduces worker alienation (Heller 1998). Another imbalance can occur when members favor one kind of practice at the expense of other practices. For example, members might focus on the implementation of bureaucratic practices and fail to invest the time and effort needed to mature participatory decision making (Stohl and Cheney 2001). Or collectivist and bureaucratic practices can combine to intensify overorganizing extremes by consolidating coercive control, creating totalitarian organizations (e.g., Barker 1993, 1999).

In previous chapters, I suggested specific ways of avoiding under- and overorganizing. Additional activities can sustain the synergistic effects of bureaucratic and collectivist practices, fostering an enabling organization. Organizations can balance expectations, facilitate true participation, engage in reflexive dialogue, encourage experimentation, supply sufficient resources, uphold inclusivity, advance their legitimacy, or set precedents.

Balance expectations. Sociologists use the term "total institution" to describe extreme organizations that engulf all aspects of their members' lives: communes, mental institutions, prisons, and the military (Goffman 1961). However, even conventional workplaces and voluntary associations can operate like such "greedy institutions" (Coser 1974) when their practices discourage members from fulfilling other responsibilities. While members' commitment to their organization may increase because they no longer can pursue other interests or responsibilities (Iannaccone 1994), members may also experience burnout, disillusionment, and alienation (Kunda 1992; Lalich 2004). Over-organizing can arise when practices push members to contribute without considering their interests.

Balancing expectations about organizational participation can prevent organizations from making excessive demands of members. For example, one worker cooperative developed a philosophy that explicitly stated that its employees should maintain a balance between work and personal pursuits. This helped protect members against obligations to undertake too many workplace responsibilities (Jackall 1984). Similarly, Burning Man coordinators encouraged members to share their load and recuperate, rather than pressuring individuals to work as much as possible.[8] Firms like Patagonia have introduced flexible hours and job sharing; they also fund leaves and encourage workers to participate in recreational activities and voluntary associations (Chouinard 2005).[9]

Such balancing of expectations should not be limited to a few, progressive organizations. Currently, Americans spend more time at their workplaces than on any other commitment (Jacobs and Gerson 2004; Schor 1991). As worker productivity has become difficult to assess, employers measure "face time," or time spent at the workplace (Bailyn 2006), to determine employee retention, compensation, and promotions. Such actions reinforce a distorted ideal that employees should not have other commitments to family or community. These expectations allow bosses to insist that their employees labor past official work hours and cut vacations short (Perlow 1998), encourage employment discrimination against women with families (Correll, Benard, and Paik 2007), justify a gendered division of labor in household and childcare tasks (Blair-Loy 2003; Hochschild [1983] 2003), and preclude participation in civic affairs (Jacobs and Gerson 2004). Similarly, voluntary associations can impose such heavy demands that members no longer can keep up with friends or family, much less have a life outside their organizations (Iannaccone 1994; Lalich 2004).

In the United States, the intensification of work has encouraged a widespread division of labor. For those who can afford the expense, specialists can take responsibility for childcare, housework, and even civic participation (Hochschild [1983] 2003; Lee 2007). While some welcome this dispersion of responsibilities, the displacement of such work onto individuals who are often underpaid and vulnerable widens social inequality (Hondagneu-Sotelo 2001). As a society, we need to reconsider whether demanding such organizational commitment is warranted or desirable and act accordingly, whether this involves increasing support of workers or scaling back organizational demands.

Facilitate true participation. In overorganized organizations, a large power imbalance ensures that front-line workers' input will not be supported or valued by management (Vallas 2006). In underorganized groups, members do not know how to advance their views, and a lack of specified practices allows well-connected or charismatic individuals to dominate decision making (Freeman 1973). These issues deprive organizations of the innovation and direction that divergent perspectives could add. Moreover, members do not gain experience with organizing themselves, undercutting learning that some view as crucial to a healthy democratic society (Fisher 2006; Skocpol 2003).

Previous research has claimed that bureaucratization supports organizational maintenance efforts, such as recruiting members and securing resources, at the expense of member-driven innovation, while collectivist practices cultivate innovative organizing tactics at the expense of organizational maintenance (Staggenborg 1989). In contrast, the Burning Man organization suggests that combined collectivist and bureaucratic practices can allow for simultaneous organizational maintenance and innovation: bureaucratic practices such as hierarchy and a division of labor differentiated the responsibilities of members and leaders while collectivist practices invited members to create roles and contribute their expertise and perspective. Rather than regressing into passivity or arguing over whether their views were adequately represented, members could redress their bugaboos or initiate pet projects; some members even started their own local organizations and events with the blessings and support of the Burning Man organization.

The implementation of such practices requires a fundamental reconceptualization of members' activities beyond strictly delineated, hierarchical roles. Supervisors and members have to understand that an enabling organization entails sharing control and accepting greater uncertainty. Members must also be prepared to take a more active role by applying their front-line experience and expertise to identifying problems and brainstorming solutions, rather than waiting for top-down orders. Under these conditions, members may experience more meaningful and productive work (Hodson 2001; Zell 1997), and organizational productivity can also benefit from this more thorough tapping of members' potential. With such practices in place, Burning Man members' endeavors exceeded the expectations of fellow members and external parties.

Engage in reflexive dialogue. Organizations benefit from regular discussions about whether practices are necessary or need adjustments. Burning Man organizers collectively examined the assumptions underlying practices when evaluating whether particular policies or activities were still needed. Based on these discussions, organizers also made changes that enhanced their organization's flexibility and responsiveness. If organizations overlook or suppress such dialogue, they risk retaining problematic organizing practices that can lead to suboptimal or even fatal outcomes (Vaughn 1996).

Reflexive dialogue can help members assess the benefits and drawbacks of particular arrangements and investigate alternatives. These discussions can raise awareness about whether members are reproducing practices by rote, particularly in introducing bureaucratic forms of control (Barker 1993, 1999). By stimulating discussions of aims and practices, an organization can more closely serve its members' interests (Rothschild and Leach 2006; Osterman 2006). Exposure to dissenting views can provoke in-depth discussion and reexamination of assumptions, preventing individual members from uncritically conforming to a majority view (Nemeth and Staw 1989).

Encourage experimentation. Burning Man evidences how organizing involves experimental actions and constant adjustments for changes in organizational conditions and individuals' situations. Burning Man's challenging desert location and other issues such as political contention reminded members of the limits to rational planning. Given time and support, members transformed seeming disasters into creative endeavors, as illustrated by the conversion of underorganized ice sales into the booming Camp Arctica. Such openness to experimentation can generate practices that better serve both members' and organizational interests. For instance, members convinced the media to prepare and participate with playful rituals and procedures, rather than deferring to the media's demands for standard public relations practices. By combining collectivist and bureaucratic practices, members aimed to facilitate coverage that would help, rather than hurt, the event.

Experimentation can involve struggle and conflict, particularly given pressures to produce on a set schedule (Zell 1997). While some view conflicts as abnormal or undesirable, such stressors can introduce mindfulness and opportunities for reflection that can help push an organization out of a comfortable rut of conventional but suboptimal practices. Play and experimentation can reinvigorate attentiveness to whether organizing practices serve intended purposes. In supporting experimentation, organizations should refrain from treating setbacks and failures as grounds for punishment; otherwise, members may engage in deception to avoid censure (Shulman 2007). By treating such bumps as learning opportunities, members can deepen their expertise and enhance goal attainment.

Supply sufficient resources. As the Burning Man organization matured, its organizers could better support members' efforts with resources, including materials, training, and time. In particular, organizers and volunteer coordinators educated members about collectivist practices. Without sufficient training or grounding, members may not understand why they should carry out such practices, particularly if they lack prior experience with these practices. Otherwise, members may reproduce familiar practices without considering their effects and appropriateness (Barker 1993, 1999; DiMaggio and Powell 1983; Snook 2000). Constant coaching and training thus are essential for implementing unfamiliar practices and adjusting to new situations (Hackman 2002).

Organizations also need to provide sufficient resources, such as labor, supplies, equipment, and workspace. While members with a strong work ethic or a fear of losing their livelihood will compensate for inadequate resources, their heroic efforts can hasten their burnout and turnover, thus affecting organizational survival (Swidler 1979; Weinberg 2003). Therefore, management has a special responsibility of ensuring that members have sufficient resources and support to do their work (Hackman 2002). Shirking this responsibility is neither sustainable nor ethical; it is a marker of mismanagement (Hodson 2001).

In comparison with other organizations, the Burning Man organization had an advantageous position in that organizers could secure resources with revenues drawn from ticket sales and donations. Some organizations, particularly voluntary associations and nonprofits, have more difficulties obtaining needed resources, as they may have to adopt undesired practices or moderate their goals in exchange for governmental funding or bank loans (Cress 1997; Matthews 1994; Rothschild and Whitt 1986). Should institutions withhold resources, organizations face closure (Duckles et al. 2005; Hager, Galaskiewicz, and Larson 2004). Increasingly, nonprofit organizations undertake commercial activities to decrease such dependencies (Grams 2008). Other organizations, especially for-profits, may not have problems with securing resources, but they must decide how to allocate resources. As CEO compensation has skyrocketed, the accompanying disparities in wages and working conditions among lower-level workers raise questions about whether such for-profit firms adequately support their personnel (Khurana 2002).

Uphold inclusivity. Previous research has advised that organizations stay small and selective about member recruitment if they want to retain their alternative practices and survive (e.g., Rothschild and Whitt 1986). While maintaining a small, homogenous membership can enhance organizational survival, a more expansive, heterogeneous membership is another possible path. Under the principle of "radical inclusion," the Burning Man organization promoted the inclusion, rather than the exclusion, of members, thus diversifying a once insular group. Collectivist practices reinforced the premise that organizational imperatives should not displace members' interests. These practices helped codify acceptance of the challenges and variable outcomes associated with working in a more expansive group.

As organizations diversify their membership along dimensions such as gender, race, and sexual orientation, conflicts over organizing practices and aims or divisions among groups can arise (Allmendinger and Hackman 1995; Kanter 1977). Given such issues, members who are "different" are more likely to leave their organizations than those who are similar, intensifying the homogeneity of members (Popielarz and McPherson 1995) and segregation of networks (McPherson, Smith-Lovin, and Cook 2001). The Burning Man organization instituted practices that counteracted tendencies toward homogeneity. For instance, when members expressed annoyance about event "newbies" who flouted norms about appropriate conduct, such complaints could have easily solidified divisions between self-described old-timers and newcomers and dissuaded both groups from returning. Instead, under the mandate of "radical inclusion," members brainstormed creative ways of educating newcomers on how to participate, transforming a potentially divisive gripe into a challenge that united members with actionable steps.

In general, a diverse membership body can offer resources, skills, and perspectives that can enhance an organization's resilience. Had the Burning Man organization recruited only the "groovy granola type"[10] or anarchists, it is less likely that members would have had access to the wide range of expertise and resources needed to handle various challenges, such as relations with the media, local law enforcement, and the federal government. Burning Man's inclusiveness also elicited member devotion and appreciation. Indeed, studies have shown that organizations can better weather changes with a devoted corps of volunteers (Hager et al. 2004).

Advance legitimacy. When entrenched in daily survival activities, developing organizations may overlook the importance of promoting their practices and goals as legitimate and appropriate in their fields. Such inattention can cripple an organization, as a failure to legitimate practices and activities can invite state repression (Cunningham 2004) or result in the loss of competitive advantage (Murmann 2003). In addition, actors such as the state or resource providers can demand that an organization adopt problematic practices or goals, or other entities may even abscond with an organization's resources and outputs for their own benefit. To counter such pressures, Burning Man members engaged in concerted public relations work and cooperative endeavors to promote their activities as acceptable. Such efforts involved fending off and redirecting efforts by the media and governmental agencies to use Burning Man for other purposes. Other organizations may have to initiate more extensive activities such as lobbying or entering coalitions with similar organizations to advance their legitimacy (Aldrich and Ruef 2006; Disney and Gelb 2000; Galaskiewicz 1985; Hoffman 1999; Kaplan and Harrison 1993; Miles 1982; Murmann 2003).

An organization may also have to protect its name, reputation, and outputs against being exploited by others. But, the risk of backlash increases should individuals perceive the organization as exerting coercive control. A few eBay vendors protested Burning Man's e-mails about dropping names from titles, and documentary makers chafed against organizers' requests to cut material. Nevertheless, Burning Man supporters seemed to understand how commercial encroachment and misrepresentation could detrimentally impact the event's unique tenets of a gift economy and participation. In contrast, other organizations, particularly those that are for-profit, might have greater difficulties posing convincing moral arguments about why they need to protect their products or services against trademark infringement.[11] Such organizations may have to, as Burning Man members did, pick their battles rather than pursue all violations.[12]

Set precedents. Given the few precedents for managing a temporary city in the desert, Burning Man had to develop and promote its own organizing standards. Uncertainty and a lack of precedents increase the chances that organizations can advocate practices that serve their interests: "When organizational fields are unstable and established practices are ill-formed, successful collective action often depends upon defining and elaborating widely accepted rules of the game" (DiMaggio and Powell 1991: 30). Rather than allowing others to define organizing standards, the Burning Man organization developed departments and implemented bureaucratic practices to promote coordination with other parties. Collectivist practices, particularly a commitment to a mission and values, provided a rationale and guide for deflecting external entities' demands for other practices. Burning Man organizers also set precedents for other groups by sharing their organizing experiences in newsletters and detailed reports on a public Web site and training members on how to carry out practices and uphold principles. As other groups emulate and adapt these practices for other settings, they afford Burning Man an increasingly taken-for-granted status.

Such influence is not limited to organizations in developing fields, as new ways of organizing can arise in seemingly established fields. Even familiar, accepted organizational forms can be used to serve new ends. For example, during the late nineteenth through early twentieth centuries, women used the existing organizational forms of clubs, parliaments, unions, and corporations as new venues for political activities. This appropriation of familiar forms for other purposes allowed an otherwise marginalized group to participate in politics (Clemens 1993). Alternatively, groups can promote the acceptance of their organizational practices by showing how these uphold accepted societal beliefs (Ruef 2000). Some organizations may have to downplay controversial activities in favor of accepted activities (Lune 2002; Matthews 1994) as Burning Man did to some degree, but organizations can still promote new activities and refashioned beliefs about appropriate organizing practices (DiMaggio 1988).

The Future of Organizing

Interviews and observations revealed that the Burning Man organizers recognized that their membership ranks and organization would not endure for perpetuity, particularly as members age and their interests change, or as new challenges threaten to derail the Burning Man endeavor.[13] Rather than focusing efforts on maintaining their organization, the Burning Man organizers have also recognized the large-scale impact of educating individuals on how to organize their own communities and events. With the Burning Man organization's support, regionals now span five continents, and Burning Man-inspired events continue to appear around the world.[14] Given these developments, it seems likely that the Burning Man mission of producing an arts community can endure even if its underlying organization dissolves. By launching and supporting individuals on other organizing journeys, Burning Man has demonstrated its full capacity as an enabling organization.

Overall, this research suggests how organizations can serve rather than rule us. We can take collective responsibility for designing organizations that provide enough structure and coordination, without excessive control, to facilitate the pursuit of organizational objectives and incorporate members' interests. In doing so, we need to consider the tradeoffs of combining organizing practices, which can include ambiguity, divergent perspectives, and conflict. Making these assessments requires intensive involvement and effort that not all individuals are able or willing to expend, particularly when some view current organizational structures as a fait accompli. Those who undertake these responsibilities allow for a wider range of experiences and outcomes, including failures and triumphs. Transformed by these experiences, individuals may be inspired to undertake more endeavors.

Under such conditions, organizations can reach their full potential as tools that can help us realize particular objectives, whether these include making products or services, promoting social change, or enhancing meaningfulness, fulfillment, or connection with others. When supported by enabling organizations, we can realize ideals both massive and minute, as exemplified by Burning Man's annual, fiery, creative chaos in the Black Rock Desert.

Appendix 1

Ethnography and Qualitative Research

Sweat trickled down my forehead as I tugged on the stuck restroom door. Moments before, I had been relieved to find this restroom, an amenity in a bare-bones club consisting of a concrete floor, single light bulb, and dilapidated couches. As music by the featured performers drowned out my yelps for help, my mind turned to the band's fire dancer. When I last saw her, she was waving open flames near the sound insulation on the club's ceiling. As my panicked imagination considered this fire hazard, I regretted my decision to observe this Burning Man–bound troupe's performance. Finally, someone heard my frantic knocks and pushed the door open; I stumbled outside the club, where I met a fellow audience member who was equally unnerved by the performance.

This was one of my first evenings in the field researching organizing activities behind the Burning Man event. As an organizational ethnographer, I immersed myself in the Burning Man milieu by conducting such observations, along with participant observations, interviews, and archival research of official Burning Man organizing activities. My research delved into the regular activities that power organizations; researchers contend that we need to better understand these actions (Clemens and Minkoff 2004).

My adventures started in May 1998, when I sent an e-mail requesting access to the Burning Man organization via Marian Goodell, the most visible contact listed on Burning Man's Web site and newsletter listserv. After consulting with other organizers, Goodell granted my request and suggested that I join the Media Mecca team, which she oversaw. By July 1998, I had moved to San Francisco for the first of several intensive rounds of participant observations and observations of organizational activities. These observations covered the busiest organizing periods in the organization's production cycle, namely, the summer months preceding the 1998, 1999, and 2000 Burning Man events. In addition, I observed and participated in activities during the five months immediately following the 2000 Burning Man event and conducted follow-up participant observations in the months before the 2001 event. The eight months of concentrated observations spanning 2000–2001 culminated in my almost daily presence in the Burning Man headquarters during the summer preceding the 2000 event. Comparison of participant observations and observations over the years helped pinpoint changes in organizing activities. This method also helped identify everyday organizing routines (Schwartzman 1993).

During observations, I took field notes in real time, often typing them on my laptop.[1] My most comprehensive observations covered weekly senior staff meetings, where organizers discussed policies, goals, progress, challenges, and departmental activities. I also observed a staff retreat to understand how staffers debriefed from the 2000 event, and I followed up by observing meetings from December 2000 through January 2001, when staffers worked on a budget and reorganized departmental structures and functions. In addition, I shadowed several organizers' activities at the office and their homes. Informal conversations with organizers and members revealed some of the behind-the-scenes action, including phone or e-mail conversations that I did not observe first-hand.

I also participated in or observed at least one meeting, training orientation, and gathering of eight volunteer departments and their subunits and committees. These observations revealed discussions about how to motivate and coordinate members and departments in the Black Rock Rangers and its various subdivisions, Media Mecca, the *Black Rock Gazette,* Greeters, Check Point Salon (now Playa Info), Earth Guardians, the Art team, and the Technical ("Tech") team. My most consistent observations were of Media Mecca's meetings and online discussions, which informed chapter 6's analysis of how this department worked with the media. I did not observe departments such as the Gate (which lacked face-to-face meetings since members resided all over the United States), the Web team, commissary, Camp Arctica (ice sales), the Café, and Department of Public Works (DPW). For these underrepresented groups, I relied on interviews and reports at other meetings about their activities. I also observed department-wide meetings.

In addition, I observed and participated in year-round formal and informal Burning Man–related events, such as the town hall meetings, gallery openings, fund-raisers, performances, and parties for volunteers and participants in the San Francisco Bay area and in the Reno area of Nevada. Since such events attracted a broader cross-section of members, they provided data on cross-departmental interactions and the presentation of policies to a larger public. I also observed two meetings between Burning Man organizers and federal and local officials in Nevada. Other meetings between organizers and agencies were closed to outsiders, so I relied on the accounts provided by Burning Man organizers, as well as interviews with a few outside officials and archival research.

I also monitored a constant stream of e-mails and electronic newsletters. I followed eight years of *Jack Rabbit Speaks,* the official e-mail newsletter that disseminates communication from the Burning Man organization to a large audience of subscribed readers. Departmental and theme camp e-mail lists, which often included exchanges among their subscribers, recounted organizers' and volunteers' perspectives on issues, activities, and relevant information. I examined eight years of the Media Mecca list, six months of the Tech team list, four years of the Burning Man staff list, and one to two years of two theme camps lists.

I participated in nine Burning Man events in the Black Rock Desert between 1998 and 2008, excluding 2004 and 2006. In 1998, 2000, and 2001, I participated in and observed on-site organizing activities before the event's official start. During all attended events, excluding 2008, I volunteered for Media Mecca by bartending, driving reporters and supplies around in a golf cart, and registering people. At two events, I also volunteered at Check Point Salon by answering inquiries at the information desk. In addition, I attended on-site meetings during the 2000 event. To understand other Burning Man–related activities, I briefly observed and participated in the activities of two theme camps, Cataclysmic Megashear Ranch in 1998–1999 and Motel 666 in 1999–2000, and a Burning Man funded art project coordinated by artist Davy Normal in 2000.[2] I attended their organizational meetings and workdays and later camped with the two theme camps and attended the art project's performance at the Burning Man events. I selected these groups because of their San Francisco area locations and their members' involvement with the Burning Man organization.

In addition, I conducted interviews with individuals about their Burning Man experiences. I completed seventy-eight semistructured interviews of eighty persons in the few weeks before and the four months after the 2000 event, and I added a seventy-ninth interview of the eighty-first individual after the 2001 event. I interviewed all of the LLC members, all of the senior staff and some of their support staff, and almost all of the department heads or leads who were active in the organization during 2000. I also interviewed at least one Bay Area–based volunteer in each department; for several departments, I interviewed additional volunteers who held leadership positions.[3] I also interviewed two artists and two heads of regional Burning Man groups. Of the two artist interviewees, one was local to the San Francisco Bay area, while the other was not. Based on the recommendation of Marian Goodell, who oversaw the regionals, I interviewed the heads of the most active chapters of New York City and Austin, Texas.

To reconstruct the organizational history, I interviewed organizers who were no longer involved with the organization. These interviews included a cofounder of the original 1986 Burning Man event and leaders who were pivotal in the late 1980s through 1996 events. Based on my archival research, I identified some of the past organizers, which I confirmed by gathering recommendations of past and present organizers and other interviewees. To examine how relations with the Burning Man organization had changed over time, I interviewed representatives of agencies or organizations who had worked with it. I was not able to interview representatives from all agencies, particularly local law enforcement, and thus had to rely on the reports of Burning Man informants and newspaper accounts for local perspectives and activities. However, I was able to interview a few local Nevada residents who were active in the Gerlach General Improvement District and the Gerlach-Empire Citizen Advisory Board for the year 2000. In addition, I interviewed two Bureau of Land Management officials who were closely involved with the permit administration for the event's site.

I interviewed most individuals at the Burning Man office, their homes, restaurants, coffee shops, or my home. Due to distance or time constraints, I conducted fifteen interviews over the phone. Three of the interviews were conducted both over the phone and in person because of time constraints. Two of the interviews involved jointly interviewing two persons, or couples who volunteered for the same department. Interviews lasted from thirty minutes to four and a half hours. All but two interviews were tape-recorded and transcribed.

To establish a historical context, I examined the organization's developing archives and the personal archives of two individuals who had collected memos, budgets, fliers, and press clippings from Burning Man's earlier years. These provided information on dates of events, names of members, pertinent issues, and codified policies, as well as material intended for external consumption, such as promotional postcards and memorabilia from theme camps or art projects. In addition, I regularly perused the organization's official Web site, which features a searchable index of images of artwork, transcribed speeches, interviews, and articles. I also examined the organization's collection of press clippings, which showed how the local, national, and international media portrayed issues, as well as how some coverage distorted facts or cribbed from the Burning Man Web site.[4] In addition, I viewed press footage and documentaries that were available in the organization's video archives; these helped to reconstruct the event and organizational history, particularly the earliest and middle years of the event.

Preliminary analyses of the 1998 and 1999 data helped inform frameworks that oriented the collection and the analysis of the 2000 data. I flagged themes relevant to the research questions in the field notes, interviews, and archives and gradually built up concepts. To achieve construct validity, I triangulated multiple sources of evidence to provide greater depth and accuracy (Yin 1994).

Conducting a case study had several advantages in collecting rich data on complex phenomena. As a revelatory case, this research provided "an opportunity to examine previously inaccessible phenomena"[5] (Yin 1994: 40), namely, the daily operations of a contemporary organization. This in-depth study on how members navigated various organizing issues develops a rich, informed basis for analytic generalization.[6] This foundation launches a deeper theoretical understanding and conceptualization of under- and overorganizing by grounding future efforts to conduct larger comparative studies. Furthermore, this case study suggests paths for modifying and extending existing organizational research and concepts.

Research Issues

Setting organizational boundaries. One major issue in conducting this research concerned the boundaries of the Burning Man organization. Like the Burning Man organizers,[7] I defined the Burning Man organization as including obvious members, such as organizers and volunteers, and the more than 47,000 persons who attend the Burning Man event but do not volunteer, as all are involved in the production of the event. But rather than representing all organizational members or the assumed "average" event attendee,[8] I focused on those who contributed regularly to the organization as head organizers and volunteers. Their activities provided guidelines for lower levels of organizing among volunteers and event participants.

My initial difficulties in bounding the Burning Man phenomena are not unusual. As formal organizations become more ubiquitous, determining whether an individual is a part of an organization cannot always be established by consulting a membership list. Organizational boundaries have become more diffuse, such that temporary workers, contractors, and representatives of other organizations regularly cooperate with or work alongside "regular" organizational members to coordinate complex outputs (Scott and Davis 2007). As we move toward a more systems-based understanding of organizations and their environments (Scott and Davis 2007), determining whether an individual is part of an organization may be less useful than understanding how that individual's activities and life chances are affected by their involvement and interactions with a constellation of organizations.

Juggling multiple roles. Throughout my research, I was aware of how my multiple roles as a researcher, member, and individual overlapped and, at times, limited my activities. During meetings and informal chats with Burning Man members, I did not participate as freely or as actively as others, given my research responsibilities. I refrained from taking on volunteer responsibilities such as leadership positions despite my deepening knowledge and increasing experience, and I did not fully participate in discussions for fear of "contaminating" them with my views or inadvertently sharing privileged information. These self-imposed constraints ensured that I could not "go native," although my research colleagues flagged a few instances in which my analyses were too accepting of members' claims.

At the same time, I could not remain a complete outsider with my intimate understanding of organizing processes and my deepening relationships with members. I had access to organizational knowledge and history that newcomers and even long-time members lacked and sought. My presence sometimes fostered others' introspection and even jokes about my note taking on seemingly mundane activities and decision making. A few members reported that they initially felt self-conscious about my presence, confessing that I made them reflect more upon their actions. As revealed by the following exchange in the office, members were sometimes mystified by my research activities:

DAVE THORNTON, A.K.A. THORNY: Are you writing everything down that we say?

KATHERINE CHEN: Only things I catch. The trouble is figuring out when you're joking.

THORNTON: Yeah, I know.

ANDIE GRACE, A.K.A. ACTIONGRL [*refers to an earlier vehement discussion about a volunteer*]: I wasn't kidding about Brian, though.

For the most part, members became accustomed enough to my presence to occasionally solicit my opinions on various issues. A few members requested information or help with mediating interpersonal disputes or gaining access to organizational resources. I usually redirected these individuals toward more appropriate channels. In a few cases, contact with informants evolved into friendships that continued after I left the field.

Repeated observations. Because of other obligations, I followed Burning Man's development in intensive periods over several years, rather than confining participant observations and observations to one time period. This continual research necessitated reentry rituals and troubleshooting practicalities (i.e., contacting organizers, learning new members' names and responsibilities, finding an affordable place to live in a tight rental market), but yielded rich data about the organization's development over time. In particular, comparative time periods made it easier to identify changes in organizing routines that might otherwise have gone unnoticed. In addition, repeated observations helped me understand subtleties that might have been misinterpreted if I had less experience with the organization. For instance, Burning Man organizers often engaged in ironic banter that could have easily been mistaken for boorishness by those unfamiliar with the organizational milieu.

Revealing names and identities. Given the distinctiveness of the Burning Man event, I decided it was neither feasible nor useful to disguise the name and characteristics of the Burning Man organization and its organizers to avoid identification by readers. For consistency, I used informants' real names with their permission unless they requested anonymity. I also asked interviewees to identify information that they wanted kept confidential, which several did. I disguised characteristics and names for a few instances in which quoted information might invite repercussions or hurt feelings. However, I did not think that this was necessary for those who were openly critical of the event and organization, as their views were well known among organizers. By triangulating reports with archival accounts and observations, I could verify the veracity or accuracy of an individual's account as needed, which eliminated concerns about self-aggrandizing or misrepresentative reports.

The future of ethnographic research on organizations. Looking back, I still marvel over Burning Man members' willingness to give me access to their activities and lives.[9] Other organizations are not so amenable in allowing for intensive participant observations, observations, and interviews. Another issue concerns the ratcheting demands of academia. Conducting and analyzing extended ethnographic research is challenging and time-consuming, especially when accompanied by other responsibilities; taking into account the time needed to produce publications, other research approaches may seem more appealing because of their relative flexibility. Nevertheless, given the little we know about the inner workings of entities that impact so many aspects of our lives, I hope that others will continue to benefit from research experiences like mine. The more we learn about organizing, perhaps the closer we will get to sustaining enabling organizations.

Appendix 2

Interview Protocols

I. Interview Protocol for Volunteers

Introductory script:

Thank you for agreeing to be interviewed for my research on the development of the Burning Man organization. In this interview, we will discuss how the Burning Man organization has developed over time, as well as your role as volunteer and member in this development. This research will be incorporated into my dissertation manuscript and may eventually be published in academic journal articles or books. In general, I will keep your responses confidential from others in the organization. In writing up this research, I will also construct a pseudonym and alter your identifying characteristics instead of using your real name if you prefer. If you convey any particular information that you would especially like to keep confidential, please say so during or after the interview. May I have your permission to tape this interview? Thank you.

Event participation:

How did you hear about the Burning Man event?
When did you first go to a Burning Man event?

What convinced you to go?

Did you go with any friends, or did you go by yourself?

What made you decide to return for subsequent events?

Have you convinced any of your friends, family, or coworkers to go to Burning Man?

Have any of your friends, family, or coworkers joined you at Burning Man?

Do they plan to return to future Burning Mans?

What do you like about Burning Man?

How have your experiences with Burning Man differed over the years?

What do you hope never changes about Burning Man?

What do you hope does change about Burning Man?

Organizational participation:

When did you join the Burning Man organization as a volunteer?

How did you join the Burning Man organization as a volunteer?

Why did you decide to join a particular volunteer group?

Did you go through an interview before joining?

What are your responsibilities as a volunteer?

What do you get out of being a volunteer?

What motivates you to contribute?

What expertise do you contribute to the organization?

What resources do you contribute to the organization?

What is your "day" job?

How does being a volunteer compare with your normal work experience?

Do you meet people from [volunteer group] to socialize informally? What types of events are these?

How would you prioritize how much you value Burning Man relative to other activities, such as your work/career, your family, your friends, your significant other(s), and your other recreational activities and hobbies?

What motivates you to contribute as a volunteer?

Have you been responsible for heading any committees?

If so, how do you ensure that the work gets done by the committee members?

What's the most enjoyable part about being a volunteer?

What's the least enjoyable part about being a volunteer?

Do you volunteer for any other groups besides Burning Man, or do you perform any volunteer work?

If so, which ones?

Are you a member of any extra-curricular groups besides Burning Man?

If so, which ones?

Burning Man policies and viewpoints:

What do you think are the biggest challenges facing Burning Man?
Would you change anything about how the organization is organized?
How do you think the organization can manage its growth?
Why do you think the Burning Man event has survived?
Are you a member of a theme camp?
Which one?
How did you decide to join this particular theme camp?
How long have you been a member?
What motivates you to contribute to this theme camp?
Are you a member of an art project?
Which one / what is it?

Networks:

Think of your three closest friends. Are any of these friends involved in
    Burning Man?
Did you make any of these friends through Burning Man?
Do you have friends outside of Burning Man with whom you socialize on
    a regular basis?

Basic statistics:

What is your age?
What is your highest level of education?
What is your mother's highest level of education?
What is your father's highest level of education?
What is your primary occupation?
What is your secondary occupation, if any?
How many years have you attended Burning Man?

Closing script:

Again, is there anything that you would like to keep confidential?
Would you prefer that I use a pseudonym if I refer to your comments in
    my manuscript?
Thank you for your help with my dissertation project. Would you mind
    reading over and signing the following, which gives your permission for
    me to use your interview as data in my research?
Would you like a copy of the permission form? Here is your copy.

II. Interview Protocol for Core Organizers

Introductory script:

Thank you for agreeing to be interviewed for my research on the Burning Man organization. In this interview, we will discuss how the Burning Man organization has developed over time, as well as your role as an organizer in this development. This research will be incorporated into my dissertation manuscript and may eventually be published in academic journal articles or books. In general, I will keep your responses confidential from others in the organization. In writing up this research, I will also construct a pseudonym and alter identifying characteristics instead of using your real name if you prefer. If you convey any particular information that you would especially like to keep confidential, please say so during or after the interview. May I have your permission to tape this interview? Thank you.

Participation:

What was your background before you became an organizer?
How did you get involved with Burning Man?
Did you join the Burning Man organization as a volunteer before becoming an organizer?
How did you join the Burning Man organization as a volunteer?
When did you start as an organizer?
What were your responsibilities at the time?
Have your responsibilities changed?
What are your current responsibilities as an organizer?
What groups of people do you oversee?
How do you and others evaluate your performance?

Organizational history:

What was the organization like when you first joined as an organizer?
What kind of models do you use, if any, in organizing? Other organizations? Books? Principles? Past experiences?
How does organizing the Burning Man organization compare with organizing other groups that you've participated in?

Challenges:

What do you view as the biggest challenges facing this organization today?
What steps has Burning Man taken to address these challenges?

Organizational decisions:

How are decisions made in this organization?
Who makes sure that the decision is carried out?
What kinds of incentives do you use to ensure that a decision is
    carried out?

Communication:

How do you pass along information to fellow organizers?
How do you pass along knowledge and information to future Burning
    Man organizers?
How do you pass along information to volunteers?
How do you pass along information to participants?
How effective is e-mail as far as finding answers/getting input/delegating
    tasks?

Volunteers:

How do you recruit volunteers?
In what situations do you decide to use volunteers?
In what situations do you decide to use paid workers?
What are the advantages of using volunteers?
What are the disadvantages of using volunteers?
What are the advantages of using paid workers?
What are the disadvantages of using paid workers?
How do you motivate volunteers to complete tasks?
How do you oversee volunteers?
Has asking people to pay for tickets affected what people are willing to
    contribute to the organization as a volunteer?
What is the turnover rate like among your volunteers?
What do you like about Burning Man?
How have your experiences with Burning Man differed over the years?
What do you hope never changes about Burning Man?
What do you hope does change about Burning Man?

For initial organizers:

How did you select co-organizers?
What were you hoping to achieve at the time?

For those organizers who joined later:

How did you hear about the Burning Man event?
When did you first go to a Burning Man event?
What convinced you to go?
Did you go with any friends, or did you go by yourself?
What made you decide to return for subsequent events?
Have you convinced any of your friends, family, or coworkers to go to
     Burning Man?
Have any friends, family, or coworkers joined you at Burning Man?
Do they plan to return to future Burning Mans?

Basic statistics:

Male, female
Ethnicity
What is your age?
What is your highest level of education?
What is your mother's highest level of education?
What is your father's highest level of education?
What is your primary occupation?
What is your secondary occupation, if any?
How many years have you attended Burning Man?

Closing script:

Again, is there anything that you would like to keep confidential?
Would you prefer that I use a pseudonym if I refer to your comments in
     my manuscript?
Thank you for your help.

Notes

Chapter 1

1. The U.S. Department of Interior (2000) describes this designated National Conservation Area: "The Black Rock Desert Playa (ply-yah, Spanish for Intermittent dry lake) is a basin surrounded by several mountain ranges with elevations from 4,800 to 8,400 feet."

2. See Jones (1980) and U.S. Department of the Interior (2000) for more information about the Black Rock Desert.

3. For additional research on these aspects of the Burning Man event, see Kozinets (2002) and Gilmore and Van Proyen (2005).

4. Organizers define interactive art as "art that generates social participation." Marian Goodell, "Black Rock Arts Foundation Needs Your Help," *Jack Rabbit* e-mail newsletter, October 11, 2001, 6:2.

5. These descriptions depict large-scale art installations that have appeared at past Burning Man events: Jim Mason's *Temporal Decomposition*, Burning Man 1997; Hendrik Hackl's *Das Ammoniten Projeckt*, Burning Man 1997 and 2000; Dan Das Mann's *Last Stand*, Burning Man 2002; Finley Fryer's *Plastic Chapel*, Burning Man 2000; Jenne Giles and Philip Bonham's *Ribcage/Birdcage*, Burning Man 2000; Dana Albany's *"Laughing Sal,"* Burning Man 2005; David Best's *Temple of Stars, Temple of Honor, Temple of Joy, Temple of Tears, Temple of the Mind,* Burning Man 2000–2005.

6. For an insider's analysis of Burning Man art, see Kristen (2003, 2007).

7. Members, mostly old-timers, occasionally refer to the organization as the "Project." Some use the shorthand of "BMOrg." The latter reference serves as a tongue-in-cheek refer-

ence to the Borg, a relentless cyborg-alien force of Star Trek invention that absorbs individuals into its collective.

8. This figure was reported in the 2006 financial chart available at http://afterburn .burningman.com/06/financial_chart.html. However, during the time of my study, the organization's budget was considerably smaller.

9. Observation of volunteer coordinators meeting, June 26, 2000, San Francisco. See also http://www.burningman.com/participate/volunteer_faq.html#c.

10. Some Burning Man participants go by monikers instead of their formal names. I report both actual and Burning Man names of informants, unless otherwise noted.

11. Interview with Michael Mikel, November 7, 2000, San Francisco.

12. Merton (1936) popularized the term *unintended consequences* to describe unanticipated effects of actions.

13. Appendixes 1 and 2 provide more thorough descriptions of my methods.

14. A volunteer locksmith had assisted people on previous days, but he was not available on the Labor Day holiday.

15. During the 2008 Burning Man event, one individual asked Playa Info volunteers about the availability of an Internet phone and mentioned that he had borrowed one near Playa Info during a previous event. This incident evidenced a dependency upon infrastructural services that some Burning Man members wanted to discourage, especially since members disagreed over whether the Internet and other communication technologies should be accessible at the event. For instance, one Playa Info volunteer apparently refused to tell inquiring attendees about the availability of Internet access. This volunteer opined that attendees should have no contact with the outside world to preserve the Burning Man experience. Personal communication with Rob Oliver, Burning Man events, 2004, 2008.

16. Interview with Jerry James, October 19, 2000, San Francisco.

17. Interview with John Law, September 26, 2000, Oakland, California. Academics share similar concerns about the effects of organizing. Most notably, Piven and Cloward's ([1977] 1979) analyses of social movements questioned the efficacy of organizing. Building on Michels's ([1915] 1962) concept of oligarchy, Piven and Cloward critiqued the concentration of power within leadership ranks and the resulting conservatism of movement goals.

18. For critiques of Disney's "smile factory," see Raz (1999) and Van Maanen (1991).

19. Building on Weber's ([1946] 1958) work, sociologists use ideal types to categorize organizations and other phenomena. The term *ideal type* does not mean a perfect ideal or standard. Instead, an ideal type serves as an abstracted model that allows us to categorize and examine an organization through its characteristics and activities. In practice, an organization rarely exhibits all of an ideal type's traits.

20. Alternatively, prior research has categorized organizing goals and practices as instrumental and expressive (Curtis and Zurcher 1974; Gordon and Babchuk 1959), prefigurative and strategic (Breines 1982), exemplary and adversary (Starr 1979), and goal-oriented, ideological, and redemptive (Wilson [1974] 1995).

21. Coleman (1990) criticized organizational theory for not addressing how to avoid undesirable consequences: "Theoretical questions concerning social organization have seldom been couched in terms of how to best organize action in order to accomplish a specific task without generating undesirable externalities" (654). Others have similarly criticized social movements research's focus on structures, rather than decisions and agency (Cohen and Arato 1992; Jasper 2004). Recent studies (e.g., Barker 1999) have begun to elaborate the

consequences of particular organizing practices, and they propose possibilities for avoiding undesired consequences.

22. Cross-cultural studies document other organizational forms (Clegg 1990). Researchers have also noted the increasing prevalence of the network form (DiMaggio 2001; Harrison 1994; Lune 2007; Podolny and Page 1998; Powell 1990). In contrast with the top-down authority of the bureaucratic form, the network form consists of two or more actors that engage in "repeated, enduring exchange relations with one another" but lack "a legitimate organizational authority to arbitrate and resolve disputes that may arise" (Podolny and Page 1998: 59). However, the apparent rise of the network form may be an artifact of researchers shifting their studies to focus on ties among organizations.

23. Thanks to Peter Marsden's comments in honing this description.

24. Etzioni ([1961] 1975) first described normative control in his classification of organizations by the kinds of control used to elicit members' compliance. Kunda (1992) extended this concept to include organizational culture, in which leaders use symbols (i.e., corporate-specific bumper stickers, slogans, terms), rituals (i.e., managerial presentations and meetings), and acculturation activities (i.e., orientations) to cultivate employees' commitment and identification with a firm.

25. See also Swedberg's (2005) and Rothschild and Whitt's (1986) elaboration of value-rationality.

26. Here, I simplify organizing archetypes. Variations do exist. For example, a worker cooperative organized as a for-profit may rely predominantly upon collectivist practices. Or, a philanthropic organization can incorporate as a for-profit and mix collectivist and bureaucratic practices.

27. Some workplaces have recently introduced participatory practices, such as quality circles and teamwork, for the explicit purpose of improving production. However, employees do not have a corresponding ownership stake in their organization, and they do not receive a proportional share of the profits. Critics argue that in such workplaces, participatory practices do not adequately empower members (Boltanski and Chiapello 2005; Hackman and Wageman 1995; Rothschild and Ollilainen 1999).

28. Meyer and Rowan (1977) call this "decoupling."

29. Recent management guides such as *The Triple Bottom Line* identify "protecting the environment and improving the lives of those with whom it interacts" as additional responsibilities (Savitz with Weber 2006: x).

30. For example, Gumport and Snydman (2006) claim that "the nomenclature and presumed distinctions among publics, nonprofits, and for-profits are becoming less useful for understanding higher education" (473), particularly as organizations blend features.

31. See Lawrence and Lorsch's (1967) discussion of the difficulties of integrating processes across units.

32. Senate Report 109–273, Department of Homeland Security Appropriations Bill, 2007.

33. Personal communication with informant (identity withheld), 2007.

34. Personal communication with informant (identity withheld), 2002.

35. Thanks to the anonymous reviewer who suggested elaborating this table.

36. This term builds on Adler and Borys's (1996) "enabling bureaucracy."

37. Coleman (1974) wrote about the need to understand the rise of the organization, the juristic "person," particularly as it amassed power away from human individuals. See also Marsden's (2005) overview of Coleman's works.

38. Even some managers agree that employees should have this input (Freeman and Rogers [1999] 2006).

39. For instance, Putnam (2000) argues that, among other trends, shrinking membership in centralized national organizations such as the Parent-Teacher Association and fraternal associations demonstrate the decline of civic engagement in the United States. See also McPherson, Smith-Lovin, and Brashears's (2006) analysis, which shows that Americans' social networks of confidants have shrunk over the last two decades.

Chapter 2

1. *Zocaló* is a Spanish word for "town square."

2. "BM Web Site Usage Statistics–2/05," staff e-mail list, March 9, 2005.

3. Some artists partially construct their projects in advance and complete them on-site at the event.

4. Excerpted from *Black Rock City Operation Manual* 2000, 1.1.

5. Interviews with key personnel provided most of the material for this account. Print, archival, and Web-site materials, including the organization's 2000 and 2001 *Black Rock City Operation Manuals* and the online publication of the "Afterburn Report 2001," a comprehensive description of the organization's activities, presented additional information and retrospective timelines. Observations and participant observations of the organization's operations allowed for a behind-the-scenes perspective for 1998 through 2001. To the best of my knowledge, I have provided accurate dates, although a few of these dates conflict with those in the organization's official accounts. Organizational structures have since changed, and individuals have shifted positions or left the organization. These changes reflect the dynamic nature of the organization and its membership ranks.

6. Interview with Larry Harvey, October 25, 2000, San Francisco. Interview with Jerry James, October 19, 2000, San Francisco. Interview with Dan Miller, October 24, 2000, San Francisco.

7. The event did not become known as Burning Man until around 1993 or 1994. Interview with Larry Harvey, October 25, 2000, San Francisco. Press kit, 1995.

8. Interview with Larry Harvey, October 25, 2000, San Francisco.

9. The Cacophony Society members began collaborating with the Burning Man event around 1988. Although this group's members were once active in "pranking" and throwing irreverent underground events, the Burning Man event has since superseded their activities.

10. Interview with Larry Harvey, October 25, 2000, San Francisco.

11. Video footage from the 1988 Burning Man event. David Lortsher, *Tice Creek 6 minutes/ Summer Solstice @ Baker Beach '88*, Burning Man film archives.

12. Interview with Larry Harvey, October 25, 2000, San Francisco. Interview with John Law, September 26, 2000, Oakland, California. Interview with P. Segal, October 6, 2000, San Francisco.

13. "Zone Trip #4—Ascent into the Black Rock Desert," *Rough Draft* 47 (August 1990): 2.

14. This Cacophony Society tradition has continued. During one of the departmental training sessions that I observed, newly minted volunteers enacted this ritual at the Burning Man event, August 29, 2000.

15. Interview with Michael Mikel, November 7, 2000, San Francisco.

16. Interview with Michael Mikel, November 7, 2000, San Francisco.

17. Interview with John Law, September 26, 2000, Oakland, California. Documents from John Law's personal archives, 1991–1992.

18. Interview with John Law, September 26, 2000, Oakland, California.

19. Interview with Michael Mikel, November 7, 2000, San Francisco.

20. Interview with Michael Mikel, November 7, 2000, San Francisco. Press kit, 1995. The 2001 *Black Rock City Operation Manual* claims the start year as 1991. The *Black Rock Gazette* ceased publication by the time of the 2005 event.

21. Interview with Harley Dubois, December 21, 2001, San Francisco. See also Harvey (1997, 2000).

22. Because of changes in event norms, the disgruntled postal workers no longer carry loaded weapons within the city limits. Instead, they are more likely to perform community services. Interview with Naomi Pearce, December 1, 2000, Albany, California.

23. Interview with Harley Dubois, December 21, 2001, San Francisco.

24. Interview with Joe Fenton, December 16, 2000, Albany, California. Interview with John Law, September 26, 2000, Oakland, California.

25. "The Burning Man," *New York Times Magazine,* October 2, 1994, 18–19.

26. "Burning Man Project History" press kit, 1995–1996. The official timeline cites a different date.

27. Staff list, June 4, 1995, John Law's personal archives.

28. Interview with Larry Harvey, October 25, 2000, San Francisco.

29. Interview with Michael Mikel, November 7, 2000, San Francisco.

30. Interview with Larry Harvey, October 25, 2000, San Francisco. Interview with Crimson Rose, October 31, 2000, San Francisco.

31. Interview with Marian Goodell, November 12, 2000, San Francisco. Interview with Tom Smith (pseudonym), August 10, 2000, San Francisco. Daniel Glass, "It's Your Party: You Can Burn If You Want To," *Boston Phoenix,* September 25, 1998, 1, 6–8.

32. Mack Reed, "Where the Wild Things Are," *Los Angeles Times,* September 4, 1996, E1, E6. Jeff Stark, "Rumors," *SF Weekly,* November 17, 1996.

33. Interview with Marian Goodell, November 12, 2000, San Francisco. Interview with Jennifer Holmes, November 9, 2000, San Francisco. Interview with Jerry James, October 19, 2000, San Francisco. Interview with John Law, September 26, 2000, Oakland, California. D. Brian Burghart, "The Burning Question: Has Popularity Killed Northern Nevada's Biggest Art Festival?" *Reno News & Report,* February 19, 1997, 9–11.

34. Interview with Jerry James, October 19, 2000, San Francisco.

35. Interview with John Law, September 26, 2000, Oakland, California.

36. Interview with Jennifer Holmes, November 9, 2000, San Francisco.

37. Mack Reed, "Where the Wild Things Are," *Los Angeles Times,* September 4, 1996, E1, E6.

38. Interview with John Law, September 26, 2000, Oakland, California.

39. Interview with Harley Dubois, October 19, 2000, San Francisco.

40. Interview with Crimson Rose, October 31, 2000, San Francisco.

41. Interview with Joe Fenton, December 16, 2000, Albany, California.

42. Interview with John Law, September 26, 2000, Oakland, California.

43. Interview with Jennifer Holmes, November 9, 2000, San Francisco. Interview with John Law, September 26, 2000, Oakland, California. D. Brian Burghart, "The Burning Question: Has Popularity Killed Northern Nevada's Biggest Art Festival?" *Reno News & Report,* February 19, 1997, 9–11.

44. Interview with Larry Harvey, October 25, 2000, San Francisco.

45. Starting in 1991, Nevada's Revised Statutes allowed for the formation of the limited liability company (LLC). As an alternative to other legal forms of corporations and partnerships, the LLC form has been portrayed as "combining the best of both worlds, partnership taxation and limited liability" (Hamill 1996: 395).

46. Naomi Pearce, "Burning Man 1996 Redux," internal memo circulated among staff, October 18, 1996, Joe Fenton's personal archives.

47. In keeping with the event's theme of the *Inferno,* organizers developed a drama about Satan and Helco's efforts to buy out the Burning Man event. John Law and others built a multistory wooden replica of a building, which featured the letters "Helco" scavenged from a store sign. For a dramatic conclusion, Law rappelled from the top of the burning building to foil Satan's takeover bid.

48. Interview with Marian Goodell, November 6, 2000, San Francisco.

49. In previous events, entrepreneurial participants vended items such as coffee, alcohol, and burgers on a small scale. However, the 1995 *Survival Guide* had evidenced developing preferences for minimizing commercialism. Likewise, the summer 1996 Burning Man newsletter had noted that "as in the past, we request that all firearms be kept unloaded in our camp."

50. Interview with Michael Mikel, November 7, 2000, San Francisco.

51. Interview with Michael Mikel, November 7, 2000, San Francisco.

52. Burning Man organizers derisively noted that this group was funded by mining interests and staffed by former employees from the BLM. Interview with Larry Harvey, October 25, 2000, San Francisco.

53. Interview with Larry Harvey, October 25, 2000, San Francisco. Marian Goodell, "How You Can Help Make Burning Man Happen on the Black Rock Desert," *Jack Rabbit Speaks* e-mail newsletter, March 18, 1998, 2:16.

54. "Pershing County Wants to End Burning Man," *Reno Gazette-Journal,* September 16, 1996.

55. Interview with Larry Harvey, October 25, 2000, San Francisco.

56. Interview with Michael Mikel, November 7, 2000, San Francisco.

57. Interview with Larry Harvey, October 25, 2000, San Francisco. Don Cox, "Burning Man Threatens to Light Up Elsewhere," *Reno Gazette-Journal,* September 4, 1997, A1. Fiona Essa, "Quest for Fire: Burning Man Tribe Searches for a New Home," *Reno News & Review,* August 27, 1997, 10–11, 13, 15.

58. Interview with Larry Harvey, October 25, 2000, San Francisco. Don Cox, "Burning Man Site Cleanup Half Done," *Reno Gazette-Journal,* 1997, day unknown, 1A. Don Cox, "Burning Man Legacy Litters Desert," *Reno Gazette-Journal,* October 10, 1997, 1A, 11A. Don Cox, "Burning Man Seeking New Event Site," *Reno Gazette-Journal,* October 28, 1997, 1A.

59. "Survival," *Building Burning Man* print newsletter, Spring 1997.

60. Interview with Larry Harvey, October 25, 2000, San Francisco.

61. "Benefit Events," *Building Burning Man* print newsletter, Winter 1998, 5. "Cash Flow," *Building Burning Man* print newsletter, Winter 1998, 7.

62. Interview with Harley Dubois, October 19, 2000, San Francisco. Interview with Marian Goodell, November 6, 2000, San Francisco.

63. In previous years, members worked in their apartments, and they assembled in their homes or workplaces for occasional meetings. My observations included this transition from home to the Third St. office.

64. Goodell reported that the organization did not calculate a "real" budget until 1999. Interview with Marian Goodell, November 6, 2000, San Francisco.

65. Interview with Megan Beachler, December 12, 2000, San Francisco. Observation of senior staff meeting, August 4, 1998, San Francisco. In subsequent years, tickets could be purchased by money order only, decreasing such dependency on credit card firms.

66. Marian Goodell, "BLM Public Meetings–March 8, 9 & 10," "Write the BLM Now," "Write a Letter," "Extension for Letters to BLM," "BLM Public Meetings, March 8, 9 & 10 (Nevada)," *Jack Rabbit Speaks* e-mail newsletters, October 30, 1998; October 30, 1998; December 18, 1998; January 14, 1999; February 9, 1999; March 4, 1999, 3:5–10.

67. Interview with Larry Harvey, October 25, 2000, San Francisco. Observation of Media Mecca meeting, July 20, 2000, San Francisco.

68. Observation of Media Mecca meeting, October 12, 2000, San Francisco. Observation of town hall meeting, December 3, 2000, San Francisco. Marian Goodell, "Law Enforcement Presence at Burning Man 2000," *Jack Rabbit Speaks* e-mail newsletter, August 20, 2000, 5:2.

69. Observation of Burning Man event, 2001.

70. Personal communication with Larry Harvey, November 18, 2000, San Francisco.

71. Phone interview with Barbara Keleher, December 12, 2000. Personal communication with Harley Dubois, Burning Man event, 2007.

72. Interview with John Law, September 26, 2000, Oakland, California. Interview with Steve Mobia, October 4, 2000, San Francisco.

73. Interview with Molly Tirpak, August 10, 2000, San Francisco.

74. Theme camps also host local events. For example, in March 2007, the New York City–based Kostume Kult theme camp organized the Burning Ball weekend gathering in Montauk, Long Island.

75. Phone interview with Leslie Bocskor, December 13, 2000. Interview with Marian Goodell, November 12, 2000, San Francisco. Phone interview with George Paap, December 9, 2000.

76. David J. Frank suggested this analogy of the church and its congregation. Personal communication, 2002.

77. Marian Goodell, "Danger Ranger's Road Trip," *Jack Rabbit Speaks* e-mail newsletter, April 13, 2001, 5:11.

78. Interview with Larry Harvey, October 25, 2000, San Francisco.

79. Interview with Harley Dubois, December 21, 2001, San Francisco.

80. Harvey started the event in 1986; Mikel joined in 1990; Dubois joined in 1994. Rose joined the event in 1995 and the organizing staff in 1996; Rose's partner Roger joined the event in 1994 and the organizing staff in 1997. As the most recent addition of the six, Goodell joined in 1997. During 1998, one LLC board member, Carole Morrell, a lawyer who handled the organization's legal affairs, left the organization and was not replaced by another member. Instead, her responsibilities were split among several lawyers who are not members of the LLC board.

81. Interview with John Law, September 26, 2000, Oakland, California. Interview with Vicki Olds, September 29, 2000, San Francisco.

82. In comparison, the largest restaurant prepared 24,000 meals a day. Observation of senior staff meeting, July 28, 2000, San Francisco.

83. The camp's sales have benefited local organizations like the Gerlach Senior Citizen's Center, Volunteer Emergency Services, schools, and a memorial scholarship fund. Interview with Scott Shaner, December 5, 2000, San Francisco.

84. At the time of my study, Community Services included an additional department, Locksmiths, but its services are no longer offered. Nevertheless, those who are locked out of their vehicles can inquire at Playa Info about locksmiths.

85. Check Point Salon also recruited and placed volunteers.

86. *Black Rock City Operation Manual* 2000.

87. Established in the mid-1990s, the Gate had been an independent entity until its manager unexpectedly left in 1998. The Gate was then reassigned to Ranger oversight.

88. Most notably, John Rinaldi, a.k.a. Chicken John, had overseen members of his punk rock circus in cleaning up in the weeks after past events. The crew subsisted on food, liquor, and other sundries left by participants.

89. Interview with Christine Kristen, November 7, 2000, San Francisco. Interview with Crimson Rose, October 31, 2000, San Francisco.

90. One of the shortest-lived departments, the Playa Hygiene Dept. (PhD), was created in 2000 to standardize environmental conservation practices across departments. After achieving its goals and after the departure of its leader, it shut down before the 2001 event.

Chapter 3

1. "An Interesting Exchange on BM Trademark Protection," Media Mecca e-mail list, May 13, 2003.

2. Observation of senior staff meeting, June 8, 2002, San Francisco.

3. Interview with John Law, September 26, 2000, Oakland, California.

4. Interview with Jennifer Holmes, November 9, 2000, San Francisco.

5. Interview with John Law, September 26, 2000, Oakland, California.

6. Interview with Larry Harvey, October 25, 2000, San Francisco.

7. Interview with John Law, September 26, 2000, Oakland, California.

8. Citing fears about liability, several interviewees were circumspect about recounting the accidents that occurred during the 1996 event.

9. The victim and his lawyer eventually settled for the event's $1 million insurance policy, which was the highest level of insurance that the organization could afford at the time. *Daniel Reed and Pershing County vs. United States Department of the Interior, Bureau of Land Management,* CDOS 8843. Interview with John Law, September 26, 2000, Oakland, California.

10. Interview with Michael Mikel, November 7, 2000, San Francisco.

11. Interview with Larry Harvey, October 25, 2000, San Francisco.

12. Interview with Harley Dubois, October 19, 2000, San Francisco.

13. Phone interview with Joe Fenton, October 10, 2000.

14. Interview with John Law, September 26, 2000, Oakland, California.

15. Interview with John Rinaldi, November 3, 2000, San Francisco.

16. Most notably, the 1996 dramatization of the organizers' defense against Satan and Helco.

17. Silicon Satan (pseudonym), "Burning Man: A Vision of the Future," *New Mission News,* October 1999, 11.

18. Interview with John Law, September 26, 2000, Oakland, California.

19. Observation of book-signing party, Burning Man event, 2005. This metaphor referred to Mark Twain's book *The Adventures of Tom Sawyer.* When whitewashing a fence, the protagonist recruits help by convincing his friends that the work is a fun and desirable activity.

20. Posting by Hermine on a thread from http://www.urban75.net/vbulletin/show thread.php?s=&threadid=17140&highlight=burned+burn, August 23, 2002, 02:40 a.m.

21. This excerpt appeared as part of a now defunct entry on Steve Hassan's Resource Center for Freedom of Mind in 2000, http://www.freedomofmind.com/groups/burning/burning.htm, accessed July 5, 2000.

22. "Opps. Road to Ruin Redx," staff e-mail list, October 13, 2004.

23. "Calling It Quits," staff e-mail list, October 13, 2004.

24. For one insider's description of the lack of official organization backing the Rainbow Family, see http://www.welcomehome.org/rainbow/index.html, accessed March 5, 2008. See Niman (1997) for an ethnographic account of the Rainbow Family's decision making by consensus.

25. Identity of author and Web site withheld, Media Mecca e-mail list, May 13, 2003.

26. Phone interview with Jim DeLaHunt, August 13, 2000.

27. Phone interview with Jim DeLaHunt, August 13, 2000.

28. E-mail excerpted in Marian Goodell, "Where Does the Money Go?" *Jack Rabbit Speaks* e-mail newsletter, January 14, 2000, 4:9.

29. Interview with P. Segal, October 6, 2000, San Francisco.

30. Observation of senior staff meeting, June 2, 2000, San Francisco.

31. Interview with Crimson Rose, October 31, 2000, San Francisco.

32. "Re: [staff] Fwd: Re: The Safe Road to Ruin," staff e-mail list, October 14, 2004.

33. "Mommy, Make the Clown Be Quiet!" staff e-mail list, October 14, 2004.

34. See Stohl and Cheney (2001) for examples of how dissenting views can be suppressed, even under participatory practices.

35. "Re: [BManMedia] Larry's Response to New Mission Times," Media Mecca e-mail list, October 20, 1999.

36. Interview with Joseph Pred, October 18, 2000, San Francisco. Interview with Will Roger, November 10, 2000, San Francisco. Marian Goodell, "Job Opportunity," *Jack Rabbit Speaks* e-mail newsletter, January 10, 2001, 5:4.

37. Darryl Van Rhey (pseudonym for Larry Harvey), "An Economy of Gifts," 2002, interview in http://www.burningman.com/whatisburningman/2002/02_news_sum_2.html.

38. Marian Goodell, *Jack Rabbit Speaks* e-mail newsletter, June 20, 2001, 5:16. This nonprofit arm has since changed its mission to fund art outside of the Burning Man event.

39. Darryl Van Rhey (pseudonym for Larry Harvey), "Passing the Hat," *Building Burning Man* print newsletter, 1999 Special Winter Edition, 3–4.

40. Interview with Larry Harvey, October 25, 2000, San Francisco.

41. Larry Harvey, "Afterburn Report 2001: Black Rock City LLC Operating Agreement," http://afterburn.burningman.com/01/org/llc_agreement.html.

42. Marian Goodell, "Where Does the Money Go?" *Jack Rabbit Speaks* e-mail newsletter, February 14, 2000, 4:9. "Where Does All the Money Go?" *Building Burning Man* print newsletter, Spring 1997, 5. Darryl Van Rhey (pseudonym for Larry Harvey), "Passing the Hat," *Building Burning Man* print newsletter, 1999 Special Winter Edition, 3–4.

43. Marian Goodell, "Where Does the Money Go?" *Jack Rabbit Speaks* e-mail newsletter, February 14, 2000, 4:9.

44. Larry Harvey, "AfterBurn 2001 Report: Financial Summary—The Cost of Burning Man," http://afterburn.burningman.com/01/financial.html. Larry Harvey, "AfterBurn 2001 Report: Financial Chart," http://afterburn.burningman.com/01/financial_chart.html.

45. Larry Harvey, "AfterBurn 2003 Report: Financial Structure," http://afterburn.burningman.com/03/financial_structure.html.

46. Phone interview with Duane Hoover, November 2, 2000.

47. Interview with Michael Mikel, November 7, 2000, San Francisco.

48. Interview with Michael Mikel, November 7, 2000, San Francisco.

49. Interview with Chase Lehman (pseudonym), August 12, 2000, San Francisco.

50. Untitled memo, 2–3, John Law's personal archives.

51. "Re: [BManMedia] Larry's Response to New Mission Times," Media Mecca e-mail list, October 20, 1999.

52. "Philosophies?" Media Mecca e-mail list, October 20, 1999.

53. Observation of senior staff meeting, December 2, 2000, Oakland, California.

54. Harvey (2000).

55. Interview with Harley Dubois, December 21, 2001, San Francisco.

56. "Successful Volunteerism with Burningman," *Burningman Volunteer Handbook,* 2000, 14. The Web site referenced is https://www.msu.edu/~corcora5/org/consensus.html.

57. Larry Harvey, "Afterburn Report 2001: Consensus, Hierarchy, Authority, and Power," http://afterburn.burningman.com/01/org/consensus.html.

58. Observation of senior staff meeting, July 21, 2000, San Francisco.

59. Interview with Harley Dubois, October 19, 2000, San Francisco.

60. Interview with Harley Dubois, October 19, 2000, San Francisco.

61. One exception is Hernandez's (2006) work on Mexican cooperatives, where workers demanded information in advance of meetings so that they could make more informed decisions.

62. Observation of senior staff meeting, December 6, 2000, San Francisco. Interview with Harley Dubois, December 21, 2001, San Francisco.

63. Phone interview with Joe Fenton, October 10, 2000. Observations of senior staff meetings, 2000, San Francisco.

64. Interview with Joegh Bullock, October 3, 2000, San Francisco.

65. Observation of senior staff meeting, August 12, 1999, San Francisco.

66. Personal communication with Harley Dubois, July 28, 2000.

67. Observation of senior staff meeting, July 28, 2000, San Francisco.

68. Observation of senior staff meeting, December 2, 2000, San Francisco.

69. Interview with Dana Harrison, October 17, 2000, Berkeley, California.

70. Observation of senior staff meeting, July 28, 2000, San Francisco.

71. Interview with Dana Harrison, October 17, 2000, Berkeley, California.

72. Harvey (2000).

73. Interview with Dana Harrison, October 17, 2000, Berkeley, California. Interview with Harley Dubois, December 21, 2001, San Francisco. Larry Harvey, "Afterburn Report 2001: Consensus, Hierarchy, Authority, and Power," http://afterburn.burningman.com/01/org/consensus.html.

74. Interview with Molly Tirpak, August 10, 2000, San Francisco.

75. Observations of senior staff meetings, June 2000–January 2001, San Francisco.

76. Observation of senior staff meeting, June 2, 2000, San Francisco.

77. Observations of senior staff meetings, 1998–2000, San Francisco.

Chapter 4

1. Interview with Scott Shaner, December 5, 2000, San Francisco.

2. Phone interview with Kat DeLurgio, November 8, 2000. Interview with Fiona Essa, August 21, 2000, San Francisco. Interview with Rob Oliver, August 1, 2000, San Francisco. Interview with Tom Smith (pseudonym), August 10, 2000, San Francisco. Interview with Mark Warner, October 25, 2000, San Francisco.

3. Observation of volunteer coordinators meeting, June 26, 2000, San Francisco.

4. However, this productivity evens out over the long term.

5. See Granovetter (1973, 1995) for more on weak vs. strong ties.

6. Even attending the Burning Man event was difficult. Some event attendees and organizers withheld information about the event's date and location because of concerns that large numbers of newcomers would destroy the event's intimacy and exclusivity. Would-be attendees had to doggedly search for information. Interview with Marian Goodell, November 6, 2000, San Francisco. Interview with Larry Harvey, October 25, 2000, San Francisco.

7. Interview with Jennifer Vermut, September 26, 2001, San Francisco.

8. Goodell first tried to enter the organization and event without ties to the organization. She eventually gained entry through her status as the then girlfriend of organizer Larry Harvey. Interview with Marian Goodell, November 6, 2000, San Francisco.

9. Interview with Marian Goodell, November 6, 2000, San Francisco.

10. Interview with Jim Graham, September 23, 2000, San Francisco.

11. Some coordinators like Café manager Jesse Jones still insist that prospective volunteers contact them several times before getting assigned responsibilities. Interview with Jesse Jones, October 3, 2000, San Francisco.

12. Interview with Harley Dubois, December 21, 2001, San Francisco.

13. Interview with Dana Harrison, October 17, 2000, Berkeley, California.

14. Phone interview with Scott McKeown, October 3, 2000. Interview with Monica Senter, October 6, 2000, San Francisco.

15. Interview with Marian Goodell, November 6, 2000, San Francisco.

16. Observations of Burning Man office, 2000. Interviews with Molly Tirpak, September 21, 2000, and July 11, 2001, San Francisco.

17. Interview with John Nettle, August 15, 2000, San Francisco.

18. "Successful Volunteerism with Burningman," *Burningman Volunteer Handbook,* 2000, 4.

19. "Successful Volunteerism with Burningman," in the *Burningman Volunteer Handbook,* supported such recruitment.

20. Interview with Monica Senter, October 6, 2000, San Francisco. Phone interview with Scott McKeown, October 2, 2000. Observation of volunteer barbecue, July 22, 2000, San Francisco.

21. Personal communication with Jess Bobier, June 1, 2000.

22. Interview with Jess Bobier, September 20, 2000, San Francisco.

23. Interview with Jess Bobier, September 20, 2000, San Francisco. Interview with Rob Oliver, August 1, 2000, San Francisco. Interview with Steven Raspa, September 19, 2000, San Francisco.

24. Identities withheld.

25. *Black Rock City Operation Manual* 2000, 4.4.1.

26. See http://www.burningman.com/whatisburningman/about_burningman/principles.html.

27. Observation of lead meeting, July 5, 2001, San Francisco.

28. "Successful Volunteerism with Burningman," *Burningman Volunteer Handbook*, 2000, 16.

29. Observation of lead meeting, July 5, 2001, San Francisco.

30. Interview with Molly Tirpak, July 11, 2001, San Francisco.

31. Interview with Molly Tirpak, September 21, 2000, San Francisco.

32. Phone interview with Jim Lamb, August 10, 2000.

33. Observation of emergency services meeting, July 31, 2000, San Francisco.

34. Observation of Burning Man office, June 27, 2000, San Francisco.

35. "Successful Volunteerism with Burningman," *Burningman Volunteer Handbook*, 2000, 18.

36. "Successful Volunteerism with Burningman," *Burningman Volunteer Handbook*, 2000, 18.

37. "Successful Volunteerism with Burningman," *Burningman Volunteer Handbook*, 2000, 18.

38. Observation of senior staff meeting, July 21, 2000, San Francisco.

39. Observation of lead meeting, July 5, 2001, San Francisco.

40. Interview with Joe Fenton, December 12, 2000, Albany, California.

41. Interview with Naomi Pearce, December 1, 2000, Albany, California.

42. Interview with Marian Goodell, November 6, 2000, San Francisco.

43. Interview with Jennifer Vermut, September 26, 2001, San Francisco.

44. Interview with Jennifer Vermut, September 26, 2001, San Francisco.

45. Observation of volunteer coordinators meeting, June 26, 2000, San Francisco.

46. Observation of volunteer coordinators meeting, June 26, 2000, San Francisco.

47. "Successful Volunteerism with Burningman," *Burningman Volunteer Handbook*, 2000, 7.

48. "Successful Volunteerism with Burningman," *Burningman Volunteer Handbook*, 2000, 17.

49. Interview with Dana Harrison, October 17, 2000, Berkeley, California. Phone interview with Duane Hoover, November 2, 2000. Interview with Monica Senter, October 6, 2000, San Francisco.

50. Interview with Cindy Bakkum, August 8, 2000, San Francisco. Observations of Burning Man office, 2000, San Francisco.

51. Interview with Harley Dubois, October 19, 2000, San Francisco.

52. Observation of lead meeting, July 5, 2001, San Francisco.

53. Observation of LLC meeting, June 4, 2002, San Francisco.

54. Observation of lead meeting, July 5, 2001, San Francisco.

55. Interview with Harley Dubois, December 21, 2001, San Francisco. Interview with Dan Miller, October 24, 2000, San Francisco.

56. Interview with Harley Dubois, October 19, 2000, San Francisco.

57. Interview with Harley Dubois, October 19, 2000, San Francisco.

58. Interview with Jesse Jones, October 3, 2000, San Francisco.

59. Interview with Jesse Jones, October 3, 2000, San Francisco. Interview with Harley Dubois, October 19, 2000, San Francisco. Interview with Molly Tirpak, July 11, 2001, San Francisco.

60. The name Gerald Parsons is a pseudonym. Interview with Larry Harvey, October 25, 2000, San Francisco.

61. Interview with Larry Harvey, October 25, 2000, San Francisco.

62. Interview with Harley Dubois, October 19, 2000, San Francisco.

63. Interview with Larry Harvey, October 25, 2000, San Francisco.

64. Observation of senior staff meeting, June 2, 2000, San Francisco. Interview with Larry Harvey, October 25, 2000, San Francisco.

65. Identities of interviewees withheld.

66. Interview with Dana Harrison, October 17, 2000, Berkeley, California.

67. Interview with Steve Mobia, October 4, 2000, San Francisco.

68. Interview with Dana Harrison, October 17, 2000, Berkeley, California.

69. Interview with Eric Pouyoul, December 3, 2000, San Francisco.

70. Observation of Greeters meeting, June 13, 2000, San Francisco.

71. Observation of lead meeting, July 5, 2001, San Francisco.

72. Joint interview with Brien Burroughs and Rebecca Workman, August 19, 2000, San Francisco.

73. Interview with Alice Freedman (pseudonym), August 17, 2000, San Francisco.

74. Personal communication with Alice Freedman (pseudonym), June 3, 2002.

75. Observation of senior staff meeting, June 4, 2002, San Francisco. Some of the organizers may have read a conference paper that I had written about how the organization allowed individuals to form roles. It is possible that my presence as an observer primed this particular discussion's direction.

76. Observation of Tech team, June 6, 2000, San Francisco. Interview with Monica Senter, October 6, 2000, San Francisco. Interview with Marian Goodell, November 12, 2000, San Francisco. Personal communication with Marian Goodell, July 10, 2000. Interview with Joe Cordes, August 7, 2000, San Francisco. Interview with Baylor Gross (pseudonym), July 31, 200, San Francisco.

77. Observation of LLC meeting, June 4, 2002, San Francisco.

78. Interview with Chase Lehman (pseudonym), August 11, 2000, San Francisco.

79. Miner (1987, 1990) uses the term "idiosyncratic jobs" to differentiate these positions from those conceived independently of prospective candidates' interests.

80. The firm also ranked 10th place in *Fortune* magazine's "100 Best Companies to Work For" in 2007.

81. Typically, human resources departments suffer from low status, limited power, and understaffing. These conditions and a wide-ranging array of responsibilities for affirmative action, benefits, training, etc., make it difficult for such departments to realize their full potential (Finlay and Coverdill 2002).

Chapter 5

1. Interview with Dana Harrison, October 17, 2000, Berkeley, California.

2. After being struck by an automobile as she walked to work, Harrison reassessed her priorities: "There are things in this world worth dying for, and going to my corporate job at Schwab isn't one of them." Harrison quit her job and volunteered for several arts organizations. Interview with Dana Harrison, October 17, 2000, Berkeley, California.

3. Observation of lead meeting, July 5, 2001, San Francisco.

4. Two additional categories identified by these researchers, developing career-related benefits and reducing guilt through assisting the less fortunate and addressing personal problems, were not well represented in the Burning Man case, so I excluded these categories from this discussion. Schroeder et al. (1995) propose a more condensed typology of volunteer motivation: value-expressive, social adjustive, ego-defensive, and knowledge. A

detailed taxonomy of several theories of volunteer motivations, including ones described here, appears in Lette (2006: 172).

5. Kanter (1968, 1972) defines commitment as having three aspects: (1) *continuance,* or staying on as a member, (2) *cohesion,* or connection with fellow members, and (3) *control,* or adherence to the group's norms and authority.

6. Observation of senior staff meeting, December 6, 2000, San Francisco.

7. "Media Team Agenda & Pepsi Ad w/BM Image," Media Mecca e-mail list, May 21, 2003.

8. Observation of volunteer coordinators meeting, June 26, 2000, San Francisco.

9. "Successful Volunteerism with Burningman," *Burningman Volunteer Handbook,* 2000, 17.

10. Observations of meetings revealed that members carried out this routine, typically at the beginning of meetings.

11. "Successful Volunteerism with Burningman," *Burningman Volunteer Handbook,* 2000, 18.

12. "Successful Volunteerism with Burningman," *Burningman Volunteer Handbook,* 2000, 3.

13. Interview with Molly Tirpak, September 21, 2000, San Francisco.

14. "Successful Volunteerism with Burningman," *Burningman Volunteer Handbook,* 2000, 19.

15. "Successful Volunteerism with Burningman," *Burningman Volunteer Handbook,* 2000, 18.

16. "Successful Volunteerism with Burningman," *Burningman Volunteer Handbook,* 2000, 18.

17. "Successful Volunteerism with Burningman," *Burningman Volunteer Handbook,* 2000, 22.

18. Interview with Diane Whitman, August 18, 2000, San Francisco. Observation of senior staff meeting, August 12, 1999, San Francisco.

19. "Lead/Foreman Training Agenda," observation of lead meeting, July 5, 2001, San Francisco.

20. Interview with John Nettle, August 15, 2000, San Francisco.

21. Interview with Molly Tirpak, September 21, 2000, San Francisco.

22. Studies show that individuals who are asked to volunteer are more likely to volunteer than those who were not asked (Freeman 1997).

23. Interview with Simon Hagger, August 17, 2000, San Francisco. Interview with Diane Whitman, August 18, 2000, San Francisco.

24. Interview with Simon Hagger, August 17, 2000, San Francisco.

25. Joint interview with Antony "Shona" Guerra and Karina O'Connor, October 15, 2000, San Francisco.

26. Interview with Simon Hagger, August 17, 2000, San Francisco.

27. Interview with Scott Shaner, December 5, 2000, San Francisco.

28. Interview with Scott Shaner, December 5, 2000, San Francisco.

29. Interview with Fiona Essa, August 21, 2000, San Francisco.

30. Interview with Dan Miller, October 24, 2000, San Francisco. Observation of presentation of Burning Man artists at the Exploratorium, organized by YLEM, an organization devoted to "Artists Using Science and Technology," July 19, 2000, San Francisco.

31. Interview with Holly Kreuter, October 12, 2000, San Francisco.

32. Interview with Christine Kristen, November 7, 2000, San Francisco.

33. Interview with Mary Ellen Burdwood, August 14, 2000, San Francisco. Interview with Tom Smith (pseudonym), August 10, 2000, San Francisco. Interview with Molly Tirpak, July 11, 2001, San Francisco. Marian Goodell, *Jack Rabbit Speaks* e-mail newsletter, June 28, 2001, 5:18a.

34. Interview with P. Segal, October 6, 2000, San Francisco.

35. Interview with Ray Bruman, August 8, 2000, San Francisco.

36. Phone interview with Kat DeLurgio, November 8, 2000.

37. Joint interview with Antony "Shona" Guerra and Karina O'Connor, October 15, 2000, San Francisco.

38. Interview with Joe Cordes, August 7, 2000, San Francisco. Interview with Baylor Gross (pseudonym), July 31, 2000, San Francisco.

39. Phone interview with Jim Lamb, August 10, 2000.

40. Joint interview with Brien Burroughs and Rebecca Workman, August 19, 2000, San Francisco. Phone interview with Kat DeLurgio, November 8, 2000.

41. Interview with Jess Bobier, September 20, 2000, San Francisco.

42. Interview with Rob Oliver, August 1, 2000, San Francisco.

43. Phone interview with Jim Lamb, August 10, 2000.

44. Joint interview with Antony "Shona" Guerra and Karina O'Connor, October 15, 2000, San Francisco. Phone interview with George Paap, December 9, 2000. Observation of senior staff decompression, November 15, 2000, Tiburon, California.

45. Interview with Eric Pouyoul, December 3, 2000, San Francisco.

46. "Lead/Foreman Training Agenda," observation of lead meeting, July 5, 2001, San Francisco.

47. Such a practical understanding of the limits of planning contrasts with other organizations' use of planning. Planning in the form of "fantasy documents" creates the perception of control over events such as oil spills and nuclear accidents (Clarke 1999).

48. Interview with Chase Lehman (pseudonym), August 11, 2000, San Francisco.

49. Interview with Jesse Jones, October 3, 2000, San Francisco. Phone interview with Lissa Shoun, October 10, 2000.

50. Interview with Mark Warner, October 25, 2000, San Francisco.

51. Interview with Susan Barron, October 16, 2000, San Francisco. Interview with Joegh Bullock, October 3, 2000, San Francisco. Interview with Raines Cohen, August 16, 2000, San Francisco. Interview with Matt Dineen, August 14, 2000, San Francisco. Interview with Barney Ford, August 14, 2000, San Francisco. Interview with Chase Lehman (pseudonym), August 11, 2000, San Francisco. Interview with John Nettle, August 15, 2000, San Francisco. Interview with Vicki Olds, September 29, 2000, San Francisco.

52. Interview with Will Roger, November 10, 2000, San Francisco.

53. Phone interview with Jim Lamb, August 10, 2000. Phone interview with George Paap, December 9, 2000.

54. Interview with Matt Dineen, August 14, 2000, San Francisco.

55. Interview with Susan Barron, October 16, 2000, San Francisco. Interview with Fiona Essa, August 21, 2000, San Francisco. Interview with Kat DeLurgio, November 8, 2000, San Francisco. Interview with Jim Graham, September 23, 2000, San Francisco.

56. Phone interview with Susan Strahan, October 19, 2000.

57. Interview with Mike Wright, August 15, 2000, San Francisco.

58. Interview with Barney Ford, August 14, 2000, San Francisco.

59. Interview with Steve Mobia, October 4, 2000, San Francisco.

60. Interview with Rob Oliver, August 1, 2000, San Francisco.

61. Interview with Joegh Bullock, October 3, 2000, San Francisco. Joint interview with Brien Burroughs and Rebecca Workman, August 19, 2000, San Francisco. Interview with Raines Cohen, August 16, 2000, San Francisco. Interview with Barney Ford, August 14, 2000,

San Francisco. Interview with Alice Freedman (pseudonym), August 17, 2000, San Francisco. Phone interview with Jim Lamb, August 10, 2000. Interview with Rob Oliver, August 1, 2000, San Francisco.

62. Observations of Burning Man events, 1999–2002.

63. Interview with John Graham, September 18, 2000, San Francisco.

64. Interview with Mary Ellen Burdwood, August 14, 2000, San Francisco.

65. Interview with Flynn Mauthe, November 9, 2000, San Francisco.

66. Interview with Raines Cohen, August 16, 2000, San Francisco. Interview with Marian Goodell, November 6, 2000, San Francisco. Observation of Tech team meeting, June 6, 2000, San Francisco. Observation of Media Mecca meeting, August 9, 2000, San Francisco.

67. Interview with Mary Ellen Burdwood, August 14, 2000, San Francisco.

68. Phone interview with Joe Fenton, October 10, 2000.

69. Interview with Steven Raspa, September 19, 2000, San Francisco.

70. Interview with Fiona Essa, August, 21, 2000, San Francisco. Interview with Scott Shaner, December 5, 2000, San Francisco. Joint interview with Antony "Shona" Guerra and Karina O'Connor, October 15, 2000, San Francisco.

71. Phone interview with Lissa Shoun, October 10, 2000.

72. Interview with Molly Tirpak, July 11, 2001, San Francisco.

73. Observation of lead meeting, July 5, 2001, San Francisco.

74. Interview with Raines Cohen, August 16, 2000, San Francisco.

75. Interview with Dan Miller, October 24, 2000, San Francisco.

76. Observations of Burning Man events, 2000–2001.

77. Interview of Naomi Pearce, December 1, 2000, Albany, California.

78. Phone interview with Susan Strahan, October 19, 2000.

79. Interview with Harley Dubois, October 19, 2000, San Francisco.

80. Interview with Harley Dubois, October 19, 2000, San Francisco.

81. Observation of Greeters meeting, June 13, 2000, San Francisco.

82. Interview with Megan Beachler, December 12, 2000, San Francisco.

83. Greeters dubbed those who manned the transition shifts "trannies." Observation of Greeters meeting, June 21, 2000. Observation of lead meeting, July 5, 2001, San Francisco.

84. Observation of volunteer barbecue, July 22, 2000, San Francisco.

85. Phone interview with Lissa Shoun, October 10, 2000.

86. The Gate is responsible for processing attendees' tickets and searching vehicles for stowaways or banned items, such as ATVs or guns. Interview with Jeff Oushani, October 8, 2000, San Francisco. Interview with Teri Hyatt-Oushani, October 6, 2000, San Francisco.

87. Interview with Harley Dubois, December 21, 2001, San Francisco.

88. Observation of Tech team meeting, June 6, 2000, San Francisco.

89. Interview with Jeff Oushani, October 8, 2000, San Francisco. Interview with Teri Hyatt-Oushani, October 6, 2000, San Francisco.

90. Interview with Matt Dineen, August 14, 2000, San Francisco.

91. Interview with Molly Ditmore, August 16, 2000, San Francisco.

92. "Successful Volunteerism with Burningman," *Burningman Volunteer Handbook,* 2000, 21.

93. Observation of senior staff meeting, December 2, 2000, Oakland, California.

94. Interview with Barney Ford, August 14, 2000, San Francisco. Phone interview with Larry Henricks, September 19, 2000. Observation of lead meeting, July 5, 2001, San Francisco.

95. These meal passes were justified on the grounds that volunteers were unable to prepare their own meals during their shifts. Not all volunteers accepted these passes.

96. Ticket prices for the early 2000s events progressively increased from $95, $125, and $145 to over $200. A limited number of the lower-priced tickets were available by deadlines before the event. Some volunteers could purchase tickets at the lower prices even if they missed these deadlines. Volunteers who had their tickets comped typically purchased their tickets in advance and were reimbursed after the event. Some organizers asked individuals to state their justifications for receiving a comp. Staff members buy their own tickets, although some have the discretion to distribute an allotment of tickets to others.

97. "Successful Volunteerism with Burningman," *Burningman Volunteer Handbook,* 2000.

98. Observation of senior staff meeting, December 14, 2000, San Francisco.

99. Interview with Molly Tirpak, August 10, 2000, San Francisco.

100. Interview with Molly Tirpak, August 10, 2000, San Francisco.

101. Observation of Burning Man planning meeting, June 1, 2000. Interview with Molly Tirpak, August 10, 2000, San Francisco.

102. Observation of volunteer coordinators meeting, June 26, 2000, San Francisco.

103. Interview with John Law, September 26, 2000, Oakland, California. Phone interview with Joe Fenton, October 10, 2000.

104. For example, at the time of this study, a DPW line worker got $25 for a day's labor. A few volunteers in departments like Media Mecca received $500 for a year's worth of work.

105. Observation of senior staff meeting, November 29, 2000, San Francisco.

106. Observation of Burning Man office, August 9, 2000, San Francisco.

107. Interview with Marian Goodell, November 6, 2000, San Francisco. Interview with Flynn Mauthe, November 9, 2000, San Francisco.

108. Interview with Erik Waterman, November 17, 2000, San Francisco.

109. Interview with Dan Miller, October 24, 2000, San Francisco.

110. See Simmel [1978] 2004 about monetary exchange.

111. Phone interview with Kimric Smythe, October 11, 2000.

112. Phone interview with Kat DeLurgio, November 8, 2000.

113. Interview with Matt Dineen, August 14, 2000, San Francisco.

114. Observation of senior staff meeting, December 6, 2000, San Francisco.

115. Observation of senior staff meeting, December 6, 2000, San Francisco.

116. Interview with Joseph Pred, October 18, 2000, San Francisco.

117. Observation of senior staff meeting, December 6, 2000, San Francisco.

118. Interview with Joseph Pred, October 18, 2000, San Francisco.

119. Interview with Teri Hyatt-Oushani, October 6, 2000, San Francisco. Phone interview with Joe Fenton, October 10, 2000.

120. Interview with Will Roger, November 10, 2000, San Francisco.

121. Interview with Flynn Mauthe, November 9, 2000, San Francisco.

122. Interview with Flynn Mauthe, November 9, 2000, San Francisco. Interview with Will Roger, November 10, 2000, San Francisco. Observation of senior staff decompression, November 15, 2000, Tiburon, California.

123. Marian Goodell, "Job Opportunity," *Jack Rabbit Speaks* e-mail newsletter, January 10, 2001, 5:4.

124. *Black Rock City Operation Manual* 2000, 4.7.12.

125. Interview with John Law, September 26, 2000, Oakland, California. Silicon Satan (pseudonym), "Burning Man: A Vision of the Future," *New Mission News,* October 1999, 11.

126. Identities of interviewees withheld.

127. Observation of lead meeting, July 5, 2001, San Francisco.

128. Identity of interviewee withheld.

129. For example, Burning Man supporters have initiated and carried out projects such as a voter drive registration for the 2004 presidential election, the preservation of the Black Rock Desert, and the rebuilding of communities devastated by Hurricane Katrina.

Chapter 6

1. Interview with Larry Harvey, October 25, 2000, San Francisco. Zablocki (1980) has similarly noted that alternative organizations have more difficult relations with local organizations than with federal organizations.

2. Interview with Larry Harvey, October 25, 2000, San Francisco. Interview with Michael Mikel, November 7, 2000, San Francisco.

3. Interview with Larry Harvey, October 25, 2000, San Francisco.

4. Interview with Larry Harvey, October 25, 2000, San Francisco.

5. "We're Everywhere—BM in Pop Culture (Long & Rambling)," staff e-mail list, November 21, 2000.

6. For example, the Mondragón worker cooperatives established alternative financing practices, training schools, health care, and research and development organizations (Cheney 1999; Greenwood and Santos 1991; Whyte and Whyte 1988). However, by the cooperatives' fourth decade, the managers claimed that they had to mimic capitalist practices to be globally competitive. Instead of continuing with their alternative practices, the cooperatives have since centralized through a managerial superstructure, decreased the emphasis on regional-based production, and increased wage index disparities between the lowest and highest paid workers (Cheney 1999).

7. Organizational researchers often use neoinstitutionalist (e.g., DiMaggio and Powell 1991) and resource dependency (e.g., Pfeffer and Salancik 1978) theories to describe and predict how organizations will change with these relationships.

8. Because of space limitations, I have omitted two sets of cases from this discussion. I excluded suppliers that provided services such as land and equipment rentals, banking, ticketing, medical services, fire protection, and "portapotties" (portable chemical toilets) for the event, as observations and interviews indicated that such relations tended to support the predictions of resource dependency theory. Organizers were able to negotiate some of these relationships, especially when assisted by Burning Man's influential networks. However, given limited alternatives for resources like chemical toilets, the Burning Man organization had to make more concessions in these relations than in others.

I also excluded several interest groups that expressed concerns about the Burning Man event's impact on the natural environment, local community resources, and morality. These groups, which included local townspeople, environmental conservation groups, recreational visitors to the desert, and religious organizations, attempted to block Burning Man's access to the Black Rock Desert. Depending upon whether a particular group could impact Burning Man's access to resources, the organization responded by either addressing concerns or concealing nonconformity (Chen 2004).

9. According to Scott (2008), legitimacy draws on three bases: regulative, normative, and cultural-cognitive. When organizations comply with rules, they uphold the regulative aspect of legitimacy. For example, American public schools follow the federal government's No Child Left Behind Act by using annual tests to assess students' progress and hiring creden-

tialed teachers. When organizations adopt appropriate, accepted ways of operating, they demonstrate the normative aspect of legitimacy (Scott 2008). Normative legitimacy may be determined by any audience of professional groups (Deephouse and Suchman 2008). To continue with the previous example, public schools teach students using accepted pedagogical techniques. When organizations assume taken-for-granted, commonly shared beliefs, they undertake the cultural-cognitive aspect of legitimacy. For instance, schools enact a widely held belief that children should be educated. Organizations may draw on one or more bases of legitimacy, but not necessarily all three (Scott 2008).

10. For example, studies such as Greenwood and Suddaby (2006) have examined print and oral accounts to show how organizations use rhetoric (key words or phrases, themes, etc.) to promote acceptance of their activities or outputs. Fewer recent studies, such as Lune's (2002) analysis of a syringe-exchange program and Barman's (2002, 2006) analysis of the United Way charity, rely upon interviews and observations to examine organizational efforts toward securing external legitimacy.

11. To reconstruct the organization's relationships with actors over time, I relied upon interviews with informants, second-hand reports of interactions, forwarded e-mails of exchanges between Burning Man members and outside actors, newspaper reports, and observations. When possible, I interviewed agency officials and observed interagency meetings and interactions. However, outside actors' perspectives were relatively less well represented than the perspectives of those in the Burning Man organization.

12. For more on institutionalization, see Scott and Davis (2007: 73) and Scott (2008: 121–47).

13. Observation of interagency Cooperator's meeting, November 16, 2000, Reno, Nevada.

14. Phone interview with Mike Bilbo, December 12, 2000.

15. Frank Mullen, Jr., "Too-successful Burning Man Needs New Site," *Reno Gazette-Journal,* September 4, 1996, 1A, 8A.

16. The number of agencies that assist or monitor the Burning Man event has increased over the years. These groups have included the federal Bureau of Land Management, the Nevada Highway Patrol, the Nevada Department of Investigation, the Nevada Department of Transportation, the Nevada tax board, the Nevada Department of Health, Washoe County Health, the Washoe County Road Department, Washoe and Pershing County sheriffs, the Pershing County district attorney, the Gerlach General Improvement District, and the Gerlach-Empire Citizens Advisory. The mixture of agencies across the federal, state, and local levels has made negotiating and coordination efforts particularly complex, as the agencies did not always want to cooperate with each other.

17. Interview with Larry Harvey, October 25, 2000, San Francisco. Letter from Public Resource Associates to the BLM, June 4, 1996, John Law's personal archives.

18. In contrast, after wrangling with the Forest Service over "impossible permit demands" during 1976–1981, the Rainbow Gathering no longer apply for permits to host their events. They believe that the Constitution upholds their right to free assembly (Niman 1997: 187).

19. This quoted figure could also be a cheeky reference to 4:20, slang for cannabis consumption.

20. By 2008, the list had over 60,000 subscribers, and newsletters were e-mailed as frequently as once a week before the Burning Man event. http://www.burningman.com/blackrockcity_yearround/contacts/jrs_lists.html.

21. Marian Goodell, "How You Can Help Make Burning Man Happen on the Black Rock Desert," *Jack Rabbit Speaks* e-mail newsletter, March 18, 1998, 2:16.

22. Marian Goodell, "Thanks," *Jack Rabbit Speaks* e-mail newsletter, March 4, 1999, 3:10.

23. Marian Goodell, "Time for Burning Man to Really Network," *Jack Rabbit Speaks* e-mail newsletter, December 3, 2001, 6:5.

24. Media Mecca e-mail list, 1998–2000.

25. "Pershing County Wants to End Burning Man," *Reno Gazette-Journal,* September 16, 1996. "Officials Alarmed by Rituals, Drug Use at Annual Festival," *Humboldt Sun,* September 6, 1996. Frank Mullen, Jr., "Too-Successful Burning Man Needs New Site," *Reno Gazette-Journal,* September 4, 1996, 1A, 8A. Mack Reed, "Where the Wild Things Are," *Los Angeles Times,* September 4, 1996, E1, E6. Observation of interagency Cooperator's meeting, November 16, 2000, Reno, Nevada.

26. Interview with Larry Harvey, October 25, 2000, San Francisco.

27. Phone interview with Barb Keleher, December 12, 2000.

28. Interview with Joe Fenton, December 20, 2000, Albany, California. Interview with John Law, September 26, 2000, Oakland, California. Interview of Naomi Pearce, December 1, 2000, Albany, California. Interview with P. Segal, October 6, 2000, San Francisco.

29. Observation of senior staff meeting, August 5, 1999, San Francisco.

30. Members of the Rainbow Family raised similar questions about expenditures incurred by Forest Service agents and law enforcement who monitored Rainbow Gatherings; itemized charges included new uniforms, helicopter rentals, and overtime pay for personnel (Niman 1997).

31. Observation of senior staff meeting, December 2, 2000, Oakland, California.

32. Given that its goals, activities, and personnel draw upon two independent organizations, the Earth Guardians department is similar to a joint venture, or an organization formed by two preexisting organizations. The nonprofit Black Rock Solar, which formed in 2007 after my study ended, more closely approximates the joint venture form. Under the motto "Putting the Gift Economy to Work," several groups, including the Burning Man organization and a sustainable energy corporation, have collaborated to facilitate the installation of solar panels as an alternative energy source at local Nevada schools and hospitals; http://www.blackrocksolar.org/.

For more research on joint ventures, or the separate legal entities formed by commercial organizations, nonprofits, and governmental agencies, see Galaskiewicz and Colman (2006), Guo and Acar (2005), Guthrie (1999), Scott ([1981] 2003).

33. Interview with Harley Dubois, October 19, 2000, San Francisco.

34. Joint interview with Antony "Shona" Guerra and Karina O'Connor, October 15, 2000, San Francisco.

35. Phone interview with Mike Bilbo, December 12, 2000.

36. Observation of Black Rock ROM meeting, August 6, 2000, San Francisco.

37. Interview with Michael Mikel, November 7, 2000, San Francisco.

38. Interview with Michael Mikel, November 7, 2000, San Francisco.

39. Observation of Black Rock ROM meeting, August 29, 2000, Burning Man. Observation of senior staff decompression meeting, November 13, 2000, Tiburon, California. Possession of drug paraphernalia is a felony in Pershing County.

40. Interview with Jennifer Vermut, September 26, 2001, San Francisco. Christopher Smith, "Burning Man '98 Extinguished Quietly; Free-spirit Gathering in Nevada Nets Only a Few Drug Arrests, Traffic Accidents," *Salt Lake Tribune,* September 9, 1998, A3.

41. Interview with Michael Mikel, November 7, 2000, San Francisco.

42. Observation of senior staff decompression, November 14, 2000, Tiburon, California.

43. Observation of interagency Cooperator's meeting, November 16, 2000, Reno, Nevada.

44. Observation of Media Mecca meeting, October 12, 2000, San Francisco. Interview with Joe Fenton, October 10, 2000, Albany, California.

45. Interview with Joe Fenton, October 10, 2000, Albany, California.

46. Phone interview with Mike Bilbo, December 12, 2000.

47. Interview with Michael Mikel, November 7, 2000, San Francisco.

48. Interview with Harley Dubois, October 19, 2000, San Francisco.

49. Phone interview with Mike Bilbo, December 12, 2000.

50. This collaboration is similar to the participative, consensus-building activities among environmental justice groups, corporations, and the state (Pellow 1999).

51. Phone interview with Mike Bilbo, December 12, 2000.

52. Phone interview with Mike Bilbo, December 12, 2000.

53. "Palo Playa Story," Media Mecca e-mail list, September 25, 2002.

54. Observation of senior staff meeting, August 4, 1998, San Francisco.

55. Practitioners call this "brand management" or "reputation management" (Deephouse 2002).

56. Observation of Media Mecca meeting, July 20, 2000, San Francisco.

57. For sociological accounts of how the media works, see Fishman (1980), Gans (1979), Kielbowicz and Scherer (1986), and Tuchman (1978).

58. For examples, see Ryan, Anastario, and Jeffreys (2005); Smith et al. (2001).

59. See Andrews and Biggs (2006), Entman (2003), Gamson et al. (1992), Gamson and Meyer (1996), Gamson and Wolfsfeld (1993), Gitlin (2003), Jackall and Hirota (2000), Kielbowicz and Scherer (1986), Koopmans (2004), Koopmans and Olzak (2004), Ryan (1991), Ryan et al. (2005), and Shaw (1996).

60. See Blyskal and Blyskal (1985), Doorley and Garcia (2007), Fiss and Zajac (2006), Jackall and Hirota (2000), Kennedy (2008), Marchand (1998), Miller (1999), Tedlow (1979), and Weiner (2006).

61. See Gamson and Stuart (1992), Gamson and Wolfsfeld (1993), and McAdam (1996). Ryan et al.'s (2005) study provides a brief account of how a domestic violence coalition developed a public relations group to impact media coverage.

62. The social movement group Students for a Democratic Society (SDS) also lacked adequate structure, such as designated spokespersons and procedures, for dealing with the media. The subsequent media marginalization of SDS's goals and activities contributed to the decline of the organization (Gitlin 2003), illustrating the consequences of not correcting for underorganizing.

63. Interview with John Law, September 26, 2000, Oakland, California.

64. Interview with John Law, September 26, 2000, Oakland, California.

65. Other organizations share these fears about media-fueled perceptions shaping reality. For example, law schools fret over a business magazine's annual ranking of their programs, as a change in rank can affect student applications and transfers, recruitment and retention of faculty and staff, and alumni donations (Espeland and Sauder 2007; Sauder and Lancaster 2006). Similarly, media reports that mistakenly or jokingly labeled geographic areas or events as sites for "deviant" activities like drug dealing or cruising have transformed these areas into

such sites by attracting those interested in those activities: "As a joke, it was once written in a Dutch gay newspaper that the annual fair in Bergen op Zoom is a place where many homosexuals meet. Ever since, it really has been" (Lootsma 2000: 27).

66. Observation of senior staff meeting, December 2, 2000, Oakland, California.

67. Observation of senior staff meeting, December 2, 2000, Oakland, California.

68. Observation of Media Mecca meeting, August 19, 1999, San Francisco.

69. "Public Comment from the Citizens of BRC," document distributed at senior staff decompression, November 13, 2000, Tiburon, California.

70. "Public Comment from the Citizens of BRC," document distributed at senior staff decompression, November 13, 2000, Tiburon, California.

71. Similarly, governmental agencies learned to coordinate their relations with the media. BLM official Mike Bilbo explained how agencies agreed to give "the same message" for the media, as reporters will "try to play one person off the other to try to get different stories, and they always sensationalize the stuff that seems negative. . . . The media will characterize Burning Man in a certain way and then we get a lot of letters that follow the same line and then we will have to spend time trying to settle the letters that come in, and sometimes we get congressionals [Congresspersons] in." Phone interview with Mike Bilbo, December 12, 2000.

72. Such press stated: "The festival's biggest problem was the 70 to 90 people who required emergency medical treatment each day after taking LSD or Ecstasy, deputies said" and "[Washoe County sheriff's Lt. Will] McHardy said the only major problem has been the 80 to 90 people a day who have required medical treatment after taking certain drugs at the event." Martin Griffith, "Drug Problem Surfaces at Burning Man Festival," September 4, 1999; "Burning Man Arrests Down, But Drug-Related Medical Problems Up," September 5, 1999, Associated Press State & Local Wire.

73. Observation of town hall meeting, December 3, 2000, San Francisco. Marian Goodell, "Law Enforcement Presence at Burning Man 2000," *Jack Rabbit Speaks* e-mail newsletter, August 20, 2000, 5:2.

74. Observations of Media Mecca, 1998–2002. Observation of interagency Cooperator's meeting, November 16, 2000, Reno, Nevada.

75. Observation of Media Mecca meetings, August 1999 and July 20, 2000, San Francisco.

76. However, Media Mecca volunteers did help photographers get prime locations to shoot photos of the Burn. The media's dependency upon the Burning Man organization inverts some of Gamson and Wolfsfeld's (1993) predictions about how organizations interact with the media.

77. Media Mecca press kits, 1997–1998.

78. Interview of Naomi Pearce, December 1, 2000, Albany, California.

79. Interview of Naomi Pearce, December 1, 2000, Albany, California.

80. Media Mecca press kit, 1998.

81. Participant observation of Media Mecca activities at Burning Man, 2000.

82. Other researchers define a frame as a "central organizing principle" (Gamson et al. 1992: 384) for members' activities, with associated values and beliefs.

83. Social movement groups conduct similar analyses to determine whether they are effective in promoting their perspectives (Gamson et al. 1992).

84. Observation of Burning Man office, July 27, 2000, San Francisco.

85. Media coverage of social movements evidence similar treatment (Entman and

Rojecki 1993; Gitlin 2003). See also the media's role in moral panics, in which "deviant" groups are condemned for societal ills (Cohen [1972] 2003; Glassner 1999).

86. Social movement researchers have called this "value amplification" (Snow et al. 1986).

87. Gamson (1988) discussed the importance of making frames "resonant," or familiar and compatible with the beliefs of larger society, as this enhances the dissemination of frames. Other social movement researchers have called the process of explaining less familiar beliefs and values "frame extension"; they usually refer to this in the context of recruiting new members and support for a particular cause (Snow et al. 1986).

88. One reporter attributed the unrest at Woodstock '99 to attendees' unhappiness with overpriced food and water and unsanitary portable toilets (Samuels 1999).

89. Observation of Media Mecca meeting, August 19, 1999, San Francisco.

90. Personal communication with Candace Locklear, June 22, 2000. Marian Goodell, "MTV," *Jack Rabbit Speaks* e-mail newsletter, October 7, 1999, 4:3.

91. Observation of Burning Man event, 2001. Personal communication with Alexa Lee, CNN reporter.

92. Observation of Media Mecca meeting, July 22, 2000, San Francisco.

93. Observation of senior staff meeting, June 22, 2000, San Francisco. The discussed article was by Nicole Powers, "Summer 2K Essential Festival Guide," *URB,* July/August 2000, 48.

94. Organizers eventually addressed this issue by locating theme camps that hosted raves at the edges of the city and designating a quiet zone for campers who wished to escape the noise of generators and sound systems.

95. At the time, raves were perceived as promoting drug use.

96. George Post, "Eyewitness the World at Once," *Details,* August 1994, 23. "Burning Man," http://bgamedia.com/playboy/burning.html. "Party Over Here," *Stuff for Men,* April/May 2000, 96–103. Observation of Burning Man office, August 8, 2000, San Francisco. Observation of Media Mecca meeting, October 12, 2000, San Francisco.

97. "BM on "The View," Media Mecca e-mail list, February 10, 2006.

98. Observation of Media Mecca meeting, August 19, 1999, San Francisco.

99. Personal communication, identity withheld.

100. Interview with Mary Ellen Burdwood, August 14, 2000, San Francisco.

101. Observation of senior staff meeting, December 2, 2000, Oakland, California.

102. Researchers have noted similar impression-management tactics in other organizations. When confronted by unfavorable media coverage of school rankings, for example, business school students and staff emphasized alternative dimensions for rankings and proposed more "fair" or favorable comparisons (Elsbach and Kramer 1996).

103. Marian Goodell, *Jack Rabbit Speaks* e-mail newsletter, August 24, 2001, 5:30.

104. Observation of town hall meeting, December 3, 2000, San Francisco.

105. Observation of senior staff meeting, November 29, 2000, San Francisco. Observation of senior staff meeting, December 2, 2000, Oakland, California. Marian Goodell, "Ministry of Statistics 2000 URL," *Jack Rabbit Speaks* e-mail newsletter, July 26, 2001, 5:21.

106. Interview with Naomi Pearce, December 1, 2000, Albany, California.

107. Joint interview with Brien Burroughs and Rebecca Workman, August 19, 2000, San Francisco.

108. Not all vehicles are searched, but Gate personnel will often enter recreational vehicles to check for stowaways. Interview with Jeff Oushani, October 8, 2000, San Francisco.

Interview with Teri Hyatt-Oushani, October 6, 2000, San Francisco. Observations of Burning Man events, 1998–2003, 2005, 2007, 2008.

109. The press has, on occasion, resurrected this image. For example, the *London Observer* newspaper published a stock photo that portrayed event participants as young, tattooed, gunslinging Americans. See Ed Vulliamy, "Kings of the Weird Frontier," *London Observer,* December 9, 1999, 5.

110. For example, Larry Harvey has participated in panel discussions and has given talks at Harvard University, the Chicago Art Institute, the Walker Art Center in Minneapolis, and Cooper Union in New York City.

111. Interview with Michael Mikel, November 7, 2000, San Francisco.

112. In this case, Burning Man organizers gave permission to the ad agency to use the Burning Man name since Larry Harvey had given a speech for the Commonwealth Club. "Re: [media-team] Commonwealth Club Poster in Powell St. BART," Media Mecca e-mail list, April 23, 2003.

113. Observation of San Francisco MUNI buses and subway stops, 2003. The guerilla Billboard Liberation Front altered one billboard so that the text below the rather toothy model read: "I wanted to ask Larry Harvey if success is killing his original idea for Burning Man. So I bit him with my big teeth."

114. The term *commodification* draws on Marx's analysis of the development of capitalism, in which activities and relations are converted into exchange value (Marx and Engels [1848] 1978).

115. Other studies document the process by which cultural institutions and outputs such as museums, art, music, and books, are transformed into commodities that can be bought or sold, and how the introduction of more business-oriented practices can erode such cultural objects' nonmonetary value (Fine 2004; Miller 2006).

116. For example, high-status organizations guard their names. When Merrill Lynch & Co. renamed its mutual funds Princeton Portfolio Research & Management, Princeton University's lawyers pushed Merrill to choose another name (McGeehan 2006). The fund's head claimed that the name choice referred to the fund's location, which actually was in the adjacent town of Plainsboro. He noted, "Princeton has positive connotations given the prestige of the university" (Lauricella 2006). A Princeton spokesperson accused Merrill of "planning to exploit the university's name and reputation for its commercial gain" (McGeehan 2006). Blackstone's subsequent acquisition of Merrill's fund resolved the problem (Silva 2006).

117. "Nantucket Nectars-NOT!," senior staff and Media Mecca e-mail lists, August 13, 1998.

118. The 2007 Burning Man event, which promoted environmental conservation under the theme "Green Man," temporarily relaxed the event's prohibition against on-site advertising. To educate eventgoers about environmental conservation techniques, a posted sign provided information about the manufacturer for the solar panels used to power the Burning Man sculpture's neon and lights. The Burning Man organization later donated and installed these panels to generate power for a local school. In addition, in conjunction with other partners, the Burning Man organization supported a new nonprofit, Black Rock Solar, to promote the wider use of solar power. http://www.burningman.com/news/071218 _blackrocksolar.html.

119. "Comparing Burning Man to SyncFest?," Media Mecca e-mail list, October 26, 2001.

120. Interview with Joe Fenton, October 10, 2000, Albany, California. Media Mecca e-mail list, August-September 2000. Observation of Media Mecca meeting, October 12, 2000, San Francisco.

121. Observation of senior staff meeting, July 21, 1999, San Francisco.

122. Observations of Burning Man organization, 2000–2002. Evelyn Nieves, "A Festival with Nudity Sues a Sex Website," *New York Times,* July 5, 2002, A11.

123. Marian Goodell, "UFOs and more," *Jack Rabbit Speaks* e-mail newsletter, April 26, 2000, 4:15.

124. Over the years, lawyers helped develop a policy about the use of the Burning Man name. As Jim Graham explained to the Media Mecca listserv, "We'll allow the BM name to be used in a product description, so long as it doesn't misrepresent the event, but we ask any-one using it in the title of the auction to remove it." "An Interesting BM Trademark Issue," Media Mecca e-mail list, July 16, 2003.

125. "BM Street Sign Auction Pulled from eBay," Media Mecca e-mail list, September 19, 2001.

126. *Playboy,* September 2001, cover, 140–49.

127. Marian Goodell, "Burning Man Jeopardy," *Jack Rabbit Speaks* e-mail newsletter, July 26, 2001, 5:21.

128. Marian Goodell. "A Rabbit Rants a Little," *Jack Rabbit Speaks* e-mail newsletter, March 25, 2001, 5:10.

129. Richards' performance art involved wearing a protective suit and playing with elec-trical arcs generated by Tesla coils.

130. "Re: [media-team] Dr. Megavolt," Media Mecca e-mail list, December 10, 2001.

131. In recent years, the Burning Man organization has had more resources, so partici-pants could apply for funds to help build art projects for the event.

132. Observation of art placement meeting, June 21, 2000, San Francisco.

133. Interview with John Law, September 26, 2000, Oakland, California.

134. Interview with John Law, September 26, 2000, Oakland, California.

135. Unlike coverage produced by independent reporters, coverage produced by report-ers who accompanied American military units in Iraq focused on troops' hardships but ignored the war's effects upon civilians (Linder 2008).

136. For instance, in 2006, the BLM sought both to charge the Burning Man organization for local law enforcement and charge a user fee of four dollars per person per day; in previ-ous years, the BLM had paid local law enforcement from the collected per diem user fees. Burning Man organizers successfully appealed this as "double-dipping" before the Interior Board of Land Appeals, and the BLM returned the funds. http://afterburn.burningman .com/07/admin/legal.html.

137. See density-dependence arguments by Hannan and Carroll (1992).

138. Phone interview with Leslie Bocskor, December 13, 2000. Phone interview with George Paap, December 9, 2000. Observation of FIGMENT, an annual participatory arts celebration on Governors Island, New York City, June 29, 2008. See also http://figmentnyc .org/home_html/.

Chapter 7

1. Interview with Naomi Pearce, December 1, 2000, Albany, California.

2. Interview with John Law, September 26, 2000, Oakland, California.

3. Interview with John Rinaldi, November 3, 2000, San Francisco.

4. "Opposing the Merchandising Protocol," staff e-mail list, April 18, 2004.

5. Interview with John Law, September 26, 2000, Oakland, California. Interview with

John Rinaldi, November 3, 2000, San Francisco. Phone interview with Kimric Smythe, October 11, 2000.

6. Phone interview with Leslie Bocskor, December 13, 2000. Interview with Mary Ellen Burdwood, August 14, 2000, San Francisco. Interview of Joe Cordes, August 7, 2000, San Francisco. Interview with Matt Dineen, August 14, 2000, San Francisco. Interview with Harley Dubois, October 19, 2000, San Francisco. Interview with Joe Fenton, December 16, 2000, Albany, California. Interview with Jim Graham, September 23, 2000, San Francisco. Interview with Simon Hagger, August, 17, 2000, San Francisco. Interview with Flynn Mauthe, November 9, 2000, San Francisco. Interview with Michael Mikel, November 7, 2000, San Francisco. Interview with Will Roger, November 10, 2000, San Francisco. Interview with Tom Smith (pseudonym), August 10, 2000, San Francisco. Interview with Molly Tirpak, August 10, 2000, San Francisco. Phone interview with Susan Strahan, October 19, 2000.

7. Phone interview with Susan Strahan, October 19, 2000.

8. When I suggested helping out with a particular project, an organizer graciously thanked me for volunteering, but pointed out that I was working on my thesis.

9. Stone (2007), Bailyn (2006), and others make recommendations on how to carry out such changes.

10. Interview with Naomi Pearce, December 1, 2000, Albany, California.

11. For instance, the media has covered tussles between large entertainment conglomerates and small businesses and parents over the unlicensed use of birthday cake decorations and costumed cartoon characters as entertainers at children's parties. Katherine Rosman, "Why Dora the Explorer Can't Come to Your Kid's Birthday Party," *Wall Street Journal,* July 22, 2008, A1, A15. Diane Richard, "Freeze, Kid: You Need a License for That Cake," *Minneapolis/ St. Paul Business Journal,* February 28, 1997, http://twincities.bizjournals.com/twincities/stories/1997/03/03/story3.html.

12. Alternatively, organizations may try securing special legal protection for their outputs. For instance, a General Public License (GPL) allows for the dissemination and modification of code produced by Open Source projects. Subsequent users, including corporations, must allow access to modified code. This arrangement helps resolve issues about fair use for these organizations (Chen and O'Mahony, forthcoming).

13. Interview with Marian Goodell, November 12, 2000, San Francisco. Observation of senior staff meeting, December 18, 2000, San Francisco.

14. http://regionals.burningman.com/index.html.

Appendix 1

1. When other members requested my notes for meeting minutes or records, I shared a version of my field notes.

2. For the 2000 event theme of "The Body," Normal and a team of assistants and volunteers conceived and constructed an elaborate stage called the "Anus," which hosted their stage production about a constipated God, Sigmund Freud, and dancing "Poo Princesses."

3. Interviewed volunteers contributed on a year-round basis. Given their greater organizational involvement, their views and experiences may have differed from those who volunteered only during the event or on a sporadic basis.

4. Observations of Media Mecca at the Burning Man events showed how journalists struggled to file their stories by deadlines under challenging circumstances, including spotty Internet connections and dust storms that ruined cameras and other sensitive equipment.

5. Examples of seminal revelatory cases include Liebow's (1967) *Tally's Corner* and Whyte's ([1943] 1955) *Street Corner Society*.

6. Yin (1994) defined analytic generalization as using a previously developed theory as a template with which to compare the empirical results of the case study. In contrast, statistical generalization makes an inference about a population using empirical data collected from a sample.

7. The approach of adopting the views of organizational actors themselves is known as the realist approach (Laumann, Marsden, and Prensky 1983).

8. Several individuals and groups, particularly documentary makers, have attempted to construct a profile of the "average" participant. One now-defunct theme camp, the Ministry of Statistics, had relied on convenience sampling to collect statistics on attendees who were willing to complete their questionnaires. The Burning Man organization conducted its own online survey in 2002 and has collected an annual convenience sample survey of participants at the 2003 and subsequent events.

9. On a few occasions, a particular Burning Man organizer questioned my presence, but Goodell and others protected my access.

References

Adler, Paul S. 1992. "The 'Learning Bureaucracy': New United Motor Manufacturing, Inc." *Research in Organizational Behavior* 15: 111–94.

———. 1999. "Building Better Bureaucracies." *Academy of Management Executive* 13(4): 36–47.

Adler, Paul S., and Bryan Borys. 1996. "Two Types of Bureaucracy: Enabling and Coercive." *Administrative Science Quarterly* 41(1): 61–89.

Aldrich, Howard E., and C. Marlene Fiol. 1994. "Fools Rush In? The Institutional Context of Industry Creation." *Academy of Management Review* 19(4): 645–70.

Aldrich, Howard E., and Martin Ruef. 2006. *Organizations Evolving.* 2nd ed. Thousand Oaks, CA: Sage.

Alexander, Victoria D. 1998. "Environmental Constraints and Organizational Strategies." Pp. 272–90 in *Private Actions and the Public Good,* ed. Walter W. Powell and Elisabeth S. Clemens. New Haven, CT: Yale University Press.

Allahyari, Rebecca Anne. 2000. *Visions of Charity: Volunteer Workers and Moral Communities.* Berkeley: University of California Press.

Allmendinger, Jutta, and J. Richard Hackman. 1995. "The More, the Better? A Four-Nation Study of the Inclusion of Women in Symphony Orchestras." *Social Forces* 74(2): 423–60.

Andrews, Kenneth T., and Michael Biggs. 2006. "The Dynamics of Protest Diffusion: Movement Organizations, Social Networks, and News Media in the 1960 Sit-Ins." *American Sociological Review* 71(5): 752–77.

Arndt, Margarete, and Barbara Bigelow. 2000. "Presenting Structural Innovation in an Institutional Environment: Hospitals' Use of Impression Management." *Administrative Science Quarterly* 45(3): 494–522.

Ashcraft, Karen Lee. 2001. "Organized Dissonance: Feminist Bureaucracy as Hybrid Form." *The Academy of Management Journal* 44 (6): 1301–22.

Ashforth, Blake E., and Barrie W. Gibbs. 1990. "The Double-Edge of Organizational Legitimation." *Organization Science* 1(2): 177–94.

Bacharach, Samuel B., Peter A. Bamberger, and William J. Sonnensthul. 2001. *Mutual Aid and Union Renewal: Cycles of Logics of Action.* Ithaca, NY: Cornell University Press.

Bailyn, Lotte. 2006. *Breaking the Mold: Redesigning Work For Productive and Satisfying Lives.* 2nd ed. Ithaca, NY: Cornell University Press.

Balser, Deborah B. 1997. "The Impact of Environmental Factors on Factionalism and Schism in Social Movement Organizations." *Social Forces* 76(1): 199–228.

Barker, James R. 1993. "Tightening the Iron Cage: Concertive Control in Self-Managing Teams." *Administrative Science Quarterly* 38(3): 408–37.

———. 1999. *The Discipline of Teamwork: Participation and Concertive Control.* Thousand Oaks, CA: Sage.

Barley, Stephen R. 2008. "Coalface Institutionalism." Pp. 491–518 in *The Sage Handbook of Organizational Institutionalism,* ed. Royston Greenwood, Christine Oliver, Roy Suddaby, and Kerstin Sahlin. Thousand Oaks, CA: Sage.

Barman, Emily A. 2002. "Asserting Difference: The Strategic Response of Nonprofit Organizations to Competition." *Social Forces* 80(4): 1191–222.

———. 2006. *Contesting Communities: The Transformation of Workplace Charity.* Stanford, CA: Stanford University Press.

Barnard, Chester I. [1938] 1968. *The Functions of the Executive.* 30th Anniversary ed. Cambridge, MA: Harvard University Press.

Baum, Joel A. C., and Christine Oliver. 1991. "Institutional Linkages and Organizational Mortality." *Administrative Science Quarterly* 36(2): 187–218.

Baum, Joel A. C., and Christine Oliver. 1992. "Institutional Embeddedness and the Dynamics of Organizational Populations." *American Sociological Review* 57(4): 540–59.

Becker, Penny Edgell. 1999. *Congregations in Conflict: Cultural Models of Local Religious Life.* Cambridge, MA: Cambridge University Press.

Beckman, Christine M. 2006. "The Influence of Founding Team Company Affiliations on Firm Behavior." *Academy of Management Journal* 49(4): 741–58.

Bender, Courtney. 2003. *Heaven's Kitchen: Living Religion at God's Love We Deliver.* Chicago, IL: University of Chicago Press.

Benford, Robert D. 1997. "An Insider's Critique of the Social Movement Framing Perspective." *Sociological Inquiry* 67(4): 409–30.

Besharov, Marya Hill-Popper. 2008. "Mission Goes Corporate: Understanding Employee Behavior in a Mission-Driven Business." PhD dissertation, Department of Sociology, Harvard University, Cambridge, MA.

Biggart, Nicole Woolsey. 1989. *Charismatic Capitalism: Direct Selling Organizations in America.* Chicago, IL: University of Chicago Press.

Black Rock City Operation Manual. 2000. 2nd ed. San Francisco: Burning Man.

Black Rock City Operation Manual. 2001. 3rd ed. San Francisco: Burning Man.

Blair-Loy, Mary. 2003. *Competing Devotions: Career and Family among Women Executives.* Cambridge, MA: Harvard University Press.

Blyskal, Jeff, and Marie Hodge Blyskal. 1985. *PR: How the PR Industry Writes the News.* New York: W. Murrow.

Boltanski, Luc, and Ève Chiapello. 2005. *The New Spirit of Capitalism.* Translated by Gregory Elliott. London: Verso.

Bordt, Rebecca L. 1997. *The Structure of Women's Nonprofit Organizations.* Bloomington: Indiana University Press.

Borland, Elizabeth. 2005. "Central Dilemmas for the Survival and Growth of Social Movement Organizations." Presented at the annual meeting of the American Sociological Association, Aug. 15, Philadelphia, PA.

Braverman, Harry. 1974. *Labor and Monopoly Capital: The Degradation of Work in the Twentieth Century.* New York: Monthly Review Press.

Breines, Wini. 1982. *Community and Organization in the New Left: 1962–1968: The Great Refusal.* New York: Praeger.

Brody, Evelyn. 2006. "The Legal Framework for Nonprofit Organizations." Pp. 243–66 in *The Nonprofit Sector: A Research Handbook,* 2nd ed., ed. Walter W. Powell and Richard Steinberg. New Haven, CT: Yale University Press.

Burawoy, Michael. 1979. *Manufacturing Consent: Changes in the Labor Process under Monopoly Capitalism.* Chicago, IL: University of Chicago Press.

Burns, Tom, and G. M. Stalker. [1961] 1994. *Management of Innovation.* 3rd ed. New York: Oxford University Press.

Campbell, John L. 2005. "Where Do We Stand? Common Mechanisms in Organizations and Social Movements Research." Pp. 41–68 in *Social Movements and Organization Theory,* ed. Gerald F. Davis, Doug McAdam, W. Richard Scott, and Mayer N. Zald. New York: Cambridge University Press.

Cappelli, Peter, and David Neumark. 2001. "Do 'High-Performance' Work Practices Improve Establishment-Level Outcomes?" *Industrial and Labor Relations Review* 54(4): 737–75.

Caronna, Carol A. 2007. "Entrepreneurial Stories in the Non-profit Sector: A Partial Test and Extension of Cultural Entrepreneurship Theory." Presented at the annual meeting of the American Sociological Association, Aug. 12, New York, NY.

Castilla, Emilio J. 2005. "Social Networks and Employee Performance in a Call Center." *American Journal of Sociology* 110(5): 1243–83.

Chambré, Susan. 1991. "The Volunteer Response to the AIDS Epidemic in New York City: Implications for Research on Voluntarism." *Nonprofit and Voluntary Sector Quarterly* 20(3): 267–87.

———. 2006. *Fighting for Our Lives: New York's AIDS Community and the Politics of Disease.* New Brunswick, NJ: Rutgers University Press.

Chen, Katherine K. 2004. "The Burning Man Organization Grows Up." PhD dissertation, Department of Sociology, Harvard University, Cambridge, MA.

———. 2005. "Incendiary Incentives: How the Burning Man Organization Motivates and Manages Volunteers." Pp. 109–28 in *AfterBurn: Reflections on Burning Man,* ed. Lee Gilmore and Mark Van Proyen. Albuquerque: University of New Mexico Press.

Chen, Katherine K., and Siobhán O'Mahony. 2006. "The Selective Synthesis of Competing Logics." *Academy of Management Proceedings.*

———. Forthcoming. "Differentiating Organizational Boundaries." *Research in the Sociology of Organizations* 27.

Cheney, George. 1999. *Values at Work: Employment Participation Meets Market Pressure at Mondragón.* Ithaca, NY: ILR Press.

Chetkovich, Carol A., and Frances Kunreuther. 2006. *From the Ground Up: Grassroots Organizations Making Social Change*. Ithaca, NY: Cornell University.

Chouinard, Yvon. 2005. *Let My People Go Surfing: The Education of a Reluctant Businessman*. New York: Penguin Press.

Clark, Peter B., and James Q. Wilson. 1961. "Incentive Systems: A Theory of Organizations." *Administrative Science Quarterly* 6(2): 129–66.

Clarke, Lee. 1999. *Mission Improbable: Using Fantasy Documents to Tame Disaster*. Chicago, IL: University of Chicago Press.

———. 2006. *Worst Cases: Terror and Catastrophe in the Popular Imagination*. Chicago, IL: University of Chicago Press.

Clary, E. Gil, and Mark Snyder. 1991. "A Functional Analysis of Altruism and Prosocial Behavior: The Case of Volunteerism." Pp. 119–48 in *Review of Personality and Social Psychology*, ed. Margaret Clark. Newbury Park, CA: Sage.

———. 1999. "The Motivations to Volunteer: Theoretical and Practical Considerations." *Current Directions in Psychological Science* 8(5): 156–59.

Clary, E. Gil, Mark Snyder, Robert D. Ridge, John Copeland, Arthur A. Stukas, Julie Haugen, and Peter Miene. 1998. "Understanding and Assessing the Motivations of Volunteers: A Functional Approach." *Journal of Personality and Social Psychology* 74(6): 1516–30.

Clary, E. Gil, Mark Snyder, and Arthur A. Stukas. 1996. "Volunteers' Motivations: Findings From a National Study." *Nonprofit and Voluntary Sector Quarterly* 25(4): 485–505.

Clegg, Stewart R. 1990. *Modern Organizations: Organization Studies in the Postmodern World*. London: Sage.

Clemens, Elisabeth S. 1993. "Organizational Repertoires and Institutional Change: Women's Groups and the Transformation of U.S. Politics, 1890–1920." *American Journal of Sociology* 98(4): 755–98.

Clemens, Elisabeth S., and James M. Cook. 1999. "Politics and Institutionalism: Explaining Durability and Change." *Annual Review of Sociology* 25: 411–66.

Clemens, Elisabeth S., and Debra C. Minkoff. 2004. "Beyond the Iron Law: Rethinking the Place of Organizations in Social Movement Research." Pp. 155–70 in *The Blackwell Companion to Social Movements*, ed. David A. Snow, Sarah A. Soule, and Hanspeter Kriesi. Malden, MA: Blackwell.

Cloward, Richard A., and Frances Fox Piven. 1984. "Disruption and Organization: A Rejoinder [to William A. Gamson and Emilie Schmeidler]." *Theory and Society* 13(4): 587–99.

Cohen, Jean L., and Andrew Arato. 1992. *Civil Society and Political Theory*. Cambridge, MA: MIT Press.

Cohen, Stanley. [1972] 2003. *Folk Devils and Moral Panics: The Creation of the Mods and the Rockers*. 3rd ed. New York: Routledge.

Colby, Anne, and William Damon. 1992. *Some Do Care: Contemporary Lives of Moral Commitment*. New York: Maxwell Macmillan.

Coleman, James S. 1974. *Power and the Structure of Society*. New York: W. W. Norton & Co.

———. 1990. *Foundations of Social Theory*. Cambridge, MA: Belknap Press of Harvard University Press.

Colyvas, Jeannette A., and Walter W. Powell. 2006. "Roads to Institutionalization: The Remaking of Boundaries between Public and Private Science." *Research in Organizational Behavior* 27: 305–53.

Conell, Carol, and Kim Voss. 1990. "Formal Organization and the Fate of Social Movements: Craft Association and Class Alliance in the Knights of Labor." *American Sociological Review* 55(2): 255–69.

Correll, Shelley, Stephen Benard, and In Paik. 2007. "Getting a Job: Is There a Motherhood Penalty?" *American Journal of Sociology* 112(5): 1297–1338.

Coser, Lewis A. 1974. *Greedy Institutions: Patterns of Undivided Commitment*. New York: Free Press.

Craig, Tim. 1995. "Achieving Innovation through Bureaucracy: Lessons from the Japanese Brewing Industry." *California Management Review* 38(1): 8–36.

Creed, W. E. Douglas, Maureen A. Scully, and John R. Austin. 2002. "Clothes Make the Person? The Tailoring of Legitimating Accounts and the Social Construction of Identity." *Organization Science* 13(5): 475–96.

Cress, Daniel M. 1997. "Nonprofit Incorporation among Movements of the Poor: Pathways and Consequences for Homeless Social Movement Organization." *Sociological Quarterly* 38(2): 343–60.

Crozier, Michel. 1964. *The Bureaucratic Phenomenon*. Chicago, IL: University of Chicago Press.

Cunningham, David. 2004. *There's Something Happening Here: The New Left, the Klan, and FBI Counterintelligence*. Berkeley: University of California Press.

Curtis, Russell L., Jr., and Louis A. Zurcher, Jr. 1974. "Social Movements: An Analytical Exploration of Organizational Forms." *Social Problems* 21(3): 356–70.

Dalton, Melville. 1959. *Men Who Manage: Fusions of Feeling and Theory in Administration*. New York: Wiley.

Darr, Asaf. 1999. "Conflict and Conflict Resolution in a Cooperative: The Case of the Nir Taxi Station." *Human Relations* 52(3): 279–301.

Davidson, Leonard. 1983. "Countercultural Organizations and Bureaucracy: Limits on the Revolution." Pp. 162–76 in *Social Movements of the Sixties and Seventies*, ed. Jo Freeman. New York: Longman.

Deckard, Barbara S. 1979. *The Women's Movement: Political, Socioeconomic, and Psychological Issues*. New York: Harper & Row.

Deephouse, David. 2002. "The Term 'Reputation Management': Users, Uses and the Trademark Tradeoff." *Corporate Reputation Review* 5(1): 9–18.

Deephouse, David L., and Mark Suchman. 2008. "Legitimacy in Organizational Institutionalism." Pp. 49–77 in *The Sage Handbook of Organizational Institutionalism,* ed. Royston Greenwood, Christine Oliver, Roy Suddaby, and Kerstin Sahlin. Thousand Oaks, CA: Sage.

Dees, J. Gregory, and Beth Battle Anderson. 2004. "Blurring the Lines between Nonprofit and For-Profit." Pp. 51–71 in *In Search of the Nonprofit Sector,* ed. Peter Frumkin and Jonathan B. Imber. New Brunswick, NJ: Transaction.

Delago, Gary. 1986. *Organizing the Movement: The Roots and Growth of ACORN*. Philadelphia, PA: Temple University Press.

Dentler, Robert A., and Kai T. Erikson. 1959. "The Functions of Deviance in Groups." *Social Problems* 7: 98–107.

DiMaggio, Paul J. 1988. "Interest and Agency in Institutional Theory." Pp. 3–22 in *Institutional Patterns and Organizations,* ed. Lynne G. Zucker. Cambridge, MA: Ballinger.

———, ed. 2001. *The Twenty-first Century Firm: Changing Economic Organization in International Perspectives*. Princeton, NJ: Princeton University Press.

———. 2006. "Nonprofit Organizations and the Intersectoral Division of Labor in the Arts." Pp. 432–61 in *The Nonprofit Sector: A Research Handbook,* 2nd ed., ed. Walter W. Powell and Richard Steinberg. New Haven, CT: Yale University Press.

DiMaggio, Paul J., and Walter W. Powell. 1983. "The Iron Cage Revisited: Institutional Isomorphism and Collective Rationality in Organizational Fields." *American Sociological Review* 48(2): 147–60.

———, eds. 1991. *The New Institutionalism in Organizational Analysis.* Chicago, IL: University of Chicago Press.

Disney, Jennifer Leigh, and Joyce Gelb. 2000. "Feminist Organizational 'Success': The State of U.S. Women's Movement Organizations in the 1990s." *Women & Politics* 21(4): 39–76.

Djelic, Marie-Laure, and Antti Ainamo. 1999. "The Coevolution of New Organizational Forms in the Fashion Industry: A Historical and Comparative Study of France, Italy, and the United States." *Organization Science* 10(5): 622–37.

Doorley, John, and Helio Fred Garcia. 2007. *Reputation Management: The Key to Successful Public Relations and Corporate Communication.* New York: Routledge.

Dowling, John, and Jeffrey Pfeffer. 1975. "Organizational Legitimacy: Social Values and Organizational Behavior." *Pacific Sociological Review* 18(1): 122–36.

Dubin, Steven C. 1987. *Bureaucratizing the Muse: Public Funds and the Cultural Worker.* Chicago, IL: University of Chicago Press.

Duckles, Beth M., Mark A. Hager, and Joseph Galaskiewicz. 2005. "How Nonprofits Close: Using Narratives to Study Organizational Processes." Pp. 169–203 in *Qualitative Organizational Research: Best Papers from the Davis Conference on Qualitative Research,* ed. Kimberly D. Elsbach. Greenwich, CT: Information Age Publishing.

Eckstein, Susan. 2001. "Community as Gift-Giving: Collectivistic Roots of Volunteerism." *American Sociological Review* 66(6): 829–51.

Edwards, Richard C. 1979. *Contested Terrain: The Transformation of the Workplace in the Twentieth Century.* New York: Basic Books.

Ehrenreich, Barbara. 2001. *Nickel and Dimed: On (Not) Getting By in America.* New York: Henry Holt and Company.

Elsbach, Kimberly D. 1994. "Managing Organizational Legitimacy in the California Cattle Industry: The Construction and Effectiveness of Verbal Accounts." *Administrative Science Quarterly* 39(1): 57–88.

———. 2003. "Organizational Perception Management." *Research in Organizational Behavior* 25(1): 297–332.

Elsbach, Kimberly D., and Roderick M. Kramer. 1996. "Members' Responses to Organizational Identity Threats: Encountering and Countering the *Business Week* Rankings." *Administrative Science Quarterly* 41(3): 442–76.

Elsbach, Kimberly D., and Robert I. Sutton. 1992. "Acquiring Organizational Legitimacy through Illegitimate Actions: A Marriage of Institutional and Impression Management Theories." *Academy of Management Journal* 35(4): 699–738.

Entman, Robert M. 2003. *Projections of Power: Framing News, Public Opinion, and U.S. Foreign Policy.* Chicago, IL: University of Chicago Press.

Entman, Robert M., and Andrew Rojecki. 1993. "Freezing Out the Public: Elite and Media Framing of the U.S. Anti-Nuclear Movement." *Political Communication* 10: 155–73.

Espeland, Wendy Nelson. 1998. *The Struggle for Water: Politics, Rationality, and Identity in the Southwest.* Chicago, IL: University of Chicago Press.

Espeland, Wendy Nelson, and Michael Sauder. 2007. "Rankings and Reactivity: How Public Measures Recreate Social Worlds." *American Journal of Sociology* 113(1): 1–40.

Etzioni, Amitai. [1961] 1975. *A Comparative Analysis of Complex Organizations: On Power, Involvement, and Their Correlates.* Rev. ed. New York: Free Press.

Farrell, Michael P. 2001. *Collaborative Circles: Friendship Dynamics & Creative Work.* Chicago, IL: University of Chicago Press.

Feldman, Martha S., and Brian T. Pentland. 2003. "Reconceptualizing Organizational Routines as a Source of Flexibility and Change." *Administrative Science Quarterly* 48(1): 94–118.

Fennell, Mary L., and Jeffrey A. Alexander. 1993. "Perspectives on Organizational Change in the US Medical Care Sector." *Annual Review of Sociology* 19: 89–112.

Fine, Gary Alan. 2004. *Everyday Genius: Self-Taught Art and the Culture of Authenticity.* Chicago, IL: University of Chicago Press.

————. 2007. *Authors of the Storm: Meteorologists and the Culture of Prediction.* Chicago, IL: University of Chicago Press.

Finlay, William, and James E. Coverdill. 2002. *Headhunters: Matchmaking in the Labor Market.* Ithaca, NY: Cornell University Press.

Fisher, Dana R. 2006. *Activism, Inc.: How the Outsourcing of Grassroots Campaigns Is Strangling Progressive Politics in America.* Stanford, CA: Stanford University Press.

Fishman, Mark. 1980. *Manufacturing the News.* Austin: University of Texas Press.

Fiss, Peer C., and Edward J. Zajac. 2006. "The Symbolic Management of Strategic Change: Sensegiving via Framing and Decoupling." *Academy of Management Journal* 49(6): 1173–93.

Follett, Mary Parker. [1925] 1995. "Constructive Conflict." Pp. 67–87 in *Mary Parker Follett: Prophet of Management; A Celebration of Writings from the 1920s,* ed. Pauline Graham. Boston, MA: Harvard Business School Press.

Forbes, Linda C., and John M. Jermier. 2002. "The Institutionalization of Voluntary Organizational Greening and the Ideals of Environmentalism: Lessons about Official Culture from Symbolic Organization Theory." Pp. 194–213 in *Organizations, Policy, and the Natural Environment: Institutionalist and Strategic Perspectives,* ed. Andrew J. Hoffman and Marc J. Ventresca. Stanford, CA: Stanford University Press.

Forssell, Anders, and David Jansson. 1996. "The Logic of Organizational Transformation: On the Conversion of Non-Business Organizations." Pp. 93–115 in *Translating Organizational Change,* ed. Barbara Czarniawska and Guje Sevon. New York: Walter de Gruyter & Co.

Foucault, Michel. 1995. *Discipline and Punish: The Birth of a Prison.* Translated by Alan Sheridan. New York: Vintage Books.

Freeman, Jo (Joreen). 1973. "The Tyranny of Structurelessness." Pp. 285–99 in *Radical Feminism,* ed. Anne Koedt, Ellen Levine, and Anita Rapone. New York: Quadrangle Books.

————. 1976. "Trashing: The Dark Side of Sisterhood." *Ms.,* April 1976, 49–51, 92–98.

Freeman, Richard B. 1997. "Working for Nothing: The Supply of Volunteer Labor." *Journal of Labor Economics* 15(1): S140–66.

Freeman, Richard B., and Joel Rogers. [1999] 2006. *What Workers Want.* Ithaca, NY: Cornell University Press.

Frumkin, Peter. 2002. *On Being Nonprofit: A Conceptual and Policy Primer.* Cambridge, MA: Harvard University Press.

Frumkin, Peter, and Joseph Galaskiewicz. 2004. "Institutional Isomorphism and Public Sector Organizations." *Journal of Public Administration Research and Theory* 14(3): 283–307.

Frynas, Jedrzej George. 2005. "The False Developmental Promise of Corporate Social Responsibility: Evidence from Multinational Oil Companies." *International Affairs* 81(3): 581–98.

Galaskiewicz, Joseph. 1985. "Interorganizational Relations." *Annual Review of Sociology* 11: 281–304.

Galaskiewicz, Joseph, and Wolfgang Bielefeld. 1998. *Nonprofit Organizations in an Age of Uncertainty.* Hawthorne, NY: Walter de Gruyter.

Galaskiewicz, Joseph, and Michelle Sinclair Colman. 2006. "Collaboration between Corporations and Nonprofit Organizations." Pp. 180–204 in *The Nonprofit Sector: A Research Handbook,* 2nd ed., ed. Walter W. Powell and Richard Steinberg. New Haven, CT: Yale University Press.

Gamson, William A. 1988. "Political Discourse and Collective Action." *International Social Movement Research* 1: 219–44.

Gamson, William A., David Croteau, William Hoynes, and Theodore Sasson. 1992. "Media Images and the Social Construction of Reality." *Annual Review of Sociology* 18: 373–93.

Gamson, William A., and David S. Meyer 1996. "Framing Political Opportunity." Pp. 275–90 in *Comparative Perspectives on Social Movements: Political Opportunities, Mobilizing Structures, and Cultural Framings,* ed. Doug McAdam, John D. McCarthy, and Mayer N. Zald. New York: Cambridge University Press.

Gamson, William A., and David Stuart. 1992. "Media Discourse as a Symbolic Contest: The Bomb in Political Cartoons." *Sociological Forum* 7(1): 55–86.

Gamson, William A., and Gadi Wolfsfeld. 1993. "Movements and Media as Interacting Systems." *Annals of the American Academy of Political and Social Science* 528: 114–25.

Gans, Herbert J. 1979. *Deciding What's News: A Study of CBS Evening News, NBC Nightly News, Newsweek, and Time.* New York: Pantheon Books.

Gilmore, Lee, and Mark Van Proyen, eds. 2005. *Afterburn: Reflections on Burning Man.* Albuquerque: New Mexico Press.

Gitlin, Todd. 2003. *The Whole World is Watching: Mass Media in the Making and Unmaking of the New Left.* Berkeley: University of California Press.

Glassner, Barry. 1999. *The Culture of Fear: Why Americans are Afraid of the Wrong Things.* New York: Basic Books.

Goffman, Erving. 1961. *Asylums: Essays on the Social Situation of Mental Patients and Other Inmates.* Garden City, NY: Anchor Books.

———. 1974. *Frame Analysis: An Essay on the Organization of Experience.* New York: Harper & Row.

Gordon, C. Wayne, and Nicholas Babchuk. 1959. "A Typology of Voluntary Associations." *American Sociological Review* 24(1): 22–29.

Gouldner, Alvin W. 1954. *Patterns of Industrial Bureaucracy.* New York: Free Press.

Graham, Laurie. 1995. *On the Line at Subaru-Isuzu: The Japanese Model and the American Worker.* Ithaca, NY: ILR Press.

Grams, Diane. 2008. "Building Arts Participation through Transactions, Relationships, or Both." Pp. 13–37 in *Entering Cultural Communities: Diversity and Change in the Nonprofit Arts,* ed. Diane Grams and Betty Farrell. New Brunswick, NJ: Rutgers University Press.

Granovetter, Mark S. 1973. "The Strength of Weak Ties." *American Journal of Sociology* 78(6): 1360–80.

———. 1995. *Getting a Job: A Study of Contacts and Careers.* Chicago, IL: University of Chicago Press.

Greenberg, Edward S. 1984. "Producer Cooperatives and Democratic Theory: The Case of the Plywood Firms." Pp. 171–214 in *Worker Cooperatives in America,* ed. Robert Jackall and Henry M. Levin. Berkeley: University of California Press.

Greenwood, Davydd J., and José Luis González Santos. 1991. *Industrial Democracy as Process: Participatory Action Research in the Fagor Cooperative Group of Mondragón.* Assen, Sweden: Van Gorcum & Comp B.V.

Greenwood, Royston, and Roy Suddaby. 2006. "Institutional Entrepreneurship in Mature Fields: The Big Five Accounting Firms." *Academy of Management Journal* 49(1): 27–48.

Greiner, Larry E. 1972. "Evolution and Revolution as Organizations Grow." *Harvard Business Review* 50: 37–46.

Griswold, Wendy. 1994. *Cultures and Societies in a Changing World.* Thousand Oaks, CA: Pine Forge Press.

Gumport, Patricia J., and Stuart K. Snydman. 2006. "Higher Education: Evolving Forms and Emerging Markets." Pp. 462–84 in *The Nonprofit Sector: A Research Handbook,* 2nd ed., ed. Walter W. Powell and Richard Steinberg. New Haven, CT: Yale University.

Guo, Chao, and Muhittin Acar. 2005. "Understanding Collaboration among Nonprofit Organizations: Combining Resource Dependency, Institutional, and Network Perspectives." *Nonprofit and Voluntary Sector Quarterly* 34(3): 340–61.

Guthrie, Doug. 1999. *Dragon in a Three-Piece Suit: The Emergence of Capitalism in China.* Princeton, NJ: Princeton University Press.

Hackman, J. Richard. 2002. *Leading Teams: Setting the Stage for Great Performances.* Boston, MA: Harvard Business School Press.

Hackman, J. Richard, and Greg R. Oldham. 1980. *Work Redesign.* Reading, MA: Addison-Wesley.

Hackman, J. Richard, and Ruth Wageman. 1995. "Total Quality Management: Empirical, Conceptual, and Practical Issues." *Administrative Science Quarterly* 40(2): 309–42.

Hager, Mark A., Joseph Galaskiewicz, and Jeff A. Larson. 2004. "Structural Embeddedness and the Liability of Newness among Nonprofit Organizations." *Public Management Review* 6(2): 159–88.

Hall, John R., with Philip D. Schuyler and Sylvaine Trinh. 2000. *Apocalypse Observed: Religious Movements and Violence in North America, Europe, and Japan.* New York: Routledge.

Hamill, Susan Pace. 1996. "The Limited Liability Company: A Catalyst Exposing the Corporate Integration Question." *Michigan Law Review* 95(2): 393–446.

Hamper, Ben. 1991. *Rivethead: Tales from the Assembly Line.* New York: Warner Books.

Hannan, Michael T., and Glenn R. Carroll. 1992. *Dynamics of Organizational Populations: Density, Legitimation, and Competition.* New York: Oxford University Press.

Harrison, Bennett. 1994. *Lean and Mean: The Changing Landscape of Corporate Power in the Age of Flexibility.* New York: Basic Books.

Harvey, Larry. 1997. "Not Art about Society: Art That Generates Society: The Burning Man—An Oral History." Pp. 132–34 in *Burning Man,* ed. Brad Wieners. San Francisco: HardWired.

———. 2000. "La Vie Bohème: Bohemian Values, Populist Politics, and the New Avant-Garde." Transcribed talk, February 24, Walker Art Center, Minneapolis, Minnesota. Accessed at http://www.burningman.com/whatisburningman/lectures/la_vie.html; http://www.burningman.com/whatisburningman/lectures/la_vie2.html; http://

www.burningman.com/whatisburningman/lectures/la_vie3.html; and http://www
.burningman.com/whatisburningman/lectures/la_vie4.html.

Haveman, Heather A., and Hayagreeva Rao. 1997. "Structuring a Theory of Moral Senti-
ments: Institutional and Organizational Coevolution in the Early Thrift Industry." *American Journal of Sociology* 102(6): 1606–51.

Healy, Kieran. 2004. "Altruism as an Organizational Problem: The Case of Organ Procure-
ment." *American Sociological Review* 69(3): 387–404.

———. 2006. *Last Best Gifts: Altruism and the Market for Human Blood and Organs.* Chicago, IL:
University of Chicago Press.

Heckscher, Charles. 1994. "Defining the Post-Bureaucratic Type." Pp. 14–62 in *The Post-
Bureaucratic Organization: New Perspectives on Organizational Change,* ed. Charles Heckscher and Anne Donnellon. Thousand Oaks, CA: Sage Publications.

Heller, Frank. 1998. "Playing the Devil's Advocate: Limits to Influence Sharing in Theory
and Practice." Pp. 144–89 in *Organizational Participation: Myth and Reality,* ed. Frank
Heller, Eugen Pusic, George Strauss, and Bernhard Wilpert. Oxford: Oxford University
Press.

Heller, Frank, Eugen Pusic, George Strauss, and Bernhard Wilpert, eds. 1998. *Organizational
Participation: Myth and Reality.* Oxford: Oxford University Press.

Hernandez, Sarah. 2006. "Striving for Control: Democracy and Oligarchy at a Mexican
Cooperative." *Economic and Industrial Democracy* 27(1): 105–35.

Hewlett, Sylvia Ann, and Carolyn Buck Luce. 2005. "Off-Ramps and On-Ramps: Keeping
Talented Women on the Road to Success." *Harvard Business Review* 83(3): 43–46, 48,
50–54.

Hochschild, Arlie Russell. 1983. *The Managed Heart: Commercialization of Human Feeling.*
Berkeley: University of California Press.

———. [1983] 2003. *The Second Shift.* New York: Penguin.

Hodson, Randy. 2001. *Dignity at Work.* New York: Cambridge University Press.

Hodson, Randy, and Vincent J. Roscigno. 2004. "Organizational Success and Worker Dignity:
Complementary or Contradictory?" *American Journal of Sociology* 110(3): 672–708.

Hodson, Randy, Vincent J. Roscigno, and Stephen H. Lopez. 2006. "Chaos and the Abuse
of Power: Workplace Bullying in Organizational and Interactional Context." *Work and
Occupations* 33(4): 382–416.

Hoffman, Andrew J. 1999. "Institutional Evolution and Change: Environmentalism and the
U.S. Chemical Industry." *Academy of Management Journal* 42(4): 351–71.

———. 2001. *From Heresy to Dogma: An Institutional History of Corporate Environmentalism.*
Stanford, CA: Stanford University Press.

Hoffman, Elizabeth A. 2006. "The Ironic Value of Loyalty: Dispute Resolution Strategies in
Worker Cooperatives and Conventional Organizations." *Nonprofit Management & Leadership* 17(2): 163–77.

Hondagneu-Sotelo, Pierrette. 2001. *Doméstica: Immigrant Workers Cleaning and Caring in the
Shadows of Affluence.* Berkeley: University of California Press.

Hsu, Greta, and Michael T. Hannan. 2005. "Identities, Genres, and Organizational Forms."
Organization Science 16(5): 474–90.

Hunt, Jennifer. 1985. "Police Accounts of Normal Force." *Urban Life* 13(4): 315–41.

Hyde, Lewis. [1979] 1983. *The Gift: Imagination and the Erotic Life of Property.* New York:
Random House.

Iannaccone, Laurence R. 1994. "Why Strict Churches Are Strong." *American Journal of Sociology* 99(5): 1180–211.

Iannello, Kathleen P. 1992. *Decisions Without Hierarchy: Feminist Interventions in Organization Theory and Practice.* New York: Routledge.

Jackall, Robert. 1978. *Workers in a Labyrinth: Jobs and Survival in a Bank Bureaucracy.* Montclair, NJ: Allanheld, Osmun & Co.

———. 1984. "Paradoxes of Collective Work: A Study of the Cheeseboard, Berkeley, California." Pp. 109–35 in *Worker Cooperatives in America,* ed. Robert Jackall and Henry M. Levin. Berkeley: University of California Press.

———. 1988. *Moral Mazes: The World of Corporate Managers.* New York: Oxford Press.

Jackall, Robert, and Joyce Crain. 1984. "The Shape of the Small Worker Cooperative Movement." Pp. 88–108 in *Worker Cooperatives in America,* ed. Robert Jackall and Henry M. Levin. Berkeley: University of California Press.

Jackall, Robert, and Janice M. Hirota. 2000. *Image Makers: Advertising, Public Relations, and the Ethos of Advocacy.* Chicago, IL: University of Chicago Press.

Jacobs, Jerry A., and Kathleen Gerson. 2004. *The Time Divide: Work, Family, and Gender Inequality.* Cambridge, MA: Harvard University Press.

Janis, Irving. 1982. *Group-think: Psychological Studies of Policy Decisions and Fiascos.* 2nd ed. Boston, MA: Houghton Mifflin.

Jasper, James M. 2004. "A Strategic Approach to Collective Action: Looking for Agency in Social-Movement Choices." *Mobilization: An International Journal* 9(1): 1–16.

———. 2006. *Getting Your Way: Strategic Dilemmas in the Real World.* Chicago, IL: University of Chicago Press.

Johnson, Victoria. 2007. "What Is Organizational Imprinting? Cultural Entrepreneurship in the Founding of the Paris Opera." *American Journal of Sociology* 113(1): 97–127.

Jones, Derek C., and Donald J. Schneider. 1984. "Self-Help Production Cooperatives: Government-Administered Cooperatives during the Depression." Pp. 57–84 in *Worker Cooperatives in America,* ed. Robert Jackall and Henry M. Levin. Berkeley: University of California Press.

Jones, Peggy McGuckian. 1980. *Emigrant Trails in the Black Rock Desert: A Study of the Fremont, Applegate-Lassen, and Nobles' Routes in the Winnemucca District.* Technical Report no. 6. U.S. Department of the Interior Bureau of Land Management.

Kalleberg, Arne L., Peter V. Marsden, Jeremy Reynolds, and David Knoke. 2006. "Beyond Profit? Sectoral Differences in High-Performance Work Practices." *Work and Occupations* 33(3): 271–302.

Kaminer, Wendy. 1984. *Women Volunteering: The Pleasure, Pain, and Politics of Unpaid Work from 1830 to the Present.* Garden City, NY: Anchor.

Kanter, Rosabeth Moss. 1968. "Commitment and Social Organization: A Study of Commitment Mechanisms in Utopian Communities." *American Sociological Review* 33(4): 499–517.

———. 1972. *Commitment and Community: Communes and Utopias in Sociological Perspective.* Cambridge, MA: Harvard University Press.

———. 1977. *Men and Women of the Corporation.* New York: Basic Books.

Kaplan, Marilyn R., and J. Richard Harrison. 1993. "Defusing the Director Liability Crisis: The Strategic Management of Legal Threats." *Organization Science* 4(3): 412–32.

Kelley, Margaret S., Howard Lune, and Sheigla Murphy. 2005. "Doing Syringe Exchange:

Organizational Transformation and Volunteer Commitment." *Nonprofit and Voluntary Sector Quarterly* 34(3): 362–86.

Kennedy, Mark. 2008. "Getting Counted: Markets, Media, and Reality." *American Sociological Review* 73(2): 270–95.

Khurana, Rakesh. 2002. *Searching for a Corporate Savior: The Irrational Quest for Charismatic CEOs.* Princeton, NJ: Princeton University Press.

Kielbowicz, Richard B., and Clifford Scherer. 1986. "The Role of the Press in the Dynamics of Social Movements." *Research in Social Movements, Conflicts and Changes* 9: 71–96.

Kleinman, Sherryl. 1996. *Opposing Ambitions: Gender and Identity in an Alternative Organization.* Chicago, IL: University of Chicago Press.

Knoke, David. 1981. "Commitment and Detachment in Voluntary Associations." *American Sociological Review* 46(2): 141–58.

———. 1988. "Incentives in Collective Action Organizations." *American Sociological Review* 53(3): 311–29.

Kondo, Dorinne K. 1990. *Crafting Selves: Power, Gender, and Discourses of Identity in a Japanese Workplace.* Chicago, IL: University of Chicago Press.

Koopmans, Ruud. 2004. "Movements and Media: Selection Processes and Evolutionary Dynamics in the Public Sphere." *Theory and Society* 33(3–4): 367–91.

Koopmans, Ruud, and Susan Olzak. 2004. "Discursive Opportunities and the Evolution of Right-Wing Violence in Germany." *American Journal of Sociology* 110(1): 198–230.

Kozinets, Robert V. 2002. "Can Consumers Escape the Market? Emancipatory Illuminations from Burning Man." *Journal of Consumer Research* 29: 20–38.

Kristen, Christine. 2003. "The Outsider Art of Burning Man." *Leonardo* 36(5): 343–48.

———. 2007. "Playing with Fire." *Leonardo* 40(4): 332–37.

Kunda, Gideon. 1992. *Engineering Culture: Control and Commitment in a High-Tech Corporation.* Philadelphia, PA: Temple University Press.

Lalich, Janja. 2004. *Bounded Choice: True Believers and Charismatic Cults.* Berkeley: University of California Press.

Langer, Ellen J. 1989. *Mindfulness.* Reading, MA: Addison-Wesley.

Laumann, Edward O., Peter Marsden, and David Prensky. 1983. "The Boundary Specification Problem in Network Analysis." Pp. 18–35 in *Applied Network Analysis,* ed. Ronald S. Burt and Michael J. Minor. Beverly Hills, CA: Sage.

Lauricella, Thomas. 2006. "Merrill's Funds will Now Carry Princeton Name." *Wall Street Journal,* January 30, C9.

Lawrence, Paul R., and Jay W. Lorsch. 1967. *Organization and Environment: Managing Differentiation and Integration.* Boston, MA: Graduate School of Business Administration, Harvard University.

Lee, Caroline W. 2007. "Is There a Place for Private Conversation in Public Dialogue? Comparing Stakeholder Assessments of Informal Communication in Collaborative Regional Planning." *American Journal of Sociology* 113(1): 41–96.

Lee, Ching Kwan. 1998. *Gender and the South China Miracle: Two Worlds of Factory Women.* Berkeley: University of California Press.

Lee, Fiona, Amy Edmondson, Stefan Thomke, and Monica Worline. 2004. "The Mixed Effects of Inconsistency on Experimentation in Organizations." *Organization Science* 15(3): 310–26.

Leidner, Robin. 1991. "Stretching the Boundaries of Liberalism: Democratic Innovation in a Feminist Organization." *Signs: Journal of Women in Culture and Society* 16(2): 263–89.

———. 1993. *Fast Food, Fast Talk.* Berkeley: University of California Press.

Lette, Laura. 2006. "Work in the Nonprofit Sector." Pp. 159–79 in *The Nonprofit Sector: A Research Handbook,* 2nd ed., ed. Walter W. Powell and Richard Steinberg. New Haven, CT: Yale University Press.

Levi, Margaret, and Gillian H. Murphy. 2006. "Coalitions of Contention: The Case of the WTO Protests in Seattle." *Political Studies* 54(4): 651–70.

Lewin, Arie Y., Chris P. Long, and Timothy N. Carroll. 1999. "The Coevolution of New Organizational Forms." *Organization Science* 10(5): 535–50.

Liebow, Elliot. 1967. *Tally's Corner: A Study of Negro Streetcorner Men.* Boston, MA: Little, Brown & Co.

Linder, Andrew M. 2008. "Controlling the Media in Iraq." *Contexts* 7(2): 32–38.

Lootsma, Bart. 2000. "Erotic Maneuvers: Jan Kapsenberg's Research into Gay Software." *Hunch: The Berlage Institute Report* 2 (Summer): 20–31.

Lopez, Steven Henry. 2004. *Reorganizing the Rust Belt: An Inside Study of the American Labor Movement.* Berkeley: University of California Press.

Lounsbury, Michael, and Mary Ann Glynn. 2001. "Cultural Entrepreneurship: Stories, Legitimacy, and the Acquisition of Resources." *Strategic Management Journal* 22(6/7): 545–64.

Lounsbury, Michael, Marc Ventresca, and Paul M. Hirsch. 2003. "Social Movements, Field Frames and Industry Emergence: A Cultural-Political Perspective on US Recycling." *Socio-Economic Review* 1(1): 71–104.

Lune, Howard. 2002. "Weathering the Storm: Nonprofit Organization Survival Strategies in a Hostile Climate." *Nonprofit and Voluntary Sector Quarterly* 31(4): 463–83.

———. 2007. *Urban Action Networks: HIV/AIDS and Community Organizing in New York City.* Lanham, MD: Rowman and Littlefield Publishers.

Mansbridge, Jane J. 1983. *Beyond Adversary Democracy.* Chicago, IL: University of Chicago Press.

Marchand, Roland. 1998. *Creating the Corporate Soul: The Rise of Public Relations and Corporate Imagery in American Big Business.* Berkeley: University of California Press.

Markowitz, Lisa, and Karen W. Tice. 2002. "Paradoxes of Professionalization: Parallel Dilemmas in Women's Organizations in the Americas." *Gender & Society* 16(6): 941–58.

Marsden, Peter V. 1994. "The Hiring Process: Recruitment Methods." *American Behavioral Scientist* 37(7): 979–91.

———. 2005. "The Sociology of James S. Coleman." *Annual Review of Sociology* 31(1): 1–24.

Martin, Joanne. 1992. *Cultures in Organizations.* New York: Oxford University Press.

Martin, Joanne, Kathleen Knopoff, and Christine Beckman. 1998. "An Alternative to Bureaucratic Impersonality and Emotional Labor: Bounded Emotionality at The Body Shop." *Administrative Science Quarterly* 43(2): 429–69.

Martin, Patricia Yancey. 1990. "Rethinking Feminist Organizations." *Gender & Society* 4(2): 182–206.

———. 2005. *Rape Work: Victims, Gender, and Emotions in Organization and Community Context.* New York: Routledge.

Marwell, Nicole P. 2004. "Privatizing the Welfare State: Nonprofit Community-Based Organizations as Political Actors." *American Sociological Review* 69(2): 265–91.

———. 2007. *Bargaining for Brooklyn: Community Organizations in the Entrepreneurial City.* Chicago, IL: University of Chicago Press.

Marwell, Nicole P., and Paul-Brian McInerney. 2005. "The Nonprofit/For-Profit Continuum: Theorizing the Dynamics of Mixed-Form Markets." *Nonprofit and Voluntary Sector Quarterly* 34(1): 7–28.

Marx, Karl. [1844] 1978. "Economic and Philosophic Manuscripts of 1844." Pp. 66–125 in *The Marx-Engels Reader*, 2nd ed., ed. Robert C. Tucker. New York: W. W. Norton.

Marx, Karl, and Friedrich Engels. [1848] 1978. "Manifesto of the Communist Party." Pp. 469–500 in *The Marx-Engels Reader*, 2nd ed., ed. Robert C. Tucker. New York: W. W. Norton.

Matthews, Nancy A. 1994. *Confronting Rape: The Feminist Anti-Rape Movement and the State.* New York: Routledge.

Mayhew, Leon. 1968. "Ascription in Modern Societies." *Sociological Inquiry* 38(2): 105–20.

McAdam, Doug. 1986. "Recruitment to High-Risk Activism: The Case of Freedom Summer." *American Journal of Sociology* 92(1): 64–90.

———. 1996. "The Framing Function of Movement Tactics: Strategic Dramaturgy in the American Civil Rights Movement." Pp. 338–55 in *Comparative Perspectives on Social Movements: Political Opportunities, Mobilizing Structures, and Cultural Framings*, ed. Doug McAdam, John D. McCarthy, and Mayer N. Zald. New York: Cambridge University Press.

McGeehan, Patrick. 2006. "How to Get to Princeton? Just Try Using Its Name." *New York Times*, February 2, B4.

McPherson, Miller, Lynn Smith-Lovin, and Matthew E. Brashears. 2006. "Social Isolation in America: Changes in Core Discussion Networks over Two Decades." *American Sociological Review* 71(3): 353–75.

McPherson, Miller, Lynn Smith-Lovin, and James M. Cook. 2001. "Birds of a Feather: Homophily in Social Networks." *Annual Review of Sociology* 27: 415–44.

Merton, Robert K. 1936. "The Unanticipated Consequences of Purposive Social Action." *American Sociological Review* 1(6): 894–904.

Meyer, John, and Brian Rowan. 1977. "Institutionalized Organizations: Formal Structure as Myth and Ceremony." *American Journal of Sociology* 83(2): 340–63.

Michels, Robert. [1915] 1962. *Political Parties: A Sociological Study of the Oligarchical Tendencies of Modern Democracy.* New York: The Free Press.

Miles, Robert H. 1982. *Coffin Nails and Corporate Strategy.* Englewood Cliffs, NJ: Prentice Hall.

Miller, Karen S. 1999. *The Voice of Business: Hill & Knowlton and Postwar Public Relations.* Chapel Hill: University of North Carolina Press.

Miller, Laura J. 2006. *Reluctant Capitalists: Bookselling and the Culture of Consumption.* Chicago, IL: University of Chicago Press.

Milkman, Ruth. 1997. *Farewell to the Factory: Auto Workers in the Late Twentieth Century.* Berkeley: University of California Press.

Milofsky, Carl. 1988. "Structure and Process in Community Self-Help Organizations." Pp. 183–216 in *Community Organization: Studies in Resource Mobilization and Exchange*, ed. Carl Milofsky. New York: Oxford University Press.

Miner, Anne S. 1987. "Idiosyncratic Jobs in Formalized Organizations." *Administrative Science Quarterly* 32(3): 327–51.

———. 1990. "Structural Evolution through Idiosyncratic Jobs: The Potential for Unplanned Learning." *Organization Science* 1(2): 195–210.

Minkoff, Debra C. 1999. "Bending with the Wind: Strategic Change and Adaptation by Women's and Radical Minority Organizations." *American Journal of Sociology* 104(6): 1666–1703.

———. 2002. "The Emergence of Hybrid Organizational Forms: Combining Identity-Based Service Provision and Political Action." *Nonprofit and Voluntary Sector Quarterly* 31(3): 377–401.

Minkoff, Debra C., and Walter W. Powell. 2006. "Nonprofit Mission: Constancy, Responsiveness, or Deflection?" Pp. 591–611 in *The Nonprofit Sector: A Research Handbook,* 2nd ed., ed. Walter W. Powell and Richard Steinberg. New Haven, CT: Yale University Press.

Mintzberg, Henry. 1993. *Structure in Fives: Designing Effective Organizations.* Englewood Cliffs, NJ: Prentice-Hall.

Morrill, Calvin. 1995. *The Executive Way: Conflict Management in Corporations.* Chicago, IL: University of Chicago Press.

Morris, Aldon D. 1986. *The Origins of the Civil Rights Movement: Black Communities Organizing for Change.* New York: Free Press.

Mumby, Dennis K., and Cynthia Stohl. 1991. "Power and Discourse in Organization Studies: Absence and the Dialectic of Control." *Discourse and Society* 2(3): 313–32.

Murmann, Johann Peter. 2003. *Knowledge and Competitive Advantage: The Coevolution of Firms, Technology, and National Institutions.* New York: Cambridge University Press.

Nemeth, Charlan Jeanne, and Barry M. Staw. 1989. "The Tradeoffs of Social Control and Innovation in Groups and Organizations." *Advances in Experimental Social Psychology* 22: 175–210. New York: Academic Press.

Newman, Katherine. 1980. "Incipient Bureaucracy: The Development of Hierarchies in Egalitarian Organizations." Pp. 143–63 in *Hierarchy & Society: Anthropological Perspectives on Bureaucracy,* ed. Gerald M. Britan and Ronald Cohen. Philadelphia, PA: Institute for the Study of Human Issues.

Niman, Michael I. 1997. *People of the Rainbow: A Nomadic Utopia.* Knoxville: University of Tennessee Press.

Nyden, Philip W. 1985. "Democratizing Organizations: A Case Study of a Union Reform Movement." *American Journal of Sociology* 90(6): 1179–1203.

Oakes, Leslie S., Barbara Townley, and David J. Cooper. 1998. "Business Planning as Pedagogy: Language and Control in a Changing Institutional Field." *Administrative Science Quarterly* 43(2): 257–92.

Oerton, Sarah. 1996. *Beyond Hierarchy: Gender, Sexuality, and the Social Economy.* London: Taylor & Francis.

Ogasawara, Yuko. 1998. *Office Ladies and Salaried Men: Power, Gender, and Work in Japanese Companies.* Berkeley: University of California Press.

Oliver, Christine. 1991. "Strategic Responses to Institutional Processes." *Academy of Management Review* 16(1): 145–79.

Osterman, Paul. 2006. "Overcoming Oligarchy: Culture and Agency in Social Movement Organizations." *Administrative Science Quarterly* 51(4): 622–49.

Ostrander, Susan A. 1995. *Money for Change: Social Movement Philanthropy at Haymarket People's Fund.* Philadelphia, PA: Temple University Press.

Ostrower, Francie. 1995. *Why the Wealthy Give: The Culture of Elite Philanthropy.* Princeton, NJ: Princeton University Press.

Parks Daloz, Laurent A., Cheryl H. Keen, James P. Keen, and Sharon Daloz Parks. 1996. *Common Fire: Lives of Commitment in a Complex World.* Boston, MA: Beacon Press.

Pearce, Jone L. 1993. *Volunteers: The Organizational Behavior of Unpaid Workers.* New York: Routledge.

Pellow, David N. 1999. "Framing Emerging Environmental Movement Tactics: Mobilizing Consensus, Demobilizing Conflict." *Sociological Forum* 14(4): 659–83.

Perlow, Leslie A. 1998. "Boundary Control: The Social Ordering of Work and Family Time in a High-tech Corporation." *Administrative Science Quarterly* 43(2): 328–57.

Perrow, Charles. 1986. *Complex Organizations.* 3rd ed. New York: Random House.

Pfeffer, Jeffrey, and Gerald R. Salancik. 1978. *The External Control of Organizations: A Resource Dependence Perspective.* New York: Harper and Row.

Piven, Frances Fox, and Richard A. Cloward. [1977] 1979. *Poor People's Movements: Why They Succeed, How They Fail.* New York: Pantheon Books.

Podolny, Joel M. 2005. *Status Signals: A Sociological Study of Market Competition.* Princeton, NJ: Princeton University Press.

Podolny, Joel M., and Karen L. Page. 1998. "Network Forms of Organization." *Annual Review of Sociology* 24: 57–76.

Polletta, Francesca. 2002. *Freedom Is an Endless Meeting: Democracy in American Social Movements.* Chicago, IL: University of Chicago Press.

Pólos, László, Michael T. Hannan, and Glenn R. Carroll. 2002. "Foundations of a Theory of Social Forms." *Industrial and Corporate Change* 11(1): 85–115.

Popielarz, Pamela A., and J. Miller McPherson. 1995. "On the Edge or In Between: Niche Position, Niche Overlap, and the Duration of Voluntary Association Memberships." *American Journal of Sociology* 101(3): 698–720.

Popkin, Ann Hunter. 1978. "Bread and Roses: An Early Movement in the Development of Socialist-Feminism." PhD dissertation, Department of Sociology, Brandeis University, Waltham, MA.

Powell, Walter. 1990. "Neither Market nor Hierarchy: Network Forms of Organization." *Research in Organizational Behavior,* ed. Larry Cummings and Barry Staw, 12: 295–336. Greenwich, CT: JAI Press.

Powell, Walter W., and Rebecca Friedkin. 1987. "Organizational Change in Nonprofit Organizations." Pp. 180–92 in *The Nonprofit Sector: A Research Handbook,* 1st ed., ed. Walter W. Powell. New Haven, CT: Yale University Press.

Putnam, Robert D. 2000. *Bowling Alone: The Collapse and Revival of American Community.* New York: Simon & Schuster.

Rao, Hayagreeva. 1998. "Caveat Emptor: The Construction of Nonprofit Consumer Watchdog Organizations." *American Journal of Sociology* 103(4): 912–61.

Rao, Hayagreeva, Calvin Morrill, and Mayer N. Zald. 2000. "Power Plays: How Social Movements and Collective Action Create New Organizational Forms." *Research in Organizational Behavior* 22: 239–82.

Raz, Aviad E. 1999. *Riding the Black Ship: Japan and Tokyo Disneyland.* Cambridge, MA: Harvard University Press.

Reinelt, Claire. 1995. "Moving onto the Terrain of the State: The Battered Women's Movement and the Politics of Engagement." Pp. 84–104 in *Feminist Organizations: Harvest of the New Women's Movement,* ed. Myra Marx Ferree and Patricia Yancey Martin. Philadelphia, PA: Temple University Press.

Reskin, Barbara F., and Debra Branch McBrier. 2000. "Why Not Ascription? Organizations' Employment of Male and Female Managers." *American Sociological Review* 65(2): 210–33.

Riger, Stephanie. 1984. "Vehicles for Empowerment: The Case of Feminist Movement Organizations." Pp. 99–117 in *Studies in Empowerment: Steps toward Understanding and Action,* ed. Julian Rappaport, Carolyn Swift, and Robert Hess. New York: Haworth.

———. 1994. "Challenges of Success: Stages of Growth in Feminist Organizations." *Feminist Studies* 20(2): 275–300.

Robinson, Greg. 2001. *By Order of the President: FDR and the Internment of Japanese Americans.* Cambridge, MA: Harvard University Press.

Rojas, Fabio. 2007. *From Black Power to Black Studies: How a Radical Social Movement Became an Academic Discipline.* Baltimore, MD: John Hopkins Press.

Roscigno, Vincent J., and Randy Hodson. 2004. "The Organizational and Social Foundations of Worker Resistance." *American Sociological Review* 69(1): 14–39.

Rothschild, Joyce. 2000. "Creating a Just and Democratic Workplace: More Engagement, Less Hierarchy." *Contemporary Sociology* 29(1): 195–213.

Rothschild, Joyce, and Darcy Leach. 2006. "Avoid, Talk, or Fight: Alternative Cultural Strategies in the Battle against Oligarchy in Collectivist-Democratic Organizations." Pp. 346–61 in *Handbook of Community Movements and Local Organizations,* ed. Ram A. Cnaan and Carl Milofsky. New York: Springer.

Rothschild, Joyce, and Terance D. Miethe. 1999. "Whistle-Blower Disclosures and Management Retaliation." *Work and Occupations* 26(1): 107–28.

Rothschild, Joyce, and Carl Milofsky. 2006. "The Centrality of Values, Passions, and Ethics in the Nonprofit Sector." *Nonprofit Management & Leadership* 17(2): 137–43.

Rothschild, Joyce, and Marjukka Ollilainen. 1999. "Obscuring but Not Reducing Managerial Control: Does TQM Measure Up to Democracy Standards?" *Economic and Industrial Democracy* 20(4): 583–623.

Rothschild, Joyce, and J. Allen Whitt. 1986. *The Cooperative Workplace: Potentials and Dilemmas of Organizational Democracy and Participation.* New York: Cambridge University Press.

Roy, Donald F. 1959. "'Banana Time': Job Satisfaction and Informal Interaction." *Human Organization* 18(3): 158–68.

Ruef, Martin. 2000. "The Emergence of Organizational Forms: A Community Ecology Approach." *American Journal of Sociology* 106(3): 658–714.

Ryan, Charlotte. 1991. *Prime Time Activism: Media Strategies for Grassroots Organizing.* Boston, MA: South End Press.

Ryan, Charlotte, Michael Anastario, and Karen Jeffreys. 2005. "Start Small, Build Big: Negotiating Opportunities in Media Markets." *Mobilization: An International Journal* 10(1): 111–28.

Sager, Anthony P. 1979. "Radical Law: Three Collectives in Cambridge." Pp. 136–50 in *Co-ops, Communes & Collectives: Experiments in Social Change in the 1960s and 1970s,* ed. John Case and Rosemary C. R. Taylor. New York: Pantheon Books.

Sampson, Robert J., Heather MacIndoe, Doug McAdam, and Simón Weffer-Elizondo. 2005. "Civil Society Reconsidered: The Durable Nature and Community Structure of Collective Civic Action." *American Journal of Sociology* 111(3): 673–714.

Samuels, David. 1999. "Rock is Dead: Sex, Drugs, and Raw Sewage at Woodstock 99." *Harper's Magazine,* November 1999, 69–74, 76–82.

Sauder, Michael, and Ryon Lancaster. 2006. "Do Rankings Matter? The Effects of *U.S. News & World Report* Rankings on the Admissions Process of Law Schools." *Law & Society Review* 40(1): 105–34.

Savitz, Andrew W., with Karl Weber. 2006. *The Triple Bottom Line: How Today's Best-Run*

Companies Are Achieving Economic, Social, and Environmental Success—And How You Can Too. San Francisco: Jossey-Bass.

Schein, Edgar H. 1992. *Organizational Culture and Leadership.* San Francisco: Jossey-Bass Inc.

Schmid, Hillel. 2006. "Leadership Styles and Leadership Change in Human and Community Service Organizations." *Nonprofit Management & Leadership* 17(2): 179–94.

Schmitt, Frederika E., and Patricia Yancey Martin. 1999. "Unobtrusive Mobilization by an Institutionalized Rape Crisis Center: 'All We Do Comes from Victims.'" *Gender and Society* 13(3): 364–84.

Schofer, Evan, and Marion Fourcade-Gourinchas. 2001. "The Structural Contexts of Civic Engagement: Voluntary Association Membership in Comparative Perspective." *American Sociological Review* 66(6): 806–28.

Schor, Juliet B. 1991. *The Overworked American: The Unexpected Decline of Leisure.* New York: Basic Books.

Schroeder, David A., Louis A. Penner, John F. Dovidio, and Jane A. Piliavin. 1995. *The Psychology of Helping and Altruism: Problems and Puzzles.* New York: McGraw-Hill.

Schwartzman, Helen B. 1989. *The Meeting.* New York: Plenum Press.

———. 1993. *Ethnography in Organizations.* Newbury Park, CA: Sage.

Scott, James C. 1990. *Domination and the Arts of Resistance: Hidden Transcripts.* New Haven, CT: Yale University Press.

Scott, W. Richard. 2008. *Institutions and Organizations: Ideas and Interests.* 3rd ed. Thousand Oaks, CA: Sage.

———. [1981] 2003. *Organizations: Rational, Natural, and Open Systems.* 5th ed. Englewood Cliffs, NJ: Prentice-Hall.

Scott, W. Richard, and Gerald F. Davis. 2007. *Organizations: Rational, Natural, and Open Systems.* Upper Saddle River, NJ: Prentice-Hall.

Scott, W. Richard, Martin Ruef, Peter J. Mendel, and Carol A. Caronna. 2000. *Institutional Change and Healthcare Organizations: From Professional Dominance to Managed Care.* Chicago, IL: University of Chicago Press.

Selznick, Philip. 1949. *TVA and the Grass Roots: A Study in the Sociology of Formal Organization.* Berkeley: University of California Press.

Seo, Myeong-Gu, and W. E. Douglas Creed. 2002. "Institutional Contradictions, Praxis, and Institutional Change: A Dialectical Perspective." *Academy of Management Review* 27(2): 222–47.

Sewell, Graham. 1998. "The Discipline of Teams: The Control of Team-based Industrial Work through Electronic and Peer Surveillance." *Administrative Science Quarterly* 43(2): 397–428.

Shaw, Randy. 1996. *The Activist's Handbook: A Primer for the 1990s and Beyond.* Berkeley: University of California Press.

Sherman, Rachel. 2007. *Class Acts: Service and Inequality in Luxury Hotels.* Berkeley: University of California Press.

Shipper, Frank, and Charles C. Manz. 1992. "Employee Self-Management without Formally Designated Teams: An Alternative Road to Empowerment." *Organizational Dynamics* 20(3): 48–61.

Shulman, David. 2007. *From Hire to Liar: The Role of Deception in the Workplace.* Ithaca, NY: Cornell University Press.

Silva, Lauren Rae. 2006. "Merrill Tunnels into BlackRock." February 15, 2006. http://www.thestreet.com/pf/stocks/brokerages/10268561.html.

Simmel, Georg. [1978] 2004. *The Philosophy of Money.* 3rd ed. New York: Routledge.

Simon, John, Harvey Dale, and Laura Chisolm. 2006. "The Federal Tax Treatment of Charitable Organizations." Pp. 267–306 in *The Nonprofit Sector: A Research Handbook,* 2nd ed., ed. Walter W. Powell and Richard Steinberg. New Haven, CT: Yale University Press.

Simons, Tal, and Paul Ingram. 2003. "Enemies of the State: The Interdependence of Institutional Forms and the Ecology of the Kibbutz, 1910–1997." *Administrative Science Quarterly* 48(4): 592–621.

Sirianni, Carmen. 1984. "Learning Pluralism: Democracy and Diversity in Feminist Organizations." Pp. 554–76 in *Critical Studies in Organization & Bureaucracy,* ed. Frank Fischer and Carmen Sirianni. Philadelphia, PA: Temple University Press.

Skocpol, Theda. 2003. *Diminished Democracy: From Membership to Management in American Civic Life.* Norman: University of Oklahoma Press.

Skocpol, Theda, Marshall Ganz, and Ziad Munson. 2000. "A Nation of Organizers: The Institutional Origins of Civic Voluntarism in the United States." *American Political Science Review* 94(3): 527–46.

Smith, Jackie, John D. McCarthy, Clark McPhail, and Boguslaw Augustyn. 2001. "From Protest to Agenda Building: Description Bias in Media Coverage of Protest Events in Washington, D.C." *Social Forces* 79(4): 1397–1423.

Snook, Scott A. 2000. *Friendly Fire: The Accidental Shootdown of U.S. Black Hawks over Northern Iraq.* Princeton, NJ: Princeton University Press.

Snow, Charles C., and Scott A. Snell. 1993. "Staffing as Strategy." Pp. 448–78 in *Personnel Selection in Organizations,* ed. Neal Schmitt, Walter C. Borman, and associates. San Francisco: Jossey-Bass.

Snow, David A., E. Burke Rochford, Jr., Steven K. Worden, and Robert D. Benford. 1986. "Frame Alignment Processes, Micromobilization, and Movement Participation." *American Sociological Review* 51(4): 464–81.

Snyder, Mark, and Allen M. Omoto. 2001. "Basic Research and Practical Problems: Volunteerism and the Psychology of Individual and Collective Action." Pp. 287–307 in *The Practice of Social Influence in Multiple Cultures,* ed. Wilhelmina Wosinska, Robert B. Cialdini, Daniel W. Barrett, and Janusz Reykowski. Mahwah, NJ: Lawrence Erlbaum Associates.

Sproull, Lee, and Sara Kiesler. 1986. "Reducing Social Context Cues: Electronic Mail in Organizational Communications." *Management Science* 32(11): 1492–1512.

Staggenborg, Suzanne. 1988. "The Consequences of Professionalization and Formalization in the Pro-Choice Movement." *American Sociological Review* 53(4): 585–605.

———. 1989. "Stability and Innovation in the Women's Movement: A Comparison of Two Movement Organizations." *Social Problems* 36(1): 75–92.

———. 1995. "Can Feminist Organizations Be Effective?" Pp. 339–55 in *Feminist Organizations: Harvest of the New Women's Movement,* ed. Myra Marx Ferree and Patricia Yancey Martin. Philadelphia, PA: Temple University Press.

Stark, Rodney, and William Sims Bainbridge. 1980. "Networks of Faith: Interpersonal Bonds and Recruitment to Cults and Sects." *American Journal of Sociology* 85(6): 1376–95.

Starr, Paul. 1979. "The Phantom Community." Pp. 245–73 in *Co-ops, Communes, and Collectives: Experiments in Social Change in the 1960s and 1970s,* ed. John Case and Rosemary C. R. Taylor. New York: Pantheon.

Staw, Barry M. 1976. *Intrinsic and Extrinsic Motivation.* Morristown, NJ: General Learning Press.

Staw, Barry M., Pamela I. McKechnie, and Sheila Puffer. 1983. "The Justification of Organizational Performance." *Administrative Science Quarterly* 28(4): 582–600.

Stern, Jessica. 2003. *Terror in the Name of God: Why Religious Militants Kill*. New York: Ecco.

Stewart, Greg L., and Kenneth P. Carson. 1997. "Moving Beyond the Mechanistic Model: An Alternative Approach to Staffing for Contemporary Organizations." *Human Resource Management Review* 7(2): 157–84.

Stewart, James B. 2007. "The Kona Files." *New Yorker,* Feb. 19 & 26, 152–67.

Stinchcombe, Arthur. 1965. "Social Structure and Organizations." Pp. 142–93 in *Handbook of Organizations,* ed. James G. March. Chicago, IL: Rand McNally.

Stohl, Cynthia, and George Cheney. 2001. "Participatory Processes/Paradoxical Practices: Communication and the Dilemmas of Organizational Democracy." *Management Communication Quarterly* 14(3): 349–407.

Stone, Melissa M. 1989. "Planning as Strategy in Nonprofit Organizations: An Exploratory Study." *Nonprofit and Voluntary Sector Quarterly* 18(4): 297–315.

Stone, Pamela. 2007. *Opting Out? Why Women Really Quit Careers and Head Home*. Berkeley: University of California Press.

Strand, Kerry J. 2007. "Reframing RC: Scandal and Meaning Making in a Charismatic Social Movement." Presented at the annual meeting of the American Sociological Association, Aug. 13, New York, NY.

Suchman, Mark C. 1995. "Managing Legitimacy: Strategic and Institutional Approaches." *Academy of Management Review* 20(3): 571–610.

Suddaby, Roy, and Royston Greenwood. 2005. "Rhetorical Strategies of Legitimacy." *Administrative Science Quarterly* 50(1): 35–67.

Swedberg, Richard. 2005. *The Max Weber Dictionary: Key Words and Central Concepts*. Stanford, CA: Stanford University Press.

Swidler, Ann. 1979. *Organization Without Authority*. Cambridge, MA: Harvard University Press.

Taylor, Rosemary C. R. 1979. "Free Medicine." Pp. 17–48 in *Co-ops, Communes & Collectives: Experiments in Social Change in the 1960s and 1970s,* ed. John Case and Rosemary C. R. Taylor. New York: Pantheon Books.

Tedlow, Richard S. 1979. *Keeping the Corporate Image: Public Relations and Business, 1900–1950*. Greenwich, CT: JAI Press.

Thomas, Jan E. 1999. "'Everything about Us Is Feminist': The Significance of Ideology in Organizational Change." *Gender & Society* 13(1): 101–19.

Thornton, Patricia H. 2004. *Markets from Culture: Institutional Logics and Organizational Decisions in Higher Education Publishing*. Stanford, CA: Stanford University Press.

Tolbert, Pamela S., and Lynne G. Zucker. 1983. "Institutional Sources of Change in the Formal Structure of Organizations: The Diffusion of Civil Service Reform, 1880–1935." *Administrative Science Quarterly* 28(1): 22–39.

Troast, John G., Jr., Andrew J. Hoffman, Hannah C. Riley, and Max H. Bazerman. 2002. "Institutions as Barriers and Enablers to Negotiated Agreements: Institutional Entrepreneurship and the Plum Creek Habitat Conservation Plan." Pp. 235–61 in *Organizations, Policy, and the Natural Environment: Institutionalist and Strategic Perspectives,* ed. Andrew J. Hoffman and Marc J. Ventresca. Stanford, CA: Stanford University Press.

Tuchman, Gaye. 1978. *Making News: A Study in the Construction of Reality*. New York: Free Press.

Tuckman, Howard P., and Cyril F. Chang. 2006. "Commercial Activity, Technological Change, and Nonprofit Mission." Pp. 629–44 in *The Nonprofit Sector: A Research Handbook,* 2nd ed., ed. Walter W. Powell and Richard Steinberg. New Haven, CT: Yale University Press.

Turner, Fred. 2006. *From Counterculture to Cyberculture: Stewart Brand, the Whole Earth and the Rise of Digital Utopianism.* Chicago, IL: University of Chicago Press.

U.S. Department of the Interior. 2000. *The Black Rock Desert & Playa: Natural and Cultural History Visitor Information.* Winnemucca, NV: Bureau of Land Management, Winnemucca Field Office.

Vallas, Steven P. 2003a. "The Adventures of Managerial Hegemony: Teamwork, Ideology, and Worker Resistance." *Social Problems* 50(2): 204–25.

———. 2003b. "Why Teamwork Fails: Obstacles to Workplace Change in Four Manufacturing Plants." *American Sociological Review* 68(2): 223–50.

———. 2006. "Empowerment Redux: Structure, Agency, and the Remaking of Managerial Authority." *American Journal of Sociology* 111(6): 1677–1717.

Van Maanen, John. 1991. "The Smile Factory: Work at Disneyland." Pp. 58–76 in *Reframing Organizational Culture,* ed. Peter J. Frost, Larry F. Moore, Meryl Reis Louis, Craig C. Lundberg, and Joanne Martin. Newbury Park, CA: Sage.

Vaughn, Diane. 1996. *The Challenger Launch Decision: Risky Technology, Culture, and Deviance at NASA.* Chicago, IL: University of Chicago Press.

Videla, Nancy Plankey. 2006. "It Cuts Both Ways: Workers, Management, and the Construction of a 'Community of Fate' on the Shop Floor in a Mexican Garment Factory." *Social Forces* 84(4): 2099–2120.

Viggiani, Frances A. 1997. "Democratic Hierarchies in the Workplace: Structural Dilemmas and Organizational Action." *Economic and Industrial Democracy* 18(2): 231–60.

Voss, Glenn B., Daniel M. Cable, and Zannie Giraud Voss. 2000. "Linking Organizational Values to Relationships with External Constituents: A Study of Nonprofit Professional Theaters." *Organization Science* 11(3): 330–47.

Warren, Mark R. 2001. *Dry Bones Rattling: Community Building to Revitalize American Democracy.* Princeton, NJ: Princeton University Press.

Weber, Max. [1922] 1978. *Economy and Society: An Outline of Interpretative Sociology.* Vol. 1. Translated by Ephraim Fischoff et al. Berkeley: University of California Press.

———. [1946] 1958. "Bureaucracy." Pp. 196–244 in *Max Weber: Essays in Sociology,* ed. and trans. Hans H. Gerth and C. Wright Mills. New York: Oxford University Press.

———. [1946] 1958. "The Sociology of Charismatic Authority." Pp. 245–64 in *Max Weber: Essays in Sociology,* ed. and trans. Hans H. Gerth and C. Wright Mills. New York: Oxford University Press.

Weeks, John. 2004. *Unpopular Culture: The Ritual of Complaint in a British Bank.* Chicago, IL: University of Chicago Press.

Weick, Karl E. 1996. "Drop Your Tools: An Allegory for Organizational Studies." *Administrative Science Quarterly* 41(2): 301–13.

Weinberg, Dana Beth. 2003. *Code Green: Money-Driven Hospitals and the Dismantling of Nursing.* Ithaca, NY: ILR Press.

Weiner, Mark. 2006. *Unleashing the Power of PR: A Contrarian's Guide to Marketing and Communication.* San Francisco: Jossey-Bass.

Wharton, Carol S. 1987. "Establishing Shelters for Battered Women: Local Manifestations of a Social Movement." *Qualitative Sociology* 10(2): 146–63.

Whyte, William Foote. [1943] 1955. *Street Corner Society.* 2nd ed. Chicago, IL: University of Chicago Press.

Whyte, William Foote, and Kathleen King Whyte. 1988. *Making Mondragón: The Growth and Dynamics of the Worker Cooperative Complex.* Ithaca, NY: ILR Press.

Wilson, James Q. [1974] 1995. *Political Organizations.* Princeton, NJ: Princeton University Press.

Yin, Robert K. 1994. *Case Study Research Design and Methods.* Thousand Oaks, CA: Sage Publications.

Zablocki, Benjamin. 1980. *Alienation and Charisma: A Study of Contemporary American Communes.* New York: Free Press.

Zald, Mayer N., and Roberta Ash. 1966. "Social Movement Organizations: Growth, Decay, and Change." *Social Forces* 44(3): 327–41.

Zald, Mayer N., Calvin Morrill, and Hayagreeva Rao. 2005. "The Impact of Social Movements on Organizations." Pp. 253–79 in *Social Movements and Organization Theory,* ed. Gerald F. Davis, Doug McAdam, W. Richard Scott, and Mayer N. Zald. New York: Cambridge University Press.

Zelizer, Viviana. 1996. "Payments and Social Ties." *Sociological Forum* 11(3): 481–95.

Zell, Deone. 1997. *Changing by Design: Organizational Innovation at Hewlett-Packard.* Ithaca, NY: Cornell University Press.

Zucker, Lynne G. 1977. "The Role of Institutionalization in Cultural Persistence." *American Sociological Review* 42(5): 726–43.

———. 1983. "Organizations as Institutions." *Research in the Sociology of Organizations* 2: 1–47.

Zuckerman, Erza W. 1999. "The Categorical Imperative: Securities Analysts and the Illegitimacy Discount." *American Journal of Sociology* 104(5): 1398–1438.

Zwerdling, Daniel. [1978] 1980. *Workplace Democracy: A Guide to Workplace Ownership, Participation, and Self-Management Experiments in the United States and Europe.* New York: Harper & Row.

Index

accountability: Burning Man coordinates mobilization for agencies', 122–23, 129, 147–48; Burning Man introduces practices to increase, 45; Burning Man members' demands for, 62; collectivist practices and, 53–54; concealed hegemony and, 17; discussion of organizational practices for, 21; financial compensation for, 107, 108, 109; formalization of Burning Man strengthens, 35; incentives for, 109; incorporation as LLC and, 48, 49, 51; masked hegemony and, 14; overorganizing and lack of, 12, 13, 15; in totalitarianism, 20; of volunteer labor, 103

Adler and Borys, 181n36

admission. *See* tickets

advancing legitimacy, 161–62

advertisements: at Burning Man 2007, 202n118; Burning Man name used in, 142–43, 147

airport, 41, 99

Albany, Dana, 30

analytic generalization, 169, 205n6

anomie, 13

anonymity, 171, 173, 175, 176, 178

Aronson, Adam, 136

art: Black Rock Arts Festival, 29; Burning Man event breaks conventions regarding making and experiencing of, 2; as Burning Man mission, 93; Burning Man name associated with artworks, 145–46, 148; Burning Man organization establishes image as arts community, 34, 149; Harvey's role in Burning Man, 38, 41; large-scale installations at Burning Man, 179n5

Art Department, 41, 166

Associated Press (AP), 132, 200n72

avoidance strategy, 116

balance expectations, 156–57

Barker, James R., 16

Barman, Emily A., 197n10

Barnard, Chester, 109

Beachler, Megan (Sacred Flame), 102

Best, David, 91

Bilbo, Mike, 125, 128, 200n71

Black Rock Arts Festival, 29. *See also* Burning Man event

Black Rock Arts Foundation, 51

Black Rock City Council, 37

Black Rock City Limited Liability Company. *See* Burning Man organization

Black Rock Gazette (event newspaper), 29, 40, 79, 166

Black Rock Rangers: bureaucratic practices of, 126; and chaos of 1996 event, 45; collectivist mission of, 126; financial compensation for, 107; and law enforcement agencies, 40, 124, 125–26; meal passes for, 104; mentoring system for, 103; Mikel as leader of, 29, *39*, 77; motivation of, 98; in *Paramedics* television show proposal, 137; placement in, 73, 74; as public service, 51; recruitment for, 71

Black Rock Solar, 198n32, 202n118

BLM. *See* Bureau of Land Management (BLM)

Bobier, Jess (Nurse), 70, 95, 136

Body Shop, 11, 15

Borys, Bryan, 11

Bruman, Ray, 93–94

Bulletin Boards, 39

Bullock, Joegh, 30, 59

Burdwood, Mary Ellen (Dirtwitch), 98, 126, 139

bureaucracy: benefits of, 21, 154; blending practices to avoid under- and overorganizing extremes, 19–22, 153–54; bureaucratic practices, 7–8; Burning Man organization as blend of bureaucratic and collectivist practices, 19, 21, 44, 53, 61–62, 81, 154–56, 158; characteristics of, 6, 7; coercive overorganizing in, 12–13; concern about Burning Man organization becoming, 5; defined, 20; as end in itself, 16; external entities encourage, 115; financial compensation introduces aspects of, 105–6; increasing blending of bureaucratic and collectivist practices, 9–10, 81–82; institutionalization of, 7–8; Media Mecca's bureaucratic practices, 132, 148; member involvement affected by bureaucratic practices, 86; organizational maintenance supported over innovation in, 158; placement in, 80–81; responses to governmental agencies, media, and commodifiers, 120; sustaining volunteerism with bureaucratic and collectivist practices, 89–98, 110; unintended consequences of overorganizing in, 16–19; unintended consequences of underorganizing in, 13–15

Bureau of Land Management (BLM): asks local authorities to oversee sanitary facilities in 1996, 31; attempts to avoid cooperating with Burning Man, 122–23; author interviews officials from, 168; Burning Man event returns to BLM-managed land in 1998, 34; Burning Man organization questions standards of, 127; Burning Man organization shapes relations with, 121; Burning Man organization supports, 123–25; developing new standards for Burning Man, 128; fees, 121, 203n136; Harvey compares Washoe County with, 113; permits required from, 28, 121, 122–23; Pershing County sheriff requests to not reissue permit for 1997, 33; visits site of 1990 event, 28

Burning Man event: attempts to limit use of Black Rock Desert by, 35; authorities and, 27–28, 31, 32–33, 35, 40; the "average" participant, 205n8; budget for, 3; development of, 24–41; difficulties in attending, 189n6; distinguished from other festivals, 1–2; duration expanded to seven days, 34; as at edge of chaos, 3; as first in its field, 149; future development of, 36–37; insurance required for, 28; large-scale art installations at, 179n5; legislation proposed to limit access to event site, 123; maturing, 1998–2001, 34–35; media coverage of 1996 event, 31; moves to private land Washoe County, 33–34, 113; number of participants, 1997, 1, 26, 36, 37; opposition to, 33; organizational extremes that threaten, 3–6; origins of, 2–3, 26–27; as participatory, 1–2; population increase of, 36, *36*; reasons for attending, 65; recreation permit required for, 28; relocates to Nevada Black Rock Desert, 28–29; returns to Black Rock Desert in 1998, 34; terms used to refer to attendees and organizational members, 3; thwarted "takeover" by Satan and Helco at 1996 event, 32, 184n47. *See also* Burning Man organization; theme camps

Burning Man organization (Project; Black
Rock City Limited Liability Company)
  acting on suggestions and criticisms,
    42–63; antipathy to corporate form,
    46–50; clarifying decision making at,
    54–62; reaction to feedback by, 50–54;
    reaction to newsletter of 2000, 50
  archives of, 41, 168–69
  characteristics of: as arts community, 34,
    149; as blend of bureaucratic and col-
    lectivist practices, 19, 21, 44, 53, 61–62,
    81, 154–56, 158; boundaries of, 169–70;
    budget of, 25; diverse membership
    of, 160–61; financial and organizing
    transparency as goal of, 45, 49, 52, 62,
    155; mission statement of, 26; as "no-
    profit" business, 52; other organiza-
    tions draw on experiences of, 149–50,
    162; precedents set by, 162; primary
    objective of, 52; self-sufficiency of,
    149, 160; sufficient resources supplied
    by, 159–60; Woodstock compared
    with, 141
  headquarters of, 25–26
  history of: budgeting standardized by,
    35, 185n64; establishment of, 3; first
    headquarters of, 35; future of, 163;
    maturing, 1998–2001, 34–35; organiz-
    ers begin to work full-time for, 35;
    professionals hired by, 35; rectifying
    underorganizing, 1996–97, 30–34, 37,
    45, 154; start of formal organizing for,
    27–30
  relations with surrounding environment,
    112–50; commercial sponsorship
    eschewed by, 52, 54, 63; commodi-
    fiers' demands on, 119, 120, 141–46,
    147, 148, 162; governmental agencies'
    demands on, 119, 120, 120–29, 146, 161;
    media demands on, 119, 120, 129–41,
    146, 161; prohibition on using name
    to sell products, 43–44; vending and
    commercialism prohibited by, 2, 52,
    141, 184n49
  structure of, 37–41; board of, 26, 37–38,
    39; departments of, 38–41; incorpo-
    rates as for-profit organization, 19, 31,
    46, 47; legal partnership for, 30, 31;
    nonprofit arm added by, 51, 62; part-
    nership dissolved, 31, 46; senior staff

    of, 30, 38–39, 39; urged to incorporate
    as nonprofit organization, 49
  volunteers at: attracting and placing,
    64–82; motivating members, 84–110
  See also volunteers; and departments and
    individuals by name
Burning Man Organization Support, 40
Burning Man: Where's the Fire? (documentary),
  139
burnout, coping with, 101–2, 109
Burroughs, Brien, 74, 79
Business Management Department, 38–39

Cacophony Society, 27, 28, 182n9
Camp Arctica, 39, 65–66, 92, 159, 166
campground regulations, 128
Carpenter, Michael (Tex), 44
Cataclysmic Megashear Ranch, 167
Center Camp Café, 39, 76, 79, 91, 102, 104, 166
CEO compensation, 160
Challenger space shuttle disaster, 18
chaos, disabling, 20, 20, 44, 153
Check Point Salon (Playa Info), 4, 39, 51, 73,
  79, 97, 166, 167
Christmas Camp, 29
civil liberties, bureaucratic practices and
  coercive control endanger, 12–13
Coast Guard, 40
"code 48," 90
coercive control: with bureaucratic practices,
  16; with collectivist practices, 13, 16, 44,
  86; in culty collectives, 44, 86; motivation doesn't require, 110; in oligarchy, 44;
  organizers' concern with governmental
  agencies', 119, 124, 126; in overorganizing,
  3, 11, 12, 95, 153; participants' concern
  with organizers', 144, 146, 162; performance stifled by, 18; and prohibition
  of discussion of compensation, 108; in
  totalitarianism, 20, 89, 155, 156
Cohen, Raines, 100
Coleman, James S., 180n21, 181n37
collectivist organizations, 8–11; and anticommodification, 141, 142, 144; benefits of, 21,
  154; blending practices to avoid under-
  and overorganizing extremes, 19–22;
  Burning Man organization as blend of
  bureaucratic and collectivist practices, 19,
  21, 44, 53, 61–62, 81, 154–56, 158; decision
  making in, 6, 9, 11, 54; defining character-

collectivist organizations (*continued*)
istics of, *6,* 8–9; deflecting demands for external entities, 162; external entities encourage bureaucracy rather than, 115; and for-profit form, 47; inclusivity in, 160–61; increasing blending of bureaucratic and collectivist practices, 9–10, 81–82; Media Mecca collectivist practices, 133–34, 135, 148; member-driven innovation supported over organizational maintenance in, 158; overorganizing in, 13; placement in, 72, 75, 77, 79, 80–81; recruitment policies of, 70–72; responses to governmental agencies, media, and commodifiers, *120;* sustaining volunteerism with bureaucratic and collectivist practices, 89–98, 109, 110; training in collectivist practices, 159–60; unintended consequences of overorganizing in, 16–19; unintended consequences of underorganizing in, 13–15

commercialism. *See* commodification

commissary, 39, 166

commitment: consensus decision making enhances, 58; defined, 192n5; job versus other, 157; methods of increasing, 88; re-evaluating, 98–103, 109

commodification: Burning Man formulates policies against, 114; of cultural institutions and outputs, 202n115; defined, 114, 202n114; demands made on Burning Man, 119, *120,* 141–46, 147, 148, 162; media encouraged to focus on noncommercialism, 135; policy on using Burning Man name, 144, 203n124; vending and commercialism prohibited at Burning Man event, 2, 52, 141, 184n49

Commonwealth Club of California, 141, 202n112, 202n113

communes, 8, 66, 72, 88

Communications Department. *See* Media Mecca (Communications Department)

Community Services, 39, 70, 186n84

compensation, financial, 105–9

concealed hegemony, 17–18

conference call meetings, 96

confidentiality, 171, 173, 175, 176, 178

conformity: conformist decision making, 59, 159; internal demands for, 13, 17

consensus decision making: benefits of, 58; in Burning Man organization, 37–38, 55–62;

Burning Man organization urged to adopt, 49, 51; in collectivist organizations, 6, 9, 11, 54, 154; defined, 56; emotional stress accompanying, 59–60

conservation. *See* environment and conservation

corporate culture, 88, 181n24

culty collectives, 20, *20,* 44, 48, 86, 110

Daniel Reed and Pershing County vs. United States Department of the Interior, Bureau of Land Management, 46, 186n9

Dante, 30, 46, 184n47

Database team, 40

decision making: in bureaucratic organizations, *6,* 20; clarifying Burning Man's, 54–62; in collectivist organizations, 6, 9, 11, 54; conformist, 59, 159; in overorganized organizations, 17, 18; in underorganized organizations, 14, 15. *See also* consensus decision making

defiance strategy, 116, 121

DeLaHunt, Jim, 49

delegating, 99–100

DeLurgio, Kat, 94, 106

Department of Homeland Security, underorganizing at, 12

Department of Mutant Vehicles (DMV), 40

Department of Public Works (DPW), 40–41; financial compensation for, 41, 107, 108, 195n104; motivating volunteers at, 94, 96, 97, 98; in research for this study, 166; Roger as head of, *39*

depleted meaning, 16

dialogue, reflexive, 158–59

DiMaggio, Paul J., 162

Dineen, Matt, 106

Directory, 39

disabling chaos, 20, *20,* 44, 153

disempowered teams, 20, *20,* 110, 154, 156

Disney amusement parks, *6,* 16

dissenting views: conformism prevented by exposure to, 159; in consensus decision making, 59; in overorganized organizations, 12; underorganizing can result in lack of procedure for expressing, 15

dissipated efforts, 13–14

Ditmore, Molly, 103

diversity, 160–61

division of labor: in Black Rock Rangers, 126;

as bureaucratic practice, 6, 7; Burning Man's first, 30; external entities encourage, 115, 155; intensification of work results in greater, 157; to reduce volunteer workload, 99; and reinforced underorganizing, 15; as separating workers from effects of their contribution, 97; in totalitarian organizations, 20

do-ocracy, 55, 63

Doty, Peter, 29

DPW. See Department of Public Works (DPW)

drugs: Black Rock Rangers assist in arrest of sellers, 126; at early days of Burning Man, 32; organizer concern about media coverage of, 131, 132, 134, 135, 137, 138–39, 140; Pershing County concern about, 121

Dubois, Harley (Bierman): on bureaucratization and motivation, 89; on Burning Man board, 39; on Burning Man: Where's the Fire? documentary, 139; on burnout, 102; on consensus decision making at Burning Man, 37–38, 55–56; debate with Goodell over decision making, 56–58; on disclosing compensation, 108; on Earth Guardians, 125; as enabling volunteers, 75; on governmental agencies developing new standards for Burning Man, 128; Greeters proposal of, 76; on inclusion of volunteers, 70–71; on informal communication before meetings, 58; on job creation by organizers, 80; joins Burning Man senior staff, 30, 185n80; on locals refusing to do business with Burning Man, 46; on Miller's conservation policies department, 75–76; in recruitment, 69; on rule-breaking at meetings, 61; on sharing responsibilities, 100; "Successful Volunteerism with Burningman," 71; on tailoring placements, 76–77; takes chances placing volunteers, 78–79; takes charge of projects, 73; on volunteer's motivation, 86–87

Earth Guardians, 40, 92, 124–25, 166, 198n32

eBay, 43, 114, 144, 145–46, 162

efficiency: bureaucracy associated with, 7, 8, 21, 154; Burning Man placement not based on, 77–78; as not top priority at Burning Man, 53, 71; some Burning Man members emphasize, 5; tolerating volunteers' inefficiency, 75

efforts, dissipated, 13–14

Ehrenreich, Barbara, 17

electronic communications: Burning Man teams for, 40; Jack Rabbit Speaks e-mail newsletter, 122, 123, 140, 143–44, 144–45, 167, 197n20; Web site, 26, 40, 132, 139, 162, 168–69

embedded journalists, 148, 203n135

enabling organizations, 20, 21, 153, 155, 156–163, 171

encourage experimentation, 159

engage in reflexive dialogue, 158–59

environment and conservation: Black Rock Solar, 198n32, 202n118; Burning Man volunteers in non–Burning Man endeavors regarding, 110; Earth Guardians, 40, 92, 124–25, 166, 198n32; for-profit firms' concern with, 11, 117, 181n29; "Leave No Trace" policy, 125, 128–29; media and Burning Man's practices regarding, 135, 147; Miller's department concerned with, 75–76; opposition to Burning Man on grounds of, 33; Playa Hygiene Department, 186n90; Recycle Camp, 40, 79, 91–92

Essa, Fiona, 54, 93

Etzioni, Amitai, 181n24

Evening Magazine (television program), 56–58

excessive force by police officers, group norms encourage, 17

expectations, balancing, 156–57

experimentation, 94–96, 159

Extranet Team, 40

face time, 157

facilitate true participation, 158

Federal Bureau of Investigation (FBI), 12, 13, 149

feedback: Burning Man organization's reaction to, 50–54; for motivating members, 97–98, 109, 110

feel-good collectives, 20, 20, 86, 154

feminist organizations: bureaucratic and collectivist practices mixed in, 9–10; existing organizational forms used by, 162; external entities encourage bureaucracy in, 115; underorganizing can lead to members controlling each other, 14

Fenton, Joe (Boggmann): on Burning Man senior staff, *39;* and Nevada state tax collector, 127; on placement and expertise, 73; on reorganizing after 1996 event, 46; on semantics as important in recruitment, 72

financial compensation, 105–9

firearms (guns), 29, 31, 32, 47, 135, 140

"flake factor," 103

for-profit organizations: blurring of nonprofits and, 10–11; Burning Man organizers incorporate as, 19, 31, 46, 47; businesses organize as, 9; collectivist practices introduced in, 10; credibility problem for, 49; employee demands require consideration at, 63; resource allocation as problem for, 160; ties to nonprofit organizations, 149

frames, 134, 200n82, 201n87

Freedman, Alice, 79–80

Gate, the, 40, 73, 103, 140, 166, 186n87

General Public License (GPL), 204n12

gift economy, 2, 51, 114, 134, 135, 140, 198n32

Goodell, Marian: and Associated Press story on drug use, 132; author contacts Burning Man through, 165–66; on Bureau of Land Management and fire performances, 127; on Bureau of Land Management attempt to refuse permit, 122; on Burning Man board, *39;* on Burning Man organization as nebulous, 37; on complimentary tickets, 104; and consensus process at Burning Man, 60; on conservation, 124; debate with Dubois over decision making, 56–58; on democracy and collectivist practice, 54–55; on do-ocracy, 55; emotional displays during decision making, 59; on entry process for Burning Man organization, 68, 189n8; event promoter makes false claim of sponsorship by, 145; on financial compensation, 106–7; on financial disclosure, 52; on formalizing policy, 154; on job creation by organizers, 80; joins Burning Man organization, 185n80; on Manthey's use of Burning Man name, 144–45; on media coverage of sex and drugs, 138–39, 140; on media relations, 130; on MTV coverage, 137; in negotiations with public and private agencies, 38; on *Playboy* article, 129; on proposed legislation to limit access to event site, 123; on raves compared with Burning Man event,

138; on rule-breaking at meetings, 61; "Successful Volunteerism with Burningman," 71; takes charge of projects, 73; on Tech team task assignment, 80; on UFOs television program, 143–44

Gore, W. L., & Associates, 81–82

governmental agencies, 120–29; agencies that assist or monitor Burning Man, 197n16; Black Rock Rangers policy regarding, 40; and Burning Man cooperate to develop new standards, 127–29, 147; Burning Man coordinates mobilization for accountability of, 122–23, 129, 147–48; Burning Man organizers negotiate with, 35; Burning Man questions standards of, 127, 146; Burning Man supports, 123–26; conflict with Burning Man's global standards, 32–33; demands made on Burning Man by, 119, *120,* 161; increase their jurisdiction at 1996 event, 31; restrict activities of 1990 event, 27–28; seen as using Burning Man as "cash cow," 124; Washoe County's attitude toward Burning Man, 113–14. *See also* law enforcement agencies

Grace, Andie (Actiongrl), 55, 170

Graham, Jim (RonJon), 68, 136, 137, 142–43, 144, 203n124

Graham, John, 97–98

Grauberger, Mary, 27

Greenwood, Royston, 197n10

Greeters, 39, 76, 96, 101–2, 166

groupthink, 17, 59

Guerra, Antony "Shona," 92

Gumport, Patricia J., 181n30

guns (firearms), 29, 31, 32, 47, 135, 140

Hagger, Simon, 91–92

Harrison, Dana (BizBabe): on Burning Man sculpture posted on eBay, 146; on Burning Man senior staff, *39;* on emotion in decision making, 59–60; on modified consensus at Burning Man, 60–61; motivation for volunteering, 85–86, 191n2; on placement and efficiency, 77–78; on quirkiness of Burning Man volunteers, 78; on recruitment, 68; on *URB* magazine article, 138

Harvey, Larry: on attendees donating to 1997 event, 34; on bureaucratization and motivation, 89; on Burning Man as "no-profit" business, 52; on Burning Man board responsibilities, 37; on Burning Man organization established by, 3, 185n80; on Burning Man sculpture posted on eBay, 145–46; on Burning Man support of Bureau of Land Management, 123; in Commonwealth Club advertisement, 141, 202n112, 202n113; and consensus process at Burning Man, 60; creative role of, 38, 41; criticism of corporate model of, 47–48; on divesting Burning Man organization of property interest, 52; on do-ocracy, 55; event promoter makes false claim of sponsorship by, 145; as executive director of Burning Man, 38, 39; financial disclosure by, 52; formalizes organic decision-making, 55; on for-profit form, 46; Goodell backed on decision making by, 57; on hierarchy in decision making, 61; in legal partnership formation, 30; on media in conflict with Washoe County, 113–14; on media's potential for damage, 131; on Mikel becoming symbolic leader of Black Rock Rangers, 77; on MTV coverage, 137; on negotiations for 1997 event, 33; on newsletter of 2000, 50; in origins of Burning Man event, 26–27; on Pershing County sheriff's demands, 124; on placement, 75, 76; on *Playboy* article, 129; on promoting selected frames, 139; on providing for growth of Burning Man event, 31, 45; on recruitment, 72; on rule-breaking at meetings, 61; satirical comment about bureaucracy, 44; as speaker, 141, 202n110; on volunteer labor and gift economy, 51; on working with Washoe County, 113–14

hegemony: concealed, 17–18; masked, 14

Hernandez, Sarah, 188n61

Hewlett-Packard (HP), 17

Holmes, Jennifer, 30, 45

homogeneity, 160, 161

Hoover, Duane: on Bureau of Land Management and fire performances, 127; on Burning Man senior staff, 39; on business aspects of Burning Man, 52–53; on emotional displays during decision making, 59

human resources departments, 82, 191n81

Hyde, Lewis, 51

ideal types, 180n19

impression (perception) management, 118, 155, 201n102

inclusivity: uphold, 160–61. *See also* radical inclusion principle

individual (members') interests: in culty collectives, 20; enhancing accountability to, 21, 22, 45, 53, 62, 63, 160; matching organizational needs with, 76, 81, 82; overorganizing in suppression of, 17–18, 89; in placement, 72; reduced accountability to, 12, 15, 53, 55, 147, 154; reflected in collectivist practices, 8, 74, 90; social ties develop identity beyond, 21–22

inequalities, 14, 18, 20, 108, 156, 160

Inferno (Dante), 30, 46, 184n47

informal relations: privileged, 14, 70; suppressed, 17

Internet phone incident, 4–5, 18, 180n15

interns, 75, 105

interviews: of core organizers, 176–78; protocols for, 173–78; subjects of, 167–68; of volunteers, 173–75

"iron cage" of control, 16, 18, 62

Jackall, Robert, 101

Jack Rabbit Speaks (e-mail newsletter), 122, 123, 140, 143–44, 144–45, 167, 197n20

James, Jerry: on disorder at 1996 event, 30; on organizing affecting participation, 5; in origins of Burning Man event, 26–27; theme camps introduced by, 29

Jones, Jesse, 76

Kalleberg, Arne L., 10

Kanter, Rosabeth Moss, 192n5

Keleher, Barb, 123–24

Kleinman, Sherryl, 14

Kreuter, Holly, 93

Kristen, Christine (Lady Bee), 50, 93

Kuemmerle, Vanessa, 30

labor. *See* division of labor; volunteers

Lamb, Jim, 71, 94, 95

Lamplighters, 40, 51, 71, 74, 79, 97, 104

Langer, Ellen J., 96

Law, John: on ceasing Burning Man event, 31; on class-based labor at Burning Man, 48; on corporate form of Burning Man, 47; on insufficient organization for 1996 event, 30, 45; joins organizing team, 28; leaves Burning Man partnership, 31, 46; in legal partnership formation, 30; in thwarted "takeover" by Satan and Helco at 1996 event, 184n47 law enforcement agencies: Black Rock Rangers develop protocols and procedures for dealing with, 40, 124, 125–26; Burning Man event monitored by, 121; fear being overwhelmed by Burning Man, 124; media coverage intensifies pressure on, 132; registration of cameras and video recorders of, 134

"Leave No Trace" conservation policy, 125, 128–29

legitimacy: advancing, 161–62; bases of, 196n9; commodification seen as threat to, 119; defined, 117; media affect, 130, 148; organizations seek to secure, 117–18; ties to other organizations for increasing, 148–49

Lehman, Chase, 53

Lewis, Chris, 103

limited liability companies (LLCs), 46, 49, 51, 184n45

Locklear, Candace (Pippi), 136, 142, 145

Locksmiths, 186n84

London Observer (newspaper), 202n109

Los Angeles Times (newspaper), 30–31

Lost and Found, 40

Lune, Howard, 197n10

Mangrum, Stuart, 30, 53

manipulation strategy, 116, 121

Manthey, Jerri, 144–45

manuals, 103

Martin, Joanne, 15

Marx, Karl, 202n14

Mauthe, Flynn, *39*, 98, 107

meal passes, 104, 194n95

meaning: collectivist practices emphasize, 8, 16, 19, 21, *53*, 70, 89, 154; commodification seen as detracting from, 114, 119, 141, 147; depleted, 16; feedback for affirming, 92, 97, 109; some Burning Man members emphasize, 5

media: advance proposals required from, 135; bureaucratic routines of, 148; in Burning Man conflict with Washoe County, 113–14; Burning Man contravenes standard public relations practices, 133; coverage of 1996 event, 31; debate over *Evening Magazine* television coverage, 56–58; demands made on Burning Man by, 119, *120*, 129–41, 146, 161; difficulties in covering Burning Man, 204n4; filming and video recording of

Burning Man event, 131, 143–44; governmental agencies coordinate with, 200n71; as not primary means of achieving Burning Man mission, 130; organizations' fear of, 199n65; participation and immersion recommended for, 133–34, 148; promoting selected frames in, 134–41; registration of cameras and video recorders of, 134

Media Mecca (Communications Department): on advertisements using Burning Man name, 143; attempt to "spin" media coverage, 130; author joins, 166, 167; bureaucratic practices of, 132, 148; collectivist practices of, 133–34, 135, 148; in eBay controversy, 43; establishment of, 40; on Manthey's use of Burning Man name, 144; participation and immersion recommended for media by, 133–34, 148; professionalization and routinization of, 132; promotes selected frames, 135–36, 138; in research for this study, 166, 204n4; responsibilities of, 40; volunteer labor at, 51

members' interests. *See* individual (members') interests

memorabilia, 104, 109

Merrill Lynch & Co., 202n116

Merton, Robert K., 180n12

micromanagement, 48

Mikel, Michael (Danger Ranger): *Black Rock Gazette* initiated by, 29; on Black Rock Rangers' boundary-spanning role, 126; as Black Rock Rangers leader, 29, *39*, 77; on Burning Man board, *39*; on Burning Man event as on edge of chaos, 3; on first Black Rock Desert event, 28–29; on governmental agencies developing new standards for Burning Man, 128; on inefficiency of Burning Man, 53; on job creation by organizers, 80; joins organizing team, 28, 185n80; in legal partnership formation, 30; on limited liability company form, 46; on moving Burning Man event away from anarchist ideology, 32–33; on newsletter of 2000, 50; on Washoe County regulations, 33

military organizations: embedded journalists in Iraq, 148, 203n135; underorganizing in, 12

Miller, Dan, 30, 75–76

mindfulness, 96
Miner, Anne S., 81, 191n79
Ministry of Statistics theme camp, 140, 205n8
misdirected activities, 15
mission drift, 10, 156
Mobia, Steve, 78, 97
Mondragón worker cooperatives, 82, 110, 196n6
monetary incentives, 105–9
Morrell, Carole, 129, 185n80
Motel 666, 167
motivating members, 84–110; catalyzing networks and solidarity, 96–97; categories of motivations, 87, 191n4; coping with burnout, 101–2, 109; easing transitions, 102–3; feedback to affirm meaning and fulfillment, 97–98, 109, 110; financial compensation, 105–9; incentives in, 88; institutional cultural frames in, 87–88; limits of appreciation as motivation, 98; linking motivation with opportunities, 86–89; opportunities to contribute to a mission and enacting values, 93–94; reasons people volunteer for Burning Man, 87; re-evaluating commitment, 98–103, 109; reinforcing contributions with perks, 103–9; supporting experimentation and developing skills, 94–96, 159; sustaining volunteerism with bureaucratic and collectivist practices, 89–98, 109, 110
MTV (Music Television), 136–37

NASA, 18
National Weather Service, 12
Nettle, John, 69, 91
Network/Desktop Support, 40
network form of organization, 181n22
network ties, recruitment by, 67–68, 69–70
New York Times Magazine, 29
Nightline (television program), 114
nonprofit organizations: accountability not guaranteed in, 53–54; blurring of for-profits and, 10–11; Burning Man organization adds nonprofit arm, 51, 62; Burning Man organization urged to incorporate as, 49; challenges of large-scale production and organization, 62–63; charities organize as, 9; collectivist practices introduced in, 10; difficulties in obtaining resources, 160; prohibits redistribution of profit or

loss, 9; ties to for-profit organizations, 149
Normal, Davy, 167, 204n2
normative control, 9, 88, 89, 181n24
nudity, 32, 127, 131, 133, 135, 137, 143

O'Connor, Karina, 92, 94
oligarchy, 20, 20, 44, 48, 62, 115, 180n17
Oliver, Christine, 116
Oliver, Rob, 4, 95, 97
Open Source projects, 204n12
Oregon Country Fair, 128, 131
organizations: accepted forms used for new ends, 162; boundaries of, 169–70; categorization of, 6–7, 180n20; coercive overorganizing, 12–13; diversification in, 161; future of, 163; future of ethnographic research on, 171; increasing blending of bureaucratic and collectivist practices in, 81–82; organizing practices, 6–11; perils of under- and overorganizing, 1–22; responses to external pressures, 116–18; serving rather than ruling us, 163; unsupportive underorganizing, 11–12. See also for-profit organizations; nonprofit organizations; overorganizing; underorganizing
overorganizing, 12–13; anticommodification and, 144; blending practices as intensifying, 155, 156; blending practices to avoid under- and overorganizing extremes, 19–22, 153–54; as danger to Burning Man event, 3–6; external entities encourage, 115, 146–47; intensified, 19; media coverage and, 133; member involvement affected by, 86; motivation affected by, 95; strategies for avoiding, 156–63; true participation lacking in, 158; underorganizing can lead to triggered, 15; unintended consequences of, 16–19, 153–54

paganism, 31, 46, 135
Page, Karen L., 181n22
paid labor, 105–9
panoptic surveillance, 19
Paramedics (television program), 137
Parsons, Gerald, 76
participation, facilitate true, 158
Patagonia (firm), 157
Pearce, Naomi, 29, 31–32, 73, 100–101, 133, 140, 153

People Express airline, 15
perception (impression) management, 118, 155, 201n102
perks, reinforcing contributions with, 103–9
Pitt, Rebecca, 136, 137
Piven and Cloward, 180n17
placement, 72–80; bureaucratic versus collectivist practices in, 80–81; creating and supporting roles, 72, 73–76, 81, 155; of difficult or outdated members, 76–80; flexible policies for, 72, 76; increasing blending of bureaucratic and collectivist practices in, 81–82
planning: limits of, 95, 159, 193n47; scaling down overly ambitious plans, 100
Playa Hygiene Department (PhD), 186n90
Playa Info (Check Point Salon), 4, 39, 51, 73, 79, 97, 166, 167
Playboy (magazine), 129, 138, 144
Podolny, Joel M., 181n22
police officers: group norms encourage excessive force by, 17. *See also* law enforcement agencies
pornography, 137, 143, 148
portable toilets, 28, 36, 46, 196n8
Pouyoul, Eric, 78, 95
Powell, Walter W., 162
precedents, setting, 162
Pred, Joseph: on Burning Man senior staff, 39; on financial compensation for Black Rock Rangers, 107; on newsletter of 2000, 50; on recruitment for Black Rock Rangers, 71
press passes, 133
Princeton University, 202n116
privileged informal relations, 14, 70
product tie-ins, 141–42
Public Research Associates, 33
Putnam, Robert, 182n39

qualitative research, 165–71

radical inclusion principle: benefits of, 155; in Burning Man recruitment, 67, 70, 72, 76, 77, 81, 82; diversity promoted by, 160–61; emphasizes welcoming rather than excluding, 70; performance elicited by, 82; problems with, 77
Rainbow Family and Gathering, 48, 51, 128, 187n24, 197n18, 198n30

Raspa, Steven, 99
rationality: substantive, 16; value-, 6, 9
raves, 135, 137–38
record keeping, 103, 115
recruitment, 66–72; "Burning Man evangelists," 69–70; centralizing information about prospective volunteers, 69; collectivist policy for, 70–72; by demonstrated expertise, 68; by network ties, 67–68, 69–70; radical inclusion principle of, 67, 70, 72, 76, 77, 81, 82, 155, 160–61; routinizing, 69
Recycle Camp, 40, 79, 91–92
reflexive dialogue, 158–59
regionals, 37, 163
religious groups, 8, 9, 88
Renaissance Fair, 128
research: issues in, 169–71; qualitative, 165–71. *See also* interviews
resources, supply sufficient, 159–60
Richards, Austin (Dr. Megavolt), 145
Rinaldi, John (Chicken John), 47, 154, 186n88
Roger, Will, 39, 107, 185n80
role creation: benefits of, 154, 155; commitment heightened by, 90; defined, 72; performance elicited by, 82; in placement, 72, 73–76, 81, 155
Rose, Crimson: on Burning Man board, 39; on criticism of organizers, 50; on financial compensation and expectations, 107; joins Burning senior staff, 30, 185n80; on 1996 event as pivotal, 31; on *URB* magazine article, 138

San Francisco Examiner (newspaper), 140
San Francisco Focus (publication), 130–31
Scott, W. Richard, 196n9
Segal, P., 49–50, 93
Senter, Monica, 80, 81
set precedents, 162
Shaner, Scott, 65–66, 92
Shoun, Lissa, 99
Skinner, Ron, 31, 33, 35, 120–21
Smythe, Kimric, 106
Snow and Snell, 81
Snydman, Stuart K., 181n30
social capital, 22
social movement groups: alternative practices urged by, 147; change results from challenges to standards by, 117; collectivist

practices in, 8; increase media coverage by codifying relations and procedures, 148; on media, 130

solidarity, 14, 16, 17, 58, 92, 96–97

standards: Burning Man and governmental agencies cooperate to develop new, 127–29, 147; Burning Man develops and promotes its own, 162; Burning Man questions government agencies', 127, 146; organizational response to external, 116–18

stifled performance, overorganizing can lead to, 18–19

stipends, 105–9

Stirling, Earl (Dodger), 49

Stohl and Cheney, 19

Strahan, Susan, 97, 154

Student Nonviolent Coordinating Committee (SNCC), 13–14

Students for a Democratic Society (SDS), 199n62

substantive rationality, 16

Suchman, Mark, 117

"Successful Volunteerism with Burningman" (manual), 71–72, 74–75, 89, 90

Suddaby, Roy, 197n10

sufficient resources, supplying, 159–60

summer solstice, 27, 28

suppressed informal relations, 17

Survival Guide, 29, 184n49

Survivor II: The Australian Outback (television program), 144

SyncFest!, 142–43

System Administration, 40

tax collection, 127

Taylor, Ggreg, 50–51

teams: disempowered, 20, *20*, 110, 154, 156; increasing use of, 10; worker solidarity increased by, 17. See also *Burning Man teams by name*

Tech Team, 40, 74, 80–81, 94, 103, 107, 166

"thank you" mixers, 104

Theme Camp Placement and Villages, 39–40

theme camps: in Burning Man organization, 37; Camp Arctica as, 39, 92; coordinate to form villages, 32; that host raves, 201n94; introduction of, 29; media relations in, 140

Thornton, Dave (Thorny), *39*, 170

tickets: complimentary, 36, 104, 108, 195n96;

Harvey in price determination, 38; increasing admission prices, 36, 49, 195n96; media urged to report on buying advance, 138

Tirpak, Molly: on decision making by consensus, 61; on delegating, 99–100; on motivating volunteers, 90, 91; on perks, 104; on placement, 73–74, 79; on recruitment, 69, 71, 72; "Successful Volunteerism with Burningman," 71

total institutions, 156

totalitarianism, 20, *20*, 89, 154, 156

town hall meetings, 55, 96, 167

trademark infringement, 162, 204n11

transitions, easing, 102–3

UFOs: Best Evidence Ever Caught on Tape 2 (television program), 143–44

underorganizing, 11–12; blending practices to avoid under- and overorganizing extremes, 19–22, 153–54; Burning Man organization rectifies, 1996–97, 30–34, 37, 45, 54–55, 61, 154; as danger to Burning Man event, 3–6; member involvement affected by, 86; networked recruitment as, 70; recruitment, 67–68; reinforced, 15; relations with outside entities affected by, 115; strategies for avoiding, 156–63; true participation lacking in, 158; unintended consequences of, 13–15, 153

undesirable externalities, 7, 180n21

uphold inclusivity, 160–61

URB (magazine), 138

Valasquez, Fernando, 139

value-rationality, *6, 9*

Vermut, Jennifer, 67, 73

volunteers, 64–82; Harvey on gift economy and, 51; interview protocol for, 173–75; motivating, 84–110; non–Burning Man projects of, 110, 196n129; paid personnel seen as undercutting, 78; placement of, 72–80; recruitment of, 65–72; seen as exploited, 47–48; selectivity about their working conditions, 81

wage disparities, 160

Wal-Mart, 17

Warner, Mike, 96

Waterman, Erik, 106

Weber, Max, 7, 9, 16, 180n19
Web site (www.burningman.com), 26, 40,
    132, 139, 162, 168–69
Web Team, 40, 94, 107, 166
Weeks, John R., 62
WELL, the, 29
Westerbeke, Annie, 34
Whitman, Diane, 91
Wilcox, Russell, 48
Wired (magazine), 131, 137
women's organizations. See feminist
    organizations
Woodstock, 141, 142

Woodstock '99, 136–137, 201n8
workplaces: incentives in, 88; intensification
    of work, 157–58; normative control in,
    88; participatory, 10, 181n27; underorga-
    nized, 12
Wright, Mike, 97
written reports, 61
www.burningman.com, 26, 40, 132, 139, 162,
    168–69

Yin, Robert K., 205n6

Zablocki, Benjamin, 196n1